Deaf Transitions

Images and Origins of Deaf Families, Deaf Communities and Deaf Identities

of related interest

Counselling – The Deaf Challenge
Mairian Corker
ISBN 1 85302 321 3 pb
ISBN 1 85302 223 3 hb

Deaf Transitions

Images and Origins of Deaf Families, Deaf Communities and Deaf Identities

Mairian Corker

Jessica Kingsley Publishers
London and Bristol, Pennsylvania

Figure 1.2 is adapted from R. Dallos (1991) *Family Belief Systems, Therapy and Change* and reproduced with the kind permission of the author and the Open University Press.

Figures 1.4 and 1.5 are adapted from U. Kim (1994) *Individualism and Collectivism* and reproduced with the kind permission of Sage Publications, Inc.

First published in the United Kingdom in 1996 by
Jessica Kingsley Publishers Ltd
116 Pentonville Road
London N1 9JB, England
and
1900 Frost Road, Suite 101
Bristol, PA 19007, U S A

Copyright © 1996 Mairian Corker

Library of Congress Cataloging in Publication Data
Corker, Mairian.
Deaf transitions : images and origins of deaf families, deaf communities, and deaf identities / Mairian Corker.
p.   cm.
Includes bibliographical references.
ISBN 1-85302-326-4 (pbk.)
1. Deaf--Biography, 2. Deaf-Family relationships. 3. Deafness-
-Psychological aspects. 4. Identity (Psychology) I. Title.
HV2373.C67   1996
362.4'2--dc20   96-13415
                                                           CIP

British Library Cataloguing in Publication Data
Corker, Mairian
Deaf transitions : images and origins of deaf families,
deaf communities and deaf identities
1. Hearing impaired 2. Deafness - Social aspects 3. Deaf
4. Deaf - Social conditions
I. Title
305.9'08'162

ISBN 1-85302-326-4

Printed and Bound in Great Britain by
Cromwell Press, Melksham, Wiltshire

For my children
...and the lost children in all of us

Acknowledgements

This book could not have come to life so lucidly without the contributions of the narrators. They cannot be named, but to them go my heartfelt thanks for the time they gave, and the courage they showed in allowing me access to their life stories. I feel very privileged to have listened.

I must also thank other friends and colleagues who continue to influence me and show me new ways forward. A special mention here must go to Mika Brojer, Geraldine Davidson, Agnes Dyab, Michael and Morag Davis, Sally French, Peter Jackson, Kavita Kohli, John Ley, Anna McKenzie, Sandra Primack, Maureen Reed, David Rose, Tom Shakespeare, John Swain, Noel Traynor, Graham Turner and Mervyn Williams. My supervisor, Jan Hawkins, has provided me with a great deal of support and understanding, and Jane McIntosh continues to be invaluable to me.

Jessica Kingsley has once more been a most helpful, understanding and motivating publisher, the womens group have heightened the little grey cells and encouraged the discharge, and my fellow committee members of the Alliance of Deaf Service Users and Providers (Adsup) and Brenda Smith and colleagues at The City University have kept me on my toes by giving me plenty of other things to think about and do!

And finally, there is Janet, who I know is there for me, never wavering in her support, friendship and confidence in me...and the cat, Humpty Dumpty, who kept me company, threatened to have kittens, and tried to help me write (or not to write) this book. Fortunately, Tweedledum and Tweedledee arrived after it was written.

Contents

Acknowledgements vi

List of Figures ix

List of Boxes ix

Preface: Mirrors, Kaleidoscopes and Holograms 1

Ways of Seeing 2

Life Transitions and Developmental Stressors 8

The Structure of the Book 12

The People and their Narratives 12

Ethical Considerations 15

Understanding Narratives 17

Part 1 Exploring the Context

Chapter One: Whirlpools and Ripples 23

The Emergence of Self and Identity 26

Self and Identity in Deaf People 29

The Development of Identity in the Social Context 34

Family and Significant Others 38

Community and Society 41

Belief and Value Systems, and the Experience

of Oppression – Expanding Erikson's Framework 45

Exploring Notions of Deaf Identity 53

Identity Development – Creating the Ideal Environment 60

Part 2 The Narratives

Chapter Two: The Bubble and the Coal Hole 65

Chapter Three: Windows and Toast on Beans 83

Chapter Four: Boxes and the Bees' Hive 102

Chapter Five: Swamps and Rivers 123

Chapter Six: Underground Rivers 140

Chapter Seven: Coming Home 158

Part 3 Narratives in Context

Chapter Eight: Images of Deaf Futures 183
Identity in Relation to Deafness 185
Belonging – Family of Choice or Family of Origin? 189
Removing Developmental Constraints –
the Role of Humanistic Counselling 190
The Process of Counselling in Easing Transitions 190
Information and Awareness 192
Challenging Distorted Value Systems 195
Images of Deaf Futures 198

Bibliography 203

Index 210

Figures

1	Colours of feeling	5
2	Ways of seeing	6
3	The cycle of challenging and stereotyping	11
1.1	Ripples and whirlpools	24
1.2	Factors influencing identity development	25
1.3	Identity statuses	37
1.4	Examples of individualism	42
1.5	Examples of collectivism	44
1.6	Psychosocial conflicts, stigma and stereotyping	53
2.1	The bubble and the coal hole	66
3.1	Windows and toast on beans	84
4.1	Boxes and the bees' hive	103
5.1	Swamps and rivers	124
6.1	Krishna	142
6.2	Karen	144
6.3	Fiona	146
6.4	Andrew	151
7.1	Living in the past and coming home to the future	160
8.1	Identity configuration	187
8.2	Identity development in deaf people	191
8.3	'It's my parents' fault because they couldn't sign'	194
8.4	Constructing patterns of feelings, behaviours and communication	196

Boxes

1.1	The emergence of self in children	27
1.2	What deaf clients and counsellors say about psychological labels attributed to deaf people	31
1.3	Erikson's psychosocial stages	35
2.1	Attachment behaviours	78
3.1	An environment for building self-esteem	97
6.1	Ego states	153
8.1	Deaf transitions	199

Preface

Mirrors, Kaleidoscopes and Holograms

'Listen', F. Jasmine said. 'What I've been trying to say is this. Doesn't it strike you as strange that I am I and you are you? I am F. Jasmine Addams. And you are Berenice Sadie Brown. And we can look at each other, and stay together year in and year out in the same room. Yet always I am I and you are you. And I can't ever be anything else but you. Have you ever thought of that? And does it seem to you strange?' (McCullers 1946)

By thinking of 'being deaf' as a single unchanging, defining state of being, and becoming deaf as a one-off entry point to this state, we tend to construct meanings of deafness that deny the complexity of people's experience of it, and their capacity to move in and out of different states of being. We focus on single issues and explain apparent contradictions in terms of people's failure to adjust to single meanings in our model, rather than of our model's failure to accommodate the diversity of meanings in people's experience... A single state model of being deaf may also fail to acknowledge...the differences in control that people are, or are not, able to exercise in their lives. (Moorhead 1995, p.89)

Sometimes I have a strong urge to return to the sea, to stand on the cliff-top and gaze out over the currents of changing tides towards a horizon that seems solid and endless. The path of my vision wavers with each change of colour and movement as they are reflected in my soul, but the horizon anchors me, reminding me that on the other side of each great expanse of turbulence, I remain constant. This experience has always had something of a sobering effect on me – it provides me with a sense of proportion or an awareness of myself as a drop in the ocean which may at times cause ripples, but the ripples themselves, after a time of radiating outwards always return, carried by the currents, to their source. This is, in turn, a symbol of learning, where my experiences reach outwards, become mingled with the experience of others, and construct ever-evolving frameworks for my existence. But it also creates a picture of myself as a complex and composite being made of many streams of experience which come together in the sea of who I am. I ebb and recede, sometimes I am a raging storm, which stirs up my most deeply buried thoughts and feelings. I cannot see clearly through the gloom. Sometimes my inner tides carry a warmth which nurtures luxuriant, colourful growth and sometimes a chill breeze which warns of impending peril. And sometimes I am calm, peaceful, crystal clear, at one, a perfect image of my many layers and at harmony with myself, a frame for the pictures of my depths. Many of these processes are experienced by others also, but our currents and streams may have a long and hazardous journey through space and time before they can finally meet and join the circle.

Ways of Seeing

In the Foreword to *Counselling – The Deaf Challenge*, Dorothy Rowe stresses the importance of the counsellor's understanding of their client's 'ways of being'. By this she means that each of us 'creates our own individual structure of meaning, a structure of meaning which is…our way of being in the world [and which] is constantly adapted in order to survive, not just as a body but as a person'. She reminds us also of the penalty that is paid in terms of human experience when we attempt to impose a structure of meaning on an individual – our own or society's – which is at odds with that individual's understanding of herself or himself, in her reference to Brian Friel's play *Molly Sweeney* (1994), where a blind woman has the seeing world temporarily imposed on her through surgery. The play provides us with a poignant reference to the dichotomy between our own sense of ourselves and that which others have of us, in the words of Mr Rice, Molly Sweeney's doctor:

> In those last few months – she was living in the psychiatric hospital at that point – I knew I had lost contact with her. She had moved away from us all. She wasn't in her old blind world – she was exiled from that. And the sighted world, which she had never found hospitable, wasn't available to her anymore… My sense was that she was trying to compose another life that was neither sighted not unsighted, somewhere she hoped was beyond disappointment; somewhere she hoped, without expectation. (p.59)

and of Molly Sweeney herself:

> I think I see nothing at all now. But I'm not absolutely sure of that. Anyhow my borderline country is where I live now. I'm at home there. Well…at ease there. It certainly doesn't worry me anymore that what I think I see may be fantasy or indeed what I take to be imagined may very well be real – what's Frank's term? – external reality. Real – imagined – fact – fiction – fantasy – reality – there it seems to be. And it seems to be allright. And why should I question any of it anymore? (p.67)

Mr Rice speaks of 'losing contact' with Molly as she attempts to 'compose another life' which is 'beyond disappointment…without expectation', whereas Molly refers to 'being at home…at ease' in her 'borderline country' and there is an implicit sense of relief that she no longer has to worry about whether she can see or not. There is both commonality between Molly and Mr Rice about her search for meaning, and difference primarily about the outcome of this search. Literature is full of accounts of what happens when structures of meaning are imposed and I think we need to pay attention to them and apply them. For example, Margaret Forster, in her biography of the writer *Daphne du Maurier* (1993), describes a woman who, from a very young age, personified a struggle between society's expectations of her to be a devoted wife, mother and romantic novelist and her own powerful experience of being 'a boy-in-a-box' – a woman who was more attracted to and, from time to time, who became involved in secret romances or deep friendships with other women. So powerful was the battle between the inner self and the outer self which conformed, and so great were the risks of her real self being discovered that she managed to live a double life, channelling her self into her writing. But much of this writing was seen to be in the 'romantic novel' genre, and she felt very misunderstood as a writer, believing that her readers and critics failed to see the depth of what she wrote. With the growing recognition of the role of her writing as release of her unconscious, and where, Forster suggests, 'she bordered on madness', she began to express her hidden self more, though its reality remained essentially disguised in clichés and subter-fuge. When she gave full leash to her 'darker' self in one of her novels, mirroring the 'boy-in-the-box' in her protagonist who is a man, her readers were bewildered because it was a 'strange' novel, certainly not what the romantically inclined public wanted from her, and they therefore dismissed it as being 'out of character'. What is interesting about her story, however, is that when she is no longer able to write, she can no longer justify her existence because she has no outlet for who she perceives herself to be. She, in essence, faded away, perhaps because she suspected that if the significant others in her life had discovered who she was they would have responded with all the disgust of a society which is not at ease with itself and sets conditions of worth which challenge the unusual, the different, the unhealthy or the 'abnormal':

> It is as if such people are living according to a kind of legal contract, and that they only have to put one foot wrong for the whole weight of the law to descend on them. They struggle, therefore to keep themselves afloat by trying to do and be those things which they know elicit approval while scrupulously avoiding or suppressing those thoughts, feelings or activities which they sense will bring adverse judgement. Their sense of worth, both in their own eyes and in those of others who have been important to them, is conditional on winning approval and avoiding disapproval, and this means that their range of behaviour is severely restricted for they can only behave in ways which are sure to be acceptable to others. (Mearns and Thorne 1988)

I feel we need to be aware that we live in an age where we are increasingly controlled by others and moulded according to a particular image of how society ought to be. Counsellors often face the results of the suppression of the individual's freedom to be who they are in the problem situations that clients present. Those who have control over us claim that we are being given the freedom to choose, but what is such freedom when the choices themselves are limited to what others decide is acceptable for us all? They claim that restriction generates discipline, but how do we learn to be disciplined if we are not given the opportunity to learn from our mistakes, or always have to rely on others to control us and tell us what is right from within their frame of reference? What is freedom when individual creativity and ways of adapting are no longer necessary? What is freedom when rewards only come to those who fit the mould, and the rest are squandered – viewed as expendable? What is freedom when it interferes with the natural course of things?

There are, of course, many different ways of perceiving people. We make assessments of other people all the time – deciding what they are like, predicting what they will do, providing explanations for their behaviour (Hinton 1993). But we don't always question whether our assessments are accurate, not do we easily recognise that some means of communicating our perceptions are likely to breed such inaccuracy in a way which does people no justice or fairness. Often what we perceive is a function of *how* we see. For example, at a basic level, counsellors often talk about the process of counselling being like a mirror where the counsellor reflects the image that their clients present of themselves and thus enables them to see themselves more clearly. The glass of mirrors is sometimes flawed, however, and distortions are commonplace, particularly at the start of the counselling relationship. Sometimes they persist well into the middle, or even late stages, if the counsellor is not alert to the possibility that their own way of seeing their client is based on many different factors not all of which come from the client's fame of reference:

> I remember working with a recently 'separated' woman client. I kept waiting and expecting to see some element of sadness of loss or depression – but none came. I kept thinking that I saw hints of such emotions, but she denied these. So then I began to think that she must be blocking these things, and I tried to help her to find ways through these blocks. I think she got pretty fed up with that. It was only after some weeks of distinctly innacurate empathy that I realised that what was getting in the way was my personal theory on what recently separated people felt: that they would feel sad/lost/depressed. It had been extremely difficult for me to see this lively cheery woman who wanted a little bit of assistance with restructuring a new set of elements in her life. (Mearns and Thorne 1988, p.55)

Because there are limits to what a mirror can reflect and the angle from which the reflection can be viewed, the mirror image may in itself become an illusion, like the Gestaltist 'figure on ground', which 'can be seen as either two faces or as one vase, but both cannot be seen at one moment. When the one is figure, the other is background, and vice-versa' (Clarkson 1989). This emphasises that people themselves are not static, though we cannot always see the changes and transitions that are taking place. We may use what we learn to change, challenge or confirm our perceptions of a person but by the time we have achieved this – because it is not always easy to achieve – that person may have moved on to another niche of time and another set of circumstances which influence their inner self in subtle ways. Here, a hologram comes to mind because as we change our viewpoint, the image of the person that we hold itself changes, and, depending on where we view from, may reveal hidden layers or depth which have not been encountered before. If we were then to focus on the point at which these hidden layers reveal themselves we might get a sense of paraffin on water – fluidity, colours of the rainbow merging and

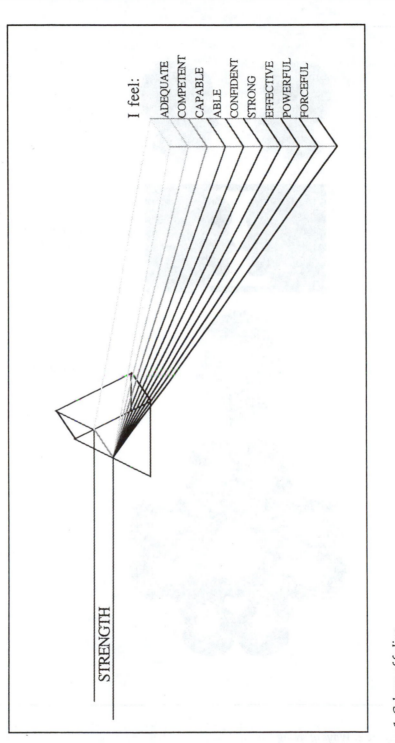

Figure 1. Colours of feeling

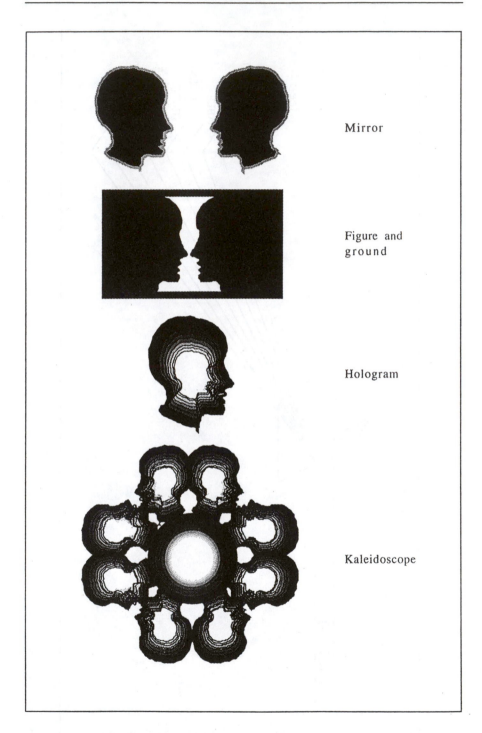

Figure 2. Ways of seeing

parting, constant changes in shape and size, lack of order and control. This recalls memories of looking through the child's kaleidoscope (Anna McKenzie 1994, personal communication) or perhaps a simple feeling passing through the glass prism of the person's soul which splits it into a rainbow of different quality, colours and intensities of feeling words (Figure 1). Kaleidoscopes themselves of course have a number of different forms. There are some, for example, where the viewer turns the end section to change the pattern and they can thus hold the pattern in one configuration to focus on and absorb the colours for as long as they wish. There are others where a rod containing coloured particles suspended in fluid is placed by the internal mirrors of the kaleidoscope and the viewer is treated to a constantly moving array of shapes, colours and patterns. In the first case, the viewer has control, in the second they have no personal control other than the ability to turn the rod upside down and start the process again. But they will probably never be able to recapture a particular image perceived in a particular movement of the fluid. They have only a transient memory.

These images are summarised in Figure 2. They are important for a number of reasons. The first reason is linked to finding a common language between counsellor and client when one or other of them is deaf,[1] and the image as a mediator of complex ways of seeing, and which cannot easily be expressed in any language, least of all the written or spoken word. This is discussed more fully in *Counselling – The Deaf Challenge*. The second is that they are symbolic of the need to move from simplistic, objectified and fixed ways of viewing people. The third is that there are different things which are relevant, meaningful and dominant in the experience of different people at different times in their lives and in different life situations. And finally, the images are representative of the *transitions* which will be explored on the following pages – transitions which take place in our individual inner worlds, in our relationships with our significant others, and the communities and societies in which we live:

> A number of social scientists...have focused more intently...on an internal (intrapsychic) developmental transformation of the sense of self and consequent ways of filtering and making sense of one's life experiences. Intrapsychic restructuring during adolescence brings identity questions to the surface; while socio-cultural factors undoubtedly may accelerate, delay or even arrest this developmental process, sequential stages in the transformation of the self and its way of understanding remain unaltered, according to this developmental perspective. (Kroger 1996, pp.5–6)

---

1   As with *Counselling – The Deaf Challenge*, I use the term 'deaf' in the broadest possible context to refer to all people for whom being deaf is an important and sometimes dominant characteristic. It may include those Deaf people who are members of the Deaf community, those who are not, and those deaf people whose relationships with both Deaf and hearing communities are not clear. The generic use of the term is not intended in any way to deny or distort the cultural conceptualisation of Deafness and Deaf People, which will be referred to using an upper-case 'D' when it is appropriate.

Life Transitions and Developmental Stressors

Counselling – The Deaf Challenge focused on the differences in the dynamics of language and communication between deaf and hearing people and on counsellor and client attitudes and characteristics which might influence the effectiveness of counselling as a 'talking through' of problem situations. As such, it is more concerned with the *issues* which are particularly relevant when *beginning* to work with deaf people and which may be overlooked for a number of different reasons. The emphasis of *Deaf Transitions* is more towards the *process* of counselling and unravelling the origins and meaning of the *content* of deaf people's narratives – both the explicit and the implicit content. This includes looking at the assumptions and misinterpretations which can be made about the meaning of personal narratives which may influence the development of trust and empathy within the counselling relationship. In this book I am assuming that we, as counsellors, *have* established a common language with our deaf clients, sufficient flexibility to modify our language as and when appropriate, and have developed a reasonable level of deaf awareness. What kind of narratives do we then explore in the counselling relationship, how do we know what they mean for our clients, and are there any further gaps in our knowledge or blocks to our understanding of these narratives which we might seek to fill or to remove? Are they fundamentally different from the narratives that we might explore with hearing clients? This represents a move from the languages used by deaf people and how they influence the dynamics of counselling as a 'talking through', to the language of counselling itself.

The desire to write *Deaf Transitions* came from an increased interest in life transitions and change, born out of a search for valid ways of *relating* deaf people to each other and to people in general, and a frustration with the stereotypes of different groups of deaf people, many of which are based on judgements and the dominance of theories which attempt to justify the divisions between them:

> Human development is interactional…a process within which the be-
> haviour of one person is meshed with the behaviour of another (Lerner
> and Spanier, 1978). It also cannot merely be confined to that time of life
> known as childhood, but has to be seen as a life-long process (Lidz,
> 1976). Not only do adults affect the development of a child but, by virtue
> of the reciprocity of interaction, a child affects the development of
> adults. From this it is a small step to note how adults, within the context
> of their relationships, affect the development of each other. Develop-
> ment is therefore a process that occurs throughout life and is of essence
> relationship bound. (Street 1989, p.74)

A particularly valuable aspect of looking at development from a life-cycle perspective is that it is something that all people appear to share as the springboard to a structure of personal and social meaning and it can therefore be the focus for exploring relationships. Although each individual is unique, there is a developmental framework of predictable stages, defined by particular developmental tasks through which *all* individuals pass as they move through life in their quest for personal meaning. In this context, whereas I do

not dispute that there is diversity amongst deaf people, I do wonder sometimes about the origin of this diversity and the wisdom of the current divisions. The term *transition* implies change and, for me, change is the source of
differences between people at any one moment in time and over time, because
it is the only thing in life that is constant. A great deal of change is influenced
by the minute-by-minute existence alongside others in a changing environment. Woolfe and Sugarman (1989) describe change as 'the basic raw material
of counselling', and go on to say that

> there is only one kind of change that can be said, with certainty, to be
> experienced by each and every human being and that is the change
> associated with aging...together with gender, race and class, age is the
> key defining characteristic of personal and social identity. (pp.28)

The concept of development as being 'relationship bound' is, I feel, a significant part of understanding any community and the individuals it comprises.
It is important at the community level because if a community is to remain
strong within itself and aware of itself as part of a wider pluralistic context,
the nature of human interaction within that community is of vital importance.
Many sociologists and psychologists would support this view. For example,
at the interpersonal level, Allport (1954) noted that prejudice and conflict are
reduced by *relating*. When common goals are pursued, persons of similar
status work together, interactions with out-group members are frequent and
varied, and stereotypes are more likely to be broken down. Rose and Kiger
(1995) have recently developed Allport's ideas with respect to deaf people.
However, at both individual and community levels, we may need to take a
broader view of the defining characteristics of personal and social identity
than suggested by Woolfe and Sugarman. Deafness and disability are, *for many
of those who are deaf and disabled and those who live and work with them*, defining
characteristics. I wonder, too, about the concept of *chronological age* as a
defining factor in a developmental process, as opposed to *life experience* or *the
gaining of wisdom*. There are many people, who, though they may be young in
years, have a depth of life experience which could be described as awesome.
The fact that this life experience is often confined to the negative aspects of
people and the pain they cause others to endure should not diminish it within
the developmental process – a process which is, after all, founded on the
transitions invoked by crisis.

From the counselling perspective, discovering how individuals within a
community can manage the continuous process of mutual adjustment and
redefinition required in social relationships without compromising their own
structure of meaning and personal power is almost a given. This management
of life transitions ultimately depends on how they can *negotiate shared meanings*
and how they *translate societal definitions* for themselves. The evidence of my
own counselling experiences is that the insidious focus on deaf people's
difference *in a negative way*, not only by hearing people in general but also by
significant others and those in their immediate socio-cultural group, is the
single most common factor that leads my clients to seek counselling. Their
family and socio-cultural environments, which should be places of safety,
have become unpredictable and uncontrollable to such an extent that their

ability to grow has become blocked and they feel totally misunderstood. This may be because when difference is viewed in a negative light, it becomes equated with isolation and marginalisation, as opposed to uniqueness. But I feel certain that it also happens because such an emphasis is one of the factors which works against the smooth progress of the developmental life cycle, and deepens the sense of crisis that clients feel when making transitions and dealing with developmental tasks. It works in this way because it is, in itself, based on a stereotyped view. In fact, whichever way we look at it, *all* the categories which are put forward as definitive statements about the nature of deafness and being deaf tend to be promoted as *universal truths* or *norms* against which deaf people are compared and by which they may be judged. We saw how judgements might show themselves in the above example of the counsellor's use of a stereotype of 'separated people' being 'sad, lost and depressed'. Each stereotyped group definition carries its own conditions of worth from the perspective of the individual who wishes to belong, and so the different categories become polarised and the relationships between them full of tension. Stereotyped world views, when they act as *stressors* (see, for example, Dallos 1991; Muncie *et al.* 1995) to individual paths to identity development, in turn influence the life cycles of the groups to which individuals belong as individuals challenge the boundaries imposed on them. The whole process, which is described in Figure 3, is reminiscent of a negative feedback loop which makes effective negotiation and translation extremely difficult and complicates the boundaries between self and others.

This negative feedback process has been described in other contexts which are also of relevance to the developmental life cycle of deaf people. For example, Carter and McGoldrick (1980, p.10) have identified a number of internal and external stressors which are associated with the development of the *family* life cycle. These include patterns of relating which are passed down over generations, family attitudes, taboos and expectations, life cycle transitions of individual family members and unpredictable events such as war, untimely death and chronic illness. Hall (1994, p.32, author's italics) describes two states of culture – tacit culture and manifest-prescriptive culture – and suggests that tacit culture can act as a stern challenge to prescribed culture:

> *Personal or tacit culture* is the antithesis of prescribed culture. It contains the paradox that even though it is shared, each person is also unique. Tacit culture is not experienced as *culture*, but simply as *being!*...We are all imprinted by personal (or tacit) culture, which is why it is so personal. It is this highly personalised experience, the 'me' quality, that makes it so difficult for people to come to grips with the reality of tacit culture. When different ethnic groups interact en masse, tacit cultural differences can be devastating.

If a stereotype does not incorporate the ability to respond to individual challenge in a positive way, then the stereotype becomes oppressive to individual freedom and structures of meaning. In this way any characteristic, attitude, behaviour or means of expression which makes up the environment surrounding each individual has the capacity both to support that individual and to act as a stressor. Understanding individuals in the counselling context

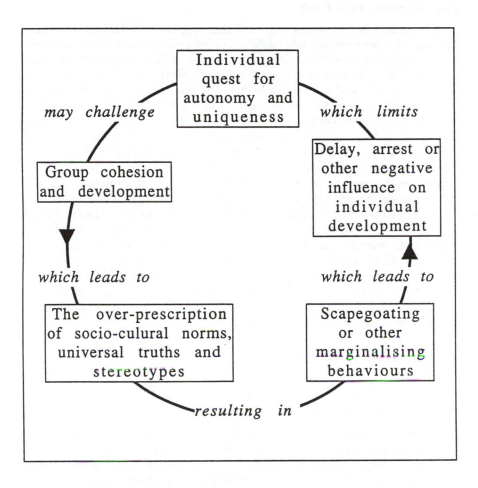

Figure 3. The cycle of challenging and stereotyping

means understanding the multitude of environmental influences, past, present and future, that make them, or may make them who they are. If they are not comfortable with who they are, it also means understanding alternative paths which they might take in self-discovery. The counsellor's role is often to highlight stressors, and, in my view, to explore with the client how negative feedback loops can be broken by considering alternative translations of societal definitions and ways in which shared meanings can be negotiated. Stressors may not always be obvious or known to the client and, for this reason, I feel that the counsellor's knowledge base must be as broad as possible in order that we can apply and relate as well as understand. There is much to be learnt from literature, philosophy, sociology and psychology, for example, which illuminates the human condition and how people come to be who they are. Such knowledge is of immense value to the process of counselling because it enables creativity, movement and growth.

The Structure of the Book

Deaf Transitions begins with a chapter discussing some of the ways in which deaf people have been or might be described and represented in developmental terms. I focus, in particular, on the concepts of self, identity and identification. We will explore some of the difficulties in making distinctions between personal identity and social identity, how the boundaries between them are blurred and how they might therefore come into conflict with each other when what the individuals want for themselves is different from what society wants from them. In the discussion on identification, we will look at the meaning of the concepts of family and community from a number of perspectives, moving into a deeper analysis of how different kinds and facets of family and community might become developmental stressors. The central chapters will follow loosely the eight stages of identity development proposed by Erikson (1968), which will be explained in more detail in chapter one. The content of each chapter will be centred upon one or more images which introduce a theme or themes dominating the chapter. These themes will be explored in the conclusion to each chapter, within the framework of the developmental life cycle and the psychosocial conflicts faced at each stage of identity development. The final chapter will bring all the various threads together, suggest some responses to the questions posed in this Preface, and explore their implications for humanistic counselling.

The People and their Narratives

The central chapters are based largely on eight life scripts or narratives which have been freely given by a variety of deaf people. I have chosen the term narrative here deliberately:

> Broadly, narrative is the telling of stories. This, however, is an inadequate definition, partly because of the low status accorded to 'story' which thus marginalises narrative...narrative is the representation of processes in time. Narrative is a moving image, a reporting of events in a sequence. While narrative speaks of time, it also normally speaks of causation, how one thing led to another... To tell a story is not just to recount indisputable and already existing facts, but to put over a message. To speak of events is simultaneously to speak of values and beliefs. It is also to take part in a real or imaginary situation. (Knights 1995, p.69)

The narrators show a significant level of emotional literacy and self-awareness; they also challenge some of the stereotyped conceptualisations that we hold of deaf people and expand our knowledge of community dynamics and developmental transitions, therefore providing some insights into how we might begin to refine our thoughts and ideas about deafness and deaf people. It must be stressed, however, that these narratives are in no way intended to present a general view of deaf people's experiences and lifestyles, nor are they necessarily representative of the deaf population. They do provide us with many examples of some of the more difficult experiences that deaf people have as they attempt to discover who they are, what or who influences the path or paths that they take to self-discovery, the kinds of barriers which can obstruct them on these paths, and the kinds of strategies they adopt to overcome these barriers. As such, they *do* represent the kinds of experiences that deaf people bring to counselling, particularly in terms of the quality of thoughts and feelings which flow between counsellor and client in the counselling relationship. For this reason, they may be difficult, even painful for some people to absorb. It is extremely important that the reader remembers this, because many of those who work with deaf people and may be interested in this book seem preoccupied with 'universal truths' about deafness and deaf people which can be empirically proven by so-called scientific method and design. The inner worlds of people are more ephemeral than that, and it is, in my experience, unusual for them to uphold these 'truths' without question when they are allowed free expression and safety. I suspect this is one reason why social 'scientists' and 'psychologists' can feel threatened by counselling. As a counsellor, it is these inner worlds that I am inextricably drawn to understanding, but in some of my other professional roles, their complexity might equally present me with problems.

The 'people' of this book will henceforth be known as Andrew, Caroline, Fiona, Joseph, Karen, Krishna, Peter and Sam, all of which are pseudonyms, and I will give no information about them other than that contained in their narratives. All are deaf and, although they all consider deafness to be a dominant aspect of their lives and describe events which have a deaf focus, their *cultural* identity is not always clear. Seven of the interviews were conducted in British Sign Language (BSL) or Sign Supported English (SSE), depending on the language preference of the interviewee, and were video-taped and translated into written English. Each interview lasted between 90 and 150 minutes. The resulting scripts were checked by the narrators, who made additions and amendments and asked for clarification where they felt it was needed. The eighth interview was a result of a written contribution which responded to a number of open questions posed by me. None of these scripts have been edited by me for content, though appropriate steps have been taken to preserve the anonymity of the interviewees by changing some of the personal details, and they have been split into sections and placed in different parts of the book. It is important to emphasise that none of these narratives come from people who are now or have been clients or students of mine. There are a number of reasons for this, the most important of which is that I find it difficult to share the *details* of my counselling sessions within the pages of a book to the depth that is required in this kind of book. Even with my clients' permission, it feels like a betrayal of their trust in me and an unhelpful exposure of the relationships I have shared with them. Moreover, I do not feel that it is always possible to successfully recreate the here-and-now of a counselling relationship when it is removed from the immediacy of the context and the environment in which it occurs. From time to time, however, throughout the following pages, I do refer to my own counsellor–client relationships but *only* where this serves to illuminate the use of a particular skill or attitude in working with a particular problem situation. These interviews were nevertheless conducted as I might work in the counselling situation. I asked only open questions, and used paraphrasing, reflecting and pinpointing skills, and I have attempted to show this in the way in which I draw the threads of the narratives together. I did find myself wanting to highlight distinctive aspects of these narratives, for example, when a particularly striking image was expressed or when poignant or deeply moving experience was related. Where this happens, I will make it clear, by giving the text of a question which I asked, for example. I did spend a high proportion of the time listening as the stories unfolded, particularly in the early stages of the narratives and, again, this is how I would ordinarily work in counselling situations. At all times, whilst wishing to facilitate free expression, I remained aware of myself in the relationships that were being developed through these interviews, and particularly of my role in the structure of the narratives that were created, and in any interpretations I subsequently made of them. This emphasises that I recognise that counselling is often a process of social construction in itself, irrespective of the approach to counselling that is used:

> There is...a strong commitment to viewing the therapeutic encounter as a milieu for the creative generation of meaning. The client's voice is not merely an auxiliary device for the vindication of the therapist's predetermined narrative, but serves in these contexts as an essential constituent of a jointly constructed reality... The emphasis then, is on the collaborative relationship between client and therapist as they strive to develop forms of narrative that may usefully enable the client to move beyond the current or continuing crisis. (Gergen and Kaye 1992, pp.174–5)

However, I am also the person who runs through all the narratives and so I form a connecting point between them, whichever way I wish to view it. In this context, the more I listened and the more the narratives developed, the more I got a sense that all these people were in the room with me together communicating with each other over time and history. Each was answering questions that others posed from their own perspective, and sometimes several viewpoints on the same issue connected the narratives in other ways. I have tried to reflect this in the structure of the book. Moreover, there were a number of occasions when the people interviewed revealed aspects of their personality which appeared to assume their own identity, and with whom they engaged in inner dialogues in an attempt to resolve some of the issues being explored. I felt, in places, that these dialogues formed a key to unlocking the narratives of deaf people's inner worlds, and so I found myself in the role of facilitator, encouraging these 'inner people' to reveal more of themselves as and when it seemed appropriate:

> We are many 'selves' each with a degree of consciousness. Our various selves may be quite dissociated and autonomous, they may be at war, or they may be more or less related, and, in an inner dialogue, move towards a harmonious community. Myself is a developing relationship between members of a community in relation to the communities of other persons. (Hobson 1989, p.157)

This description of 'communities of selves' does not refer to an identity disorder which includes the concept of multiple personality, or the psychiatric state of dissociated personality which, in itself, reflects the fluctuating fortunes in our attempts to understand the concept of identity. It is a description of the many facets of our personality, each of which seems to develop a particular role in relation to the whole, but which are usually quite spontaneously aroused by the different situations in which we find ourselves. Rowan (1990, 1993) says these facets are like moods, *transient* features – 'moments in a process of change and development which is lifelong' (1990, p.10) – of our psychological life, and which do not absolve us of personal responsibility for the actions that we take.

Ethical Considerations

There are always ethical considerations to be taken into account when writing about counselling in a way which reproduces very personal narratives. All of us who write need to be aware of this, for many different reasons. However, in this particular instance, these considerations have a further dimension which relates to a particular characteristic of the Deaf community, and at times is a source of profound despair to me as a counsellor. In Britain, the Deaf community is a very small and highly socialised community, with people travelling long distances to maintain contacts and to preserve its culture and language (Ladd 1995).[2] As with many small communities there is a tendency for everyone to know everyone else, if not directly, then through someone else, and in such circumstances, there is a lot of room for both a lack of privacy and for distorted views of individuals within the community. This is partially because Deaf people may be cut off from full access to formal, mainstream information channels, and a lot of social activities are taken up with the exchange of information about people and events in their community. Social expectations and customs mean it is quite difficult for a Deaf person to have a private self. The main channels of communication are through rumour or general hearsay, and gossip. Anthony (1992) has shown that Deaf college students who have attended residential facilities in America and use American Sign Language (ASL) were statistically more likely to be aware of rumours and to transmit rumours than students who were mainstreamed and use English-based signing systems, and which, she says, introduces culturally specific factors. She also showed that highly anxious Deaf people were more susceptible to rumour, and it is important to note that people with low self-esteem tend to be more anxious. Anthony suggests that the use of rumour and gossip may be one way through which Deaf people try to make sense of how the world works and is possibly an integral part of how Deaf people cope with an ever-changing world which at times must seem out of their control. However, as the following suggests, there is a 'flip side to the coin':

2   This may well be a cultural *expectation* rather than a cultural *reality* as socioeconomic factors and the advent of easier telecommunications for deaf people mean that social contact can now be made more easily without travel. There is evidence that the cultural dynamics of the British Deaf community are changing in some respects and this is not welcomed by all Deaf people.

One deaf [sic] writer classifies gossip as one of the mainstays of the deaf community. He also states that many deaf people are lacking in dreams and ambition. Lowered expectations have a lot to do with this. Jealousy seems to be another reason these conditions exist. The same writer describes the community as being a 'solidarity', and group loyalties have made the deaf community into a rigid conformist society. Thus, anyone trying to 'rock the boat', or attempt real achievements threatens the others. I cannot emphasise enough how widespread and infectious this is. Very little true progressive achievements can be made in the deaf community because of the excessive amount of time needed to over-come conformity. (Bertling 1994, p.93)

The disadvantages of gossip and rumour, particularly in terms of accuracy, are well documented, because every time information changes hands it risks being distorted. This may have little impact in a large community or in a small community where people generally trust each other. But they may be far-reaching in their consequences for members of a small community where the concepts of confidentiality and trust are alien to members of the community as a result of serious betrayals of trust in childhood and adolescence, for example. My despair is not with or at Deaf people, but with the systems which have created this situation and continue to reinforce it. I fear that many Deaf people still do not understand why confidentiality is an issue in the counsel-ling context, despite the growth of specialist counselling courses for Deaf people in recent years, nor why trust cannot easily be established without it. This knowledge has made me extra cautious in the way in which I have structured this book and the way in which I have used people's narratives; if I were honest, it has also made me somewhat self-defensive and protective of my work with deaf people, because I also am deaf, and subject to scrutiny by the community. It is extremely difficult to practice as a counsellor within a community where the professional skills and attitudes of counsellors are not valued by deaf people in the same way that they value communication skills, for example. This has led to growing numbers of deaf people who, with minimal training, are being encouraged to set themselves up as 'counsellors' without an understanding of or an adherence to an established Code of Practice, and without access to a level of training which will enable this understanding (Davis 1995). This should be of concern to the whole profes-sion, but, as an issue, it still tends to be marginalised by the counselling establishment, in the same way that deaf people remain marginalised and segregated, sometimes by choice, from their mainstream colleagues in coun-selling contexts. Given these difficulties, some of the narrators indicated that they were concerned they might become a 'talking point' in, or would be 'judged by' the community. Carty (1994, p.41), writing from an Australian perspective, concurs that this is an issue, and points to its origins:

Studying how Deaf identity develops is especially challenging because 90 per cent of Deaf people do not learn the essential characteristics of this identity from their families, and because the development of this identity is actively discouraged by the educational system that most

Deaf people grow up in. A further difficulty in exploring the development of this identity is that *many Deaf people have effectively blocked out
some of the painful experiences that have shaped their identities. Recalling these
experiences may be seen as risking loss of acceptance by the larger Deaf
community.* (Italics added)

Others felt that although they had reason to be very angry about some of the
things that had happened to them, they did not want to cause any pain to
their families or significant others. This latter feeling of course is not confined
to deaf people. These reservations, however, should not detract from the
quality of information given in these eight narratives.

Understanding Narratives

Humanistic psychology has traditionally been associated with dispensing
with labels and the undermining of their stereotyped use (Woolfe *et al.* 1989,
p.10). There are underlying reasons for this which might underpin many
different approaches to counselling. There are also reasons why it is important
to understand the difference between labelling *in the context of counselling* and
the kind of labelling we might engage in in everyday life:

> Labelling and diagnosing are ways of categorising people which de-
> value them and what they are saying. Labelling can be seen as a form
> of criticism, a set of presumptions, prejudgments and prejudices about
> a supposed type or stereotype of person. The person is not an individual
> in her own right, but a type of person. There are of course many such
> labels: aggressive, chauvinist, disabled, deaf, and so on, including
> derogatory, name-calling labels. It is not that labels are wrong in them-
> selves. Indeed they can be used to affirm positive identity ('Black is
> beautiful') and bring people together to challenge the discrimination
> and abuse they experience…however labelling can be a *barrier to listen-
> ing* to another person as a unique individual. (Swain 1995, p.119, italics
> added)

The key to understanding the individual structures of meaning that people
create from their life histories must lie in the images they have of their own
worlds and in their answers to the questions 'Who am I?', 'Where do I belong?'
and 'What has supported me or constrained me on my journey to self-definition?' Because *Deaf Transitions* is concerned with how *deaf* people respond to
these questions – which are fundamental questions about their identities – it
might be anticipated that their responses will include some commentary on
'What is my identity in relation to my deafness?', 'What does being deaf mean
in relation to other people?' and 'What additional tasks in the development
of my identity have I had to take on board because I am different from other
people?' In counselling, clients ascribe labels and other kinds of language to
themselves which may be chosen for their accuracy or to convey a deeply
personal meaning which signifies their history, both conscious and unconscious, and their relationships to the environment. Language may also be

ascribed in a particular way, however, because the client has expectations, real or imagined, of adverse judgements from the counsellor, who is seen to be a representative of a particular social, political, religious or cultural group which, in themselves, stem from the client's personal history.

One deaf client I recall experienced constant pain or disappointment in employment or education as a result of the reinforcement of negative attitudes towards her deafness, and she believed that such attitudes were 'the norm'. She subsequently attributed *all* misfortune in *new* employment or educational opportunities to her being deaf, and engaged in a vicious circle of self-blame which prevented her from seeking out and experimenting with such opportunities. She was unable to understand neither that her feelings about oppression were entirely justified nor that deafness can, given supportive circumstances, be viewed as an asset or as a *valuable* difference. Using particular terms and referring to particular incidents are two ways in which clients 'test trust' (Fong and Cox 1983; Corker 1994). It is very easy to give deaf people a number of familiar alternatives and ask 'Which of these do you feel "fits" you?' But their response can in some circumstances be linked to what they *know* rather than what they *feel* but cannot express. Equally, if an alternative way of describing their experience is *suggested*, it can it be absorbed and self-ascribed without thought *because it is new*, and for no other reason. For example, I recall a very difficult situation when working with a group of Deaf people. I became concerned that one group member was showing persistent homophobic feelings. I felt it was appropriate to attempt to understand where these feelings were coming from and to use the situation as an educational opportunity for the group. When I did this, he believed that I was suggesting that he *was* gay. Though I explained in great detail to them the difference between hidden worries about other people being gay and hidden fears about our own sexuality, the seed was planted. He began to put the label 'gay' on his adolescent experiences, in residential school, and to attribute the relationship problems he was having at the time to being 'gay'. The more I attempted to clarify this with him, the more every problem which arose for this man in the group became a result of 'my suggestion that he was gay'. I eventually became the archetypal 'scapegoat' who was seen as being responsible for his emotional problems.

These are only some of the dimensions to unravelling client narratives which serve to show that everything which is communicated acquires a particular psychological and emotional loading when it is framed by individual experience. Understanding how deaf clients strike a balance between self and others in the development of identity requires looking at the nature of the individual self. Exploring transitions in the client's inner world requires careful attention to the content and layers of meaning within client narratives, because these narratives are often the only evidence we have that transitions have taken or are taking place, and accurately understanding them is therefore critical. I am reminded of a long time ago when I learnt about the metamorphosis of the butterfly. I can see the physical evidence of the transitions taking place within the life cycle of the butterfly in exactly the same way in which I can observe the physical growth of human beings. But, like the microscopic, cellular changes taking place within each stage of the butterfly's metamor-

phosis, it is difficult to comprehend the extent or the nature of the psychological and emotional journeys that people undertake in order to become whole,
self-actualised human beings. That is why an awareness of different ways of
seeing became important to me. I do recognise that stereotypes and labels can
be powerful 'reservoirs of meaning' (Leyens *et al.* 1994), and I would not want
to distract from this. But I am also aware that rigid structures of meaning
which exclude or marginalise large numbers of people lead to their becoming
engaged in a tortuous and lonely struggle to create a home for themselves.
With such clients, stereotyped ways of seeing do not help me as a counsellor
to establish empathy, nor do they fully embrace the range of possibilities
which these clients need to explore in order to accept themselves. I constantly
have to remind myself of this if I am to be effective in my work.

I am clear that I do not enter a counselling relationship with a deaf person
to collude with society's polarised views of how deaf people 'ought to be', nor
to collude with the generalised view that hearing people are 'the enemy'. I
know from my own personal experience that society, and perhaps members
of the counselling profession with all their different hats, have personal
theories of how I 'ought' to be as a deaf person, and that some hearing people
are 'the enemy', though it is not necessarily because they are hearing. However, it has struck me repeatedly that in the place of safety created by the
counselling relationship, deaf clients struggle with the whole idea of 'norms'
and want to feel comfortable with themselves *as they are*. As they describe
themselves *outside* of the counselling relationship, how they behave, how they
relate to others, I sometimes get a sense of a different person to the one I know
in the counselling relationship. I feel that this may be the outcome of an
internal struggle between individual autonomy and self-esteem on the one
hand, and the power of intimacy and belonging on the other, which takes
place against a background where personal choices are limited. Different
sections of society, at different times in their history, have a series of *a priori*
narratives which impose relatively closed systems of understanding on people. When an individual is from an oppressed group they will be under
constant dual *pressures to conform* to the demands of an oppressive society
before they are granted individual status, to *'come out' as a member of that
oppressed group* and to belong to it. But this means that there must be a whole
range of intermediate ways of being. I feel we are often afraid of complexity
and of looking too deeply at the changing colours of human beings in case we
discover things which make us realise that our perceptions may be mistaken
and challenge some very fundamental beliefs that we have. The adverse
judgements, the need for approval, the scapegoating and so on are clearly
present, and, as we shall see, they are deeply embedded both within the
cultures of different communities and within individual identities. We do
need to look deeper into their origins and the contribution of individuals to
their construction in the counselling context. But what we make of our
experiences is, in the end, who we are. The question of whether 'the beast is
within or without' in the concluding chapter to *Counselling – The Deaf Challenge*
springs to mind. The beast, here, is the shadow side of everything we are and
do, which often seeks to undermine us in our search for meaning, or blocks
our paths to discovery. The answer to this question is probably that the beast

is prevalent and insidious in all of us to different degrees and in different ways, but a large part of the problem with it is either that it is driven deep underground into our unconscious urges or we cannot, or do not want to see that even our deepest shadows harbour beauty in disguise. *Deaf Transitions* seeks to liberate the beast in all of us.

Part 1

Exploring the Context

Whirlpools and Ripples

'We all of us somehow caught. We born this way or that way and we don't know why. But we caught anyhow… We each one of us somehow caught all by ourself. Is that what you was trying to say?'

'I don't know', F. Jasmine said. 'But I don't want to be caught.'

'Me neither', said Berenice. 'Don't none of us. I'm caught worse than you is.'

F. Jasmine understood why she had said this, and it was John Henry who asked in his child voice: 'Why?'

'Because I am black', said Berenice.' (McCullers 1946, p.113)

A poet is the most unpoetical of any thing in existence, because he has no identity; he is continually in for – and filling some other body.

(Keats 1818)

When I look back on my own life, there have been times when I have felt that there is this something central in me that feels 'right', calmly in control and guiding me like a beacon. I have never been able to put a name to this feeling; I am not even sure if it *is* a feeling. I just know when it is there, because I can sense it sending ripples of influence, gentle suggestions of change which radiate outwards from the core and affect everything I say and do. When I am in this state, I feel together and whole – as if I have some solidity which I can rely on and which will carry me forward on the crest of the wave. I have come, over time, to recognise that when I am 'at one' with myself, I am also 'at one' with my environment. But there have been other times when I feel this centrality being sucked downwards and inwards in a whirlpool of stress, confusion, negative forces and conditions. When this happens, I can sense a voice in my head screaming that things are getting out of control and that I am in danger of allowing the essence of my self to be dragged from its rightful home to a place where it is buried so deep that I will no longer be able to reach it.

That has frightened me because I know how much that centrality means to me and how tranquil and at peace with myself I feel as its ripples sooth away my pain, and enable me just to be, both with myself and with others. I long to have that state constantly, but at the same time, however much havoc they wreak, I probably need the eddies to remind me of how important that central feeling is to me and urge me to reclaim it. I have always had ripples and whirlpools in my life, but I have not always been able to recognise them for what they are. Often I have focused too easily on the whirlpools because it is easier to see and feel when the balance in my life is upset than to understand what it is that provides stability. I have often taken stability for granted and have used up a lot of my energy contending with the whirlpools. I can remember, too, many times in my life when stability was meaningless and everything seemed to be controlled by those around me – I became the whirlpool. The central part of me became the wishes and desires of those around me, and I did not know or understand how I could stop their control.

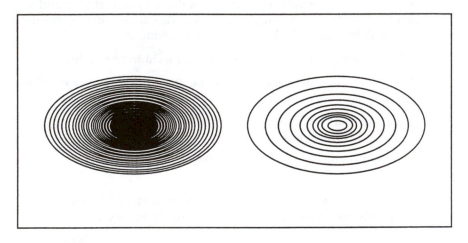

Figure 1.1 Ripples and whirlpools

Both of these images, for me, are something about self and identity. On the one hand there is a centredness which is solid and radiates outwards and beyond – 'a sea which is boundless and measureless' (Kahlil Gibran 1926), and on the other hand there is a panicky out-of-control feeling of this centredness being uprooted and drained of its influence and its energy as it gets caught up in the eddies of external forces. On the one hand there is calm and wholeness, on the other, there is conflict and division. My quest for meaning then becomes a compromise or a resolution of the two. This is of course my own perception of part of my own structure of meaning, and I would not pretend it was anything else. It also echoes some of the attempts to describe how people, including deaf people, experience and face the transitions in their lives as a result of the relationships they form with others and the influence this has on their inner worlds. Most individuals are suspended in a system which has many layers. They are part of a family, of a community and of a society and have inherited images of who they are, their belief and value blueprints and the patterns of relationships they choose from all levels of the system. This systems perspective, as it relates to identity development, is

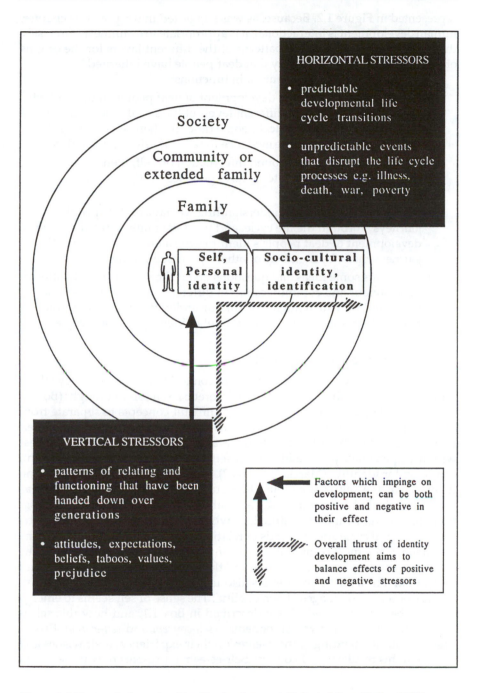

Figure 1.2 Factors influencing identity development (Adapted from Dallos 1991)

represented in Figure 1.2. Because, as was suggested in the previous chapter, human development is interactional, it is appropriate to examine more closely the structure and relationship patterns of the different layers for the origins of the images of self and identity that deaf people have inherited.

This chapter therefore has four main functions:

- It aims to look at identity development of deaf people in the context of human interaction at different levels of the social system and the different ways in which deaf people describe themselves, using this discussion to examine the evidence for a 'deaf self or personality';
- it aims to provide background information on self, identity, and identification as they relate to the experience of stigma, expectations of incompetence and loss;
- it aims to examine what understanding we have of deaf people's journeys[1] through the life cycle, and what we might infer about the development of deaf people's identities from our knowledge of the journeys made by members of other oppressed groups;
- it presents some ideas and questions about the structure and patterns of behaviour and communication in different types of families and communities, which might inform our understanding of their role as potential stressors in the development of identity in deaf people.

The Emergence of Self and Identity

Self and identity have a number of different connotations in psychology which for the most part are linked to different theoretical schools of thought (Bosma *et al.* 1994). They are, however, extremely difficult concepts to separate from a developmental perspective, though many authors suggest that the self precedes the identity in the developmental cycle and probably lies deepest within the personality – 'a solid sense of self is a necessary, but not a sufficient, condition for identity' (Marcia 1994, p.72). Another means of differentiating them is that the self is something that stays essentially the same whereas identity, as the link between the self and others, may be subject to reorganisations, redefinitions, and reconstructions which will depend on the stage in the developmental cycle and the kinds of relationships that are encountered. The definition of self most commonly used in *humanistic psychology* is that it is the 'inner core' of the personality system and the source of our mental energy and motivation. Humanistic counsellors also use terms such as 'self-awareness', 'a sense of self' and 'images of personality'. The sense of self seems to emerge in a number of stages, which are described in Box 1.1, and how this self is ultimately viewed has two components – *self-concept* and *self-esteem*. People base their understanding of themselves on their experience, their wishes and so on and this results in self-concept. Self-esteem represents how the self-con-

---

1   Journeying, here, refers to psychological and emotional journeys, rather than to physical journeys. Information about who we are can, of course, come from physical journeying, but processing and making sense of this information requires that we undertake inner journeys.

cept is evaluated. Some aspects of self-concept can be realistic whereas others can be very unrealistic. We might use the example of the tale of Cinderella. The Ugly Sisters have such inflated self-concepts that they believe the Prince will choose to marry one of them rather than marry Cinderella. They look in the mirror and see that they are desirable, but the truth is that this particular aspect of their self-concepts is so unrealistic that it amounts to self-deception, and, as Morgan (1994) says 'we are often trapped by the images we hold of ourselves'. Cinderella, however, has a realistic, if modest, self-concept that shines through whether she is a poor servant girl or a magical princess, but, at least initially, she lacks self-esteem as her appraisal of herself is of one who is too lowly for the Prince to marry.

Self-esteem comes from an appraisal of the self, according to two primary internal assessments or judgements (Harter 1988, 1990) which are related to:

- the child's experience of a discrepancy between what she would *like* to be or thinks she *ought* to be, and what she thinks she *is*;
- the general sense of support the child feels from those around her, in particular from her parents and peers.

Box 1.1 The emergence of self in children	
The symbiotic relationship	The child does not understand that her self is separate from that of her mother, and remains strongly *attached* to her mother.
A subjective sense of self	Through everyday interaction, the child begins to establish that she exists independently, that she can have effects on things or make things happen, and that she has experiences. She begins the process of *separation*.
An objective sense of self	The child realises that her self has unique properties and qualities and so she develops growing self-awareness.
Self-recognition and Self-consciousness	The child develops a desire to do things for herself, recognises herself in her reflection in the mirror or in pictures of herself and develops self-conscious or 'social' emotions such as embarrassment and empathy.
Self-definition	The child begins to define herself, to label herself in various ways and to create an internal model or image of herself, her qualities and her abilities, which affects the choices she makes and the way in which she interprets her experiences.
Self-exploration	The child tries out different experiences and being with different people, evaluates her experiences and appraises herself.
Self-concept, Self-esteem	The outcome of the development of self.

The second of these assessments makes an implicit reference to the distinction between *vertical* and *horizontal* relationships (Hartup 1989), both of which are important to and have different functions in children's development. Vertical relationships involve an attachment to someone who has greater social power or knowledge, such as a parent or teacher, and are *complementary* rather than reciprocal; that is, the adult nurtures and controls the child, while the child makes bids for attention and is dependent or obedient. Horizontal relationships are, in contrast, reciprocal and, at least potentially, equitable, and might include relationships with peers and siblings. The individuals involved are seen to have equal social power. *Both* kinds of relationship are needed for the child to develop effective social skills, the former providing protection and security and the environment in which a strong sense of self can be built, and the latter providing opportunities to try out basic skills which have been learnt and to develop skills which can be learned only in a relationship between equals, such as cooperation, competition and intimacy. The bigger the discrepancy and the lower the level of support received from vertical and horizontal relationships, the lower the self-esteem. A particularly vicious combination is when a child believes that support from her parents is dependent on good performance in some area of her life, for example in her education or the development of her social skills. If she does not measure up to the standard, she will experience both a discrepancy between her ideal and her actual achievement and a loss of support from her parents. Parental and peer values, labels and judgements help to shape the importance a child will place on some skill or quality and their self-esteem will also be affected by their direct experience of success or failure.

As was suggested earlier, many definitions of *identity* are based on a sense of something 'which remains the same despite changes', or to quote Kluckhohn in Erikson (1956): 'man [sic] is like all other men, like some men and like no other man', which brings identity closer to a sense of self:

> Compare the example of a fruit tree during the four seasons: In winter it has no leaves, in spring it blossoms and produces new green leaves, in summer it bears fruit, and in autumn its leaves turn red and ultimately fall off. Nevertheless, there is no doubt that it remains the same tree. Or take a human being: Despite the tremendous changes between conception and death, it remains the same unique person. However, despite these self-evident examples it is not at all clear what exactly the identity of the tree or that person is. And, on second thought, there is a paradox in the sense that something cannot change if it does not, in a certain respect remain the same. (Grotevant *et al.* 1994, p.8)

In placing the individual in the context of their environment and 'the tremendous changes between conception and death', an implicit distinction is made between self and others and, hence, between personal and social identity, though the two are ultimately linked:

> Identity is a constellation by which a person is known. What he or she actually is, is the self. Identity...in a psychological sense, is a person's sense of self... With respect to identity and identification, a person's identification is how he is known to others. His identity is how he is

known to himself, what he thinks and feels about himself... Identity is built from multiple identifications. (Rangell 1994, pp.27–8)

Self and Identity in Deaf People

Lane (1992) in a recent and extensive review of the literature on the personality characteristics of deaf people, points out that the list of labels associated with deaf people makes dismaying reading. We have been confronted with terms such as antisocial, dependent, immature, submissive, egocentric, naive, unintelligent, androgynous, impulsive, stubborn, depressive, neurotic, paranoid and so on. Different sections of the deaf community also have their own labels, which, as Padden and Humphries (1988) suggest with respect to the Deaf community, are not always used to establish commonality but to marginalise people who are seen to be of lesser status or undesirable. Examples based on Deaf 'norms' are DEAF-WAGE (or, in America, PEDDLER), THINK-HEARING, ORAL, MIND-RICH, ALWAYS PLAN and ORAL FAIL. All of these labels are essentially negative stereotypes of 'the deaf self', as perceived through the eyes of those Deaf people who regard themselves as a linguistic or cultural minority. These eyes, too, can have flawed lenses, distorted by their own experience of oppression. Such labels are commonly based on normative assumptions about the conditions of hearingness or Deafness, and a fixed notion of 'deaf identity'. They do not always take into account fully the origins of the conditions described, or the images that deaf people hold of themselves. I have compiled a list of responses from deaf clients and counsellors to some of the labels attributed by psychologists and other professionals which makes clear the difficulties which can happen as a result of indiscriminate and inappropriate application of labels (Box 1.2). Indeed, when I interviewed 'the people' of this book, some pointed overtly to the discrepancy between the meaning they attached to particular labels and those attached by others. Their feelings of inner conflict came from attempting to resolve this discrepancy in an environment where they were often swimming against the tide. On quite a number of occasions they point to the damage done by a failure on the part of other people to listen to and understand their structures of meaning.

KRISHNA

I realised the destructive power within a society which labels, stereotypes and devalues our experience in such a way that we actually believe in this less than positive view of ourselves. There's nothing wrong with who we are, it's how society views us and how we feel compelled to manifest their view of us. They impose their lifetime's values on us because they can't know or understand us, and they're sometimes afraid of us because we're different in some way from them. I do feel though that it is always easier for other people to label. They describe things as they see them but when you are living these conflicts inside, and living with all these different people, all with very strong views, outside, it's very hard. You feel like you just don't have that freedom of expression to define yourself in the same way that others have when they are sticking labels on you.

FIONA

For me it's like a military campaign – Deaf labelling hearing, hearing labelling Deaf. It's as if a power game is being played. In itself, this isn't a bad thing – it is part of a community finding its strength. But I feel Deaf people are losing by doing exactly the same thing to hearing as hearing people did to them – turning everything upside down.

ANDREW

All of this labelling bothers me a great deal. It's as good as saying to me that my language can only mean one thing and that is crazy. More importantly it all feels as if I am being deprived of the opportunity to use my language creatively to define myself, because the meaning that other people give to what I communicate is always stereotyped – they stereotype me. If I were to draw up a list of words which I feel describe the deaf and hearing parts of me respectively, I am quite certain that they would be hotly disputed by both Deaf and hearing people because neither accept the opposite part in me. For example, I know a lot of hearing and Deaf people who are so scared of negative feelings and so fed up with deafness being seen as a 'disease' that they can only relate to definitions of deaf people which are seen to be 'positive'. When people on occasions say to me 'You must be positive' or 'stop being so negative', I can actually feel myself flinch inside – I want to shout at them that they don't know what the words mean, and all they are trying to do is to deny the fact that I may not feel positive at that moment in time because they can't cope with it. When they meet someone like me, I become either 'hearing impaired' or 'disabled'. Well, I don't like the term hearing impaired. I am not an impaired hearing person because I know what it is to be hearing and a lot of the time I can function legitimately as a hearing person using a combination of what is accessible to me and what I have memories of. I don't need to pretend. As for 'disabled'. Yes, I am disabled – by many hearing and Deaf people who reject me, tell me I am not perfect in some way and demand that I must do *this* or be *that* if I am to be accepted. The way people label me is so simplistic. Hearing people talk about disabling explosive devices which have been found buried in order to render them 'safe', and that is exactly what they do to deaf people, try to make us 'safe' so that they minimise the chance of explosions! So what 'being positive' seems to mean is that deaf people are striving to be acceptable – that means *either* Deaf *or* hearing and certainly nothing in-between. It's as if deaf people must be seen to be uncomplicated, not complaining, doing it for themselves and being positive about it so they're no trouble any more unless of course certain people happen to think that that's not good enough because they still haven't been 'cured'. Deaf people are taught that disabled means sick or ill, that disabled people can't get involved in sport and that disabled people have no pride and no culture, and Deaf people believe it. These meanings are really meaningless for me on a personal level. But every time I venture out into the world or read a book, I see them applied to people *like* me and I feel trapped by these descriptions. Other people modify the meaning of language all the time, and that seems to be acceptable because there is a constant need to provide new editions of the various dictionaries. Yet I have to struggle for the right to use language to describe in a positive way who I feel I am, and that struggle feels like a constant attack on the sense of who I am.

These narratives and the responses shown in Box 1.2 demonstrate a reluctance to take on board narrowly conceived labels. They are saying: 'We think we

---

Box 1.2 What deaf clients and counsellors say about psychological labels attributed to deaf people

Poor Conceptual thinking, restricted reasoning, poor insight and self-awareness	We are not taught about concepts or the semantics of experience. Our education is characterised by learning about the structure of language. The deaf self is not valued and poor attempts are made to construct a contrived hearing self.
Aggressive, irritable, moody, frustrated easily, explosive	How would you feel if these labels were applied to you? It's worth bearing in mind the following simple formula;

$$\text{Severity of Problem Situation} = \text{Distress} \times \text{Uncontrollability} \times \text{Frequency}$$

Naive, credulous, childlike, dependent, submissive, suggestible, doubting, immature, lacking in initiative	Most channels of information are inaccessible; hearing people make judgements about what we ought to know; we are taught to believe and accept that everything which is thrown at us as 'right'; we are not taught how to take responsibility for ourselves, how to be independent, or how to trust, and, as if that is not enough, we have limited access to counselling.
Motor development slow, mechanically inept	How do deaf people with fluent sign language compare to hearing people who are learning it?
Paranoid, suspicious, psychotic reactions, neurotic, egocentric	Well, we do constantly wonder what people are saying to us and there are many lip patterns which look like our name. The term 'psychotic' was coined to describe the character of people in prisons. It is sometimes said that being deaf in a hearing world is like being in prison. We have to be egocentric and keep the ball in our court to manage communication better, some would say, to survive.
Possessive, rigid, stubborn	Most of us have had to fight doubly hard to achieve what we have. We are not about to give it up easily. We are not taught about the 'shades of grey' and so we can become trapped in 'black and white' thinking and behaviour.

**Box 1.2 What deaf clients and counsellors say about
psychological labels attributed to deaf people**

---

*Asocial, unsocialised,
clannish, isolated,
competitive, morally
undeveloped*

How many of you positively go out of your way to
socialise with deaf people? How many of you have
minicoms at home? How many of you go home to
switch off from deaf people? Some of our parents
believed that we were too immature to have sex
education, and that we would not be able to cope
with information about AIDS or homosexuality, for
example. Are audism, sexism, racism, religious
persecution and homophobia morally correct? (Do
we live in a morally developed society?)

*Shy, serious, shrewd,
passionate, unconfident*

Hands up whether any of these words apply to
you!

*No language, poor
language, unintelligent,
unaware*

No education, poor education. But I've got a
Masters Degree!

*Concrete, hedonistic,
androgynous*

Concrete is that stuff that they make houses and
pavements with, isn't it? Excuse me while I consult
my dictionary for the other two.

*Failure internalised,
failure externalised*

Sounds like somebody can't make their mind up!

Depend on admiration

We don't get much if these labels are anything to
go by!

---

now what you mean, but our meaning of the situations we experience, which
have led you to ascribe these labels to us, is different. We need alternative
language which reflects more accurately who we are and how we feel.'

Remvig (1971) and Basilier (1973) found that impulsiveness and rigidity,
certain narcissistic features and inclinations to concrete thinking were common in *poorly functioning* deaf children and adults, and both point out that
these characteristics could almost always be regarded as the result of communication difficulties and the ensuing social and cultural deprivation. This latter
point is in accordance with the view of Denmark (1994) in his exploration of
mental health issues in relation to deaf people. The earlier studies point to the
large numbers of deaf people who function well both at work and socially and
suggest that deafness *per se* does not cause personality disorders. In a significant British study, Gregory *et al.* (1995, pp.183–5) found little evidence for a
distinct deaf personality, and certainly not one which could be described only
in negative terms:

> It was encouraging to see that most of the young people, nearly two-
> thirds, described themselves as happy and only one in ten was not
> happy. In terms of calmness, just over one-third who answered saw
> themselves as calm, while just under one-third felt they became 'easily

worked up'. While four out of ten felt generally confident, for a further four out of ten, whether or not they felt confident depended on the situation, and one in five never felt confident. Likewise, for more than four out of ten whether or not they showed their feelings depended on the situation, although about one quarter felt they were never able to show how they felt... A picture emerges of a group of young people, of whom the majority liked themselves and felt proud of themselves, although most of them had aspects of themselves they would have liked to change. The most negative finding was that the majority did feel sorry for themselves. No consistent personality patterns appeared to emerge, and a range of personality characteristics was described, as it might be in any group of young people.

Young deaf people with low self-esteem are cited as 'a cause for concern' in this study but the authors stress that is it difficult to isolate causes of low self-worth or to make definitive statements which apply to all the young people who show lack of self-worth. Again, this might be said to be true in any group of young people. However, American researchers have suggested that one important factor in the development of a poor self-concept lies in the vertical relationships formed by deaf children, particularly when adults exercise excess control (Bell and Harper 1977) and have expectations of incompetence (Wood 1989) which results in children developing a distorted view of the nature of social relationships (Lederberg 1993). Marschark (1993, p.62, italics added) also suggests that in situations where deaf children experience horizontal relationships with others who are *similar* to them, as might happen in a residential school, for example, they experience an enhanced sense of identity:

> Although in some ways the residential school may limit children's range of experience with 'normal' aspects of social development, in other ways they are afforded opportunities of social interaction that would be missing, or at least impoverished, in a public (*mainstream*) school setting. Some of the possibilities – on both sides of the coin – may seem trivial to some investigators: hanging about in the mall, riding a bicycle to school, telling dirty jokes, and flirting in the playground. However, the implications of such behaviors for coherent social and personality development during the school years cannot be ignored. Such experiences lead directly to children's acquisition of an internal locus of control, an accurate self-image, and positive self-esteem.

Locus of control (LOC) is a term first described by Rotter (1966) to indicate the degree of responsibility which people take for themselves. Persons who tend to have a greater internal locus of control assume responsibility for their own behaviour and perceptions, are more self-confident in their decisions and less likely to seek authority for guidance. Individuals with an external LOC seldom take responsibility for their own behaviour. LOC is therefore quite a good indicator of self-esteem. Several studies (e.g. Bodner and Johns 1977; Dowaliby *et al.* 1983; Montgomery and Laidlaw 1993) suggest that deaf people tend towards being more external in their LOC than hearing people. Montgomery and Laidlaw (1993) cite the example of deaf employees who perceive responsibility for work output as externally located, as tending to treat hearing colleagues as handy full-time welfare or social workers instead of helpful workmates who have a job of their own to do. They emphasise, however, that there are those who try to get by with the least effort expended in all sectors of the population and this is not necessarily an indication of an external LOC. Further, other authors, such as Hurwitz (1992) suggest that self-determination by deaf people is a relatively recent occurrence resulting from political activity in response to oppression by hearing people. Set against this, Rodda (1966) and Gregory (1976) have indicated that deaf children are less likely than hearing children to receive explanations from parents and others about emotions, reasons for actions, role expectations and the consequences of various behaviours. This, together with the limited education they subsequently receive and the continuing lack of access to a full and fluent language, can mean that some deaf children and young people do not have enough knowledge for the cognitive, emotional and social exploration necessary for social and political action. For example, the recent British Deaf Association report *Visible Voices* (Hawcroft *et al.* 1996) showed that Deaf people need to have their skills and confidence built up before they can become fully involved in decision-making processes, and they lose interest if decisions are not made quickly.

The Development of Identity in the Social Context

Rogers (1959) and others argued that the self as a concept has meaning only in relation to others, and therefore postulated a movement away from the internal concept of self through a process of communication and social interaction. This is in keeping with the psychosocial view that we come to reflect the groups to which we belong, a view which is echoed above in Rangell's distinctions between self, identity and identification and fits with distinction between *personal* or self-identity and *social* identity originally proposed by Erikson (1959, p.102).

> The term identity expresses a mutual relation in that it connotes both a persistent sameness within oneself (self-sameness) and a persistent sharing of some kind of essential character with others... At one time it will appear to refer to a conscious sense of individual identity; at another, to an unconscious striving for a continuity of personal character; at a third, as a criterion of the silent doings of ego-synthesis; and finally, as a maintenance of inner solidarity with the group's ideals and identity.

According to Erikson's psychosocial theory (1963), identity develops through a progressive resolution of conflicts between needs and social demands. At each of eight proposed stages, conflicts must be resolved at least partially before the next set of problems can be approached. Box 1.3 describes these stages and gives some examples of successful and unsuccessful outcomes. We saw above, reference to the first stage, and it might be useful to expand on this. The child's first task is to resolve the conflict between trust and mistrust and the success with which this can be done will depend on whether they form secure attachments with their parents. Generally, those who do form

Box 1.3 Erikson's psychosocial stages

Psychosocial conflict	Key tasks and activities of the stage	Helpful outcome	Unhelpful outcome
Basic trust – mistrust	Trust in mother or primary caregiver; forming a secure attachment; trust in own ability to make things happen.	Hope; Tolerate frustration; Delay gratification	Suspicion, withdrawal
Autonomy – shame, doubt	Learning new skills which increase choices, and learning self-control and self-determination with gentle discipline; avoiding being made to feel incompetent, which leads to shame.	Self-esteem; Self-control; Will	Compulsion, irresponsibility
Initiative – guilt	Organise activities around some goal; become more assertive and aggressive. Harsh or demeaning parental response may lead to guilt.	Feeling of purpose; Enjoying achievement	Inhibition
Industry – role confusion	Take in all basic cultural skills and norms and gain recognition. If not praised for achievements will develop feelings of inadequacy and inferiority.	Competence	Inadequacy, inferiority
Identity – role confusion	The search for a continuity and sameness in oneself; understanding our gender, sexuality, race, social affiliations, values and likely occupation. If one or more of these is not resolved, role confusion can result.	Allegiance; Loyalty	Shyness, defiance, socially unacceptable behaviour
Intimacy – isolation	Form one of more intimate relationships; make commitments in relationships; form family groups. Competition form others or fear means a failure to commit, which can lead to isolation.	Love	Alienation; lack of commitment; exclusivity
Generativity – stagnation	Bear and rear children; productivity at work; creativity in one's life; educating the next generation; developing social conscience; avoiding self-absorption.	Care; Social conscience; Social justice	Rejection of others; self-indulgence
Integrity – despair	Integrate all the above and accept self; avoid regret for wasted chances and unfortunate choices which leads to despair.	Wisdom	Derision; self-disgust; arrogance

secure attachments at this stage are able then to show basic trust in their interactions with the social world as a whole. If they know their parents can be relied on they generalise these expectations onto other people:

> Gradually, a rudimentary sense of personal identity emerges. Infants realise that their memories, images and anticipated sensations are firmly linked with familiar and predictable things and people. This comfortable certainty about the world and their place in it allows babies to venture into new realms of experience. (Hoffman et al. 1994, p.207)

Marcia (1966, 1980) proposed that the process of identity formation has two parts – a *crisis*, or what he later (1994) called *exploration*, and a *commitment*. Exploration is a period of decision-making when old choices and values are reexamined, and it can occur either gradually or abruptly. It usually involves challenging childhood positions and some withdrawal from them. The outcome of this process is often a commitment to a specific role or a specific set of beliefs and values, or both. A genuine commitment is one which individuals have made for themselves and which would be abandoned by them with the greatest of reluctance. Marcia's work expanded on the description of the stages of psychosocial development put forward by Erikson, in particular at the adolescent stage where both believed that a clear sense of identity was established because all the parts which are needed for integration of the ego identity do not exist together before that time. These parts are:

- gender;
- mature physical capacities;
- sexuality;
- ability to reason beyond the concrete operational level;
- responses to social expectations to become more than a child.

He described the interaction between crisis and commitment which resulted in four possible identity statuses which *late adolescents* may be expected to be resolving (see Figure 1.3):

> The original dichotomy of Identity – Identity Diffusion (Confusion) did not capture adequately the variety of styles of identity resolution that our initial research participants described to us about themselves. Specifically, some arrived at an identity by means of an exploratory period; others just became more firmly entrenched in the identities bestowed upon them in childhood. Some seemed to have no firm identity resolution and were relatively unconcerned about this, while others, similarly unresolved, were very concerned and struggling to reach some closure on the issue. (Marcia 1994, p.72)

Different kinds of socio-cultural environments perceive individuals in very different ways and embody different relationship patterns, beliefs and values. The dominant cultural milieu may or may not be conducive to particular developmental trends, and the particular features of both the individual and their environment will lead to different experiences of being 'caught'. Most people will experience the 'crises' that Marcia (1994) describes and which

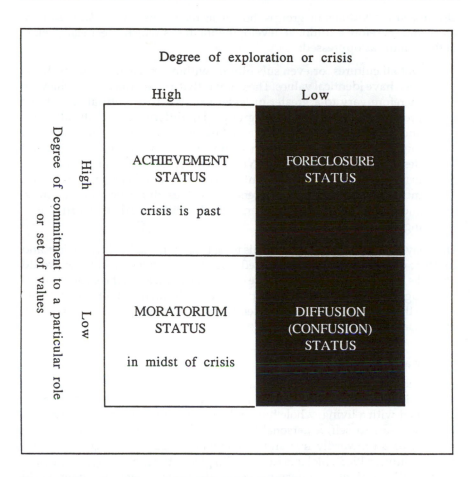

Figure 1.3 Identity statuses (adapted from Marcia 1980)

originate from the quality of their interaction with the socio-cultural environment. These might include, for example, conflicts emerging from the social
organisation of that environment and patterns of communication. Their resolution is part of the natural process of identity development. Any factor which
prevails against the integration of the parts outlined by Marcia in the above
discussion will influence the way in which identity develops. In this context,
it is important to note that:

> If the initial identity configuration attained at late adolescence is a
> self-constructed one, rather than one which has been conferred upon
> the individual, achieved rather than ascribed, successive identity refor-
> mulations can be expected throughout the life cycle as the individual
> meets and resolves the challenges involved in ego growth. Hence, the
> initial identity, if it is a self-constructed one is not the last one. (Stephen,
> Fraser and Marcia 1992)

Oppressed individuals or groups, however, may experience *additional* conflicts, and therefore additional developmental tasks which specifically relate to their status as oppressed:

> Not all cultures, or even subcultures within a particular society, however, have identical values. Those goals that are seen as worth achieving therefore vary to a greater or lesser extent across cultural and ethnic groups and even within those groups. The differences in cultural values and attitudes between deaf and hearing populations, for example, might result in deaf children having somewhat different goals and desires than hearing peers... When considering the possibility of divergence in the achievement orientations of deaf and hearing children, we must therefore consider differences in values, differences in standards, and differences in who are seen as the 'significant others' worth pleasing. (Marschark 1993, p.63)

This may cause oppressed individuals to be faced with unhealthy choices and conflicts where there is an exacerbated dissonance between what they would like to be and who they think they are on the one hand and who society thinks they 'ought' to be and who they are perceived to be on the other. We will now explore this further by a focus on different levels of the social context on which individuals are suspended.

Family and Significant Others

The critical role of the family in paving the way to the development of a healthy identity has never been disputed. Freud reminds us that 'we are concerned with a living, whole human being and how he [*sic*] can become a viable ego, a real self, a personal "I" with all his inborn energies flowing together as an inwardly free and spontaneous capacity to enjoy, love and create' (Guntrip 1968). Melanie Klein (1932) placed the roots of self very firmly in the mother–infant relationship, even to the point where the wider world was regarded as being insignificant in the development of the self. This would seem reasonable given the idea that the development of self precedes the development of identity, and it does not preclude environmental and social factors from influencing the development of identity. Further, because the developmental needs of an individual exist alongside those of other family members, who may themselves be at different developmental stages, conflicts can arise directly as a result of this. A failure to resolve these conflicts can affect the whole life span of the individual. For example, many people from oppressed minorities share childhood and adolescent histories where identity confusion or confusion about affectional needs was equated with threat or conditions (Bee 1994). Some observed oppressive behaviour directed at adults like themselves which resulted in a lingering sense of dread. The fears resulting from these situations included humiliation, lack of communication, rejection or abandonment by significant others, peers and society at large.

The family environment is often where oppression first shows itself, in part because of a parental realisation that a child who is different may make additional demands of them which means that parenthood may not follow its natural course. There are a number of suggested reasons for this, one of which is that *the life cycle of the family* falls out of synchronisation with the life cycle of individuals within the family, which places the family under greater pressure to change and reorganise itself without disintegrating. The family life cycle could be seen as a subdivision of the intimacy, generativity and integrity stages of Erikson's model. Haley (1981) identifies the critical transitional stages as:

- the courtship period
- marriage and its consequences
- childbirth and dealing with the young
- middle marriage difficulties
- weaning parents from children
- retirement and old age

These transitions relate to what might be called 'the nuclear family' of mother, father and children. However, this model applies only to 5 per cent of households at any one time. In 1980 one in five children could expect to experience the divorce of their parents (Wallerstein and Kelly 1980) and there is considerable evidence that the divorce rate has risen since then. Increasing numbers of adults decide not to have children and to emphasise generativity through their work, for example. The 1980s and 1990s have seen the rise of the much maligned single-parent family. Some single parents form new relationships following divorce or marry for the first time someone who has been divorced and has children of their own, giving rise to stepfamilies. Others do not marry but cohabit, or cannot marry because of legal constraints as in the case of gay and lesbian parents, for example. Some opt for celibate relationships and still others, because of culturally entrenched factors, live in extended families or communes. These are all examples of *societal and cultural definitions of families* and, as Dallos (1991, p.5) suggests, families must 'translate these societal definitions for themselves and the continuous processes of mutual adjustments and redefinitions that are required in order to manage family life':

> [for example] 'leaving home' is in itself culturally constructed. There are differences between various cultures and sections of a culture. In Asian societies and agricultural communities in Britain, it may be quite acceptable for the children to continue to live at home after marriage. Culture can be seen to lay down the broad brushstrokes of how things should happen in families, but each has to work out the details. (Dallos 1991, p.5)

Gunter (1992) also makes the useful distinction between a *family of choice* and a *family of origin*, which may be of particular relevance to members of oppressed or disadvantaged groups. With reference to gays and lesbians, he suggests that they often have a primary identity with the family of choice for several reasons which might include, for example, rejection of or by the family of origin, the need to identify with or establish a primary family unit and the expectations of society that people have a family identity. Gunter feels that little attention has been given to the qualitative differences between the family

of choice and family of origin and lists important factors for consideration
such as:

- formation of membership
- boundary system maintenance
- goal setting
- structural types

Despite the evidence we have of many different kinds of family, the nuclear
family configuration is still the one which people are encouraged – in some
societies, pressurised – to aspire to, even though it is impossible for some to
achieve this, and completely undesirable for others. A viable family life cycle
model must highlight the interplay between the images of the family offered
by society and the family's interpretation and internalisation of them. The
roles and experiences facing many families are highly complex, as are the
behaviours they engage in as they attempt to resolve potential conflicts. For
example, Baumrind (1967, 1971, 1973) focused on four aspects of family
functioning: nurturance or warmth, firmness and clarity of control, level of
maturity demands and the degree of communication between the parent and
the child, which tended to result in particular patterns or styles of parenting.
She identified three main patterns, *permissive*, *authoritarian* and *authoritative*,
which emphasised the interrelationships between the four aspects of family
functioning. A further category, *neglectful*, was added by Maccoby and Martin
(1983). The most consistently positive outcomes have been associated with
the authoritative pattern, in which the parents are high in both control and
warmth, setting clear limits but also responding to the child's individual
needs. Children from such families tend to show higher self-esteem, are more
independent but at the same time are more likely to comply with parent
requests, and may show more generous behaviour towards others as well.

Dallos (1991) has renewed the focus on the communicative function of
families or how families develop patterns of shared behaviour, beliefs and
emotions. He suggests that family behaviour might be described in terms of
circular causality, where communication is a never-ending, never-beginning
flow (Watzlawick, Beavin and Jackson 1967). Communication and beliefs are
interdependent, particularly in the sense that what we experience the other
person communicating is at least partially determined by what we 'expect'
them to communicate. This is as true of a counselling relationship as it is of
family relationships:

> Whenever a therapist or researcher and a family meet, both will form
> impressions about how the other sees the world, including importantly
> what they think families are and should be. None of us has a monopoly
> on this endeavour; families as much as therapists, psychologists, psy-
> chiatrists and social workers equally have the ability to construct mean-
> ings, to make sense of the world around them and what is happening
> to them. (Dallos 1991, p.2)

Each partner's behaviour can be seen to be maintained in the actions of the
other, and the way in which patterns are organised is designed to set a
dynamic equilibrium which forms the boundaries or limits for what kind of

behaviour is acceptable and allowed and represents the benchmark for family functioning. In systems theory, this dynamic equilibrium would be called *homeostasis*, and most families will go to great lengths to preserve it, *whether it is realistic or not*:

> The family...was initially encountered at a large psychiatric institute to which they had turned in their search for a remedy for five and a half year old Mary's unusual behaviour. Family members stated that Mary was a verbal and intelligent child who malingered and refused to speak in public in order to embarrass the family. Extensive clinical examination revealed Mary to be severely retarded [*sic*] and unable to perform at anywhere near the level of confidence claimed by her parents and two older siblings... Initial viewings of the videotapes suggested that family members' transactions were permeated by subtle, almost artful, practices that could function to create the image of Mary as an intelligent child. (Pollner and Wikler 1985)

There is not always conscious awareness of this, however. Active and passive expressions from primary caregivers may range from overt condemnation of difference as a deviance which cannot be tolerated, through criticism of the behaviour of adults who conform to a number of negative stereotypes of that difference, to a complete silence in the family or a denial of the existence of that difference. Other passive societal dimensions may be expressed through family expectations or assumptions of 'normality' and these can be reinforced more directly by active or passive expression of ambivalent or oppressive feelings by professionals who come into contact with the family.

Community and Society

Families are themselves suspended in a social and cultural matrix which, as was suggested above, places its own demands on the developmental life cycle of families and individuals within them. Perhaps one of the most important ways of viewing society as the origin of these demands, and one which has particular implications for counselling, lies in whether the society or community in which we live has an individualist or a collectivist world view. Hofstede (1991, p.51) defines these world views as follows:

> Individualism pertains to societies in which the ties between individuals are loose: everyone is expected to look after himself or herself and his or her own immediate family. Collectivism as its opposite pertains to societies in which people from birth onwards are integrated into strong, cohesive in-groups, which throughout people's lifetime continue to protect them in exchange for unquestioning loyalty.

The differences between individualist and collectivist societies can be described in terms of belief and value systems, and relationships between individuals and groups, in particular the fluidity or rigidity of boundaries between individuals or groups of individuals and the level of demarcation between individuals. Individualist societies emphasise 'I' consciousness, autonomy, emotional independence, individual initiative, the right to privacy, the need for specific friendship and universalism. These societies, in their

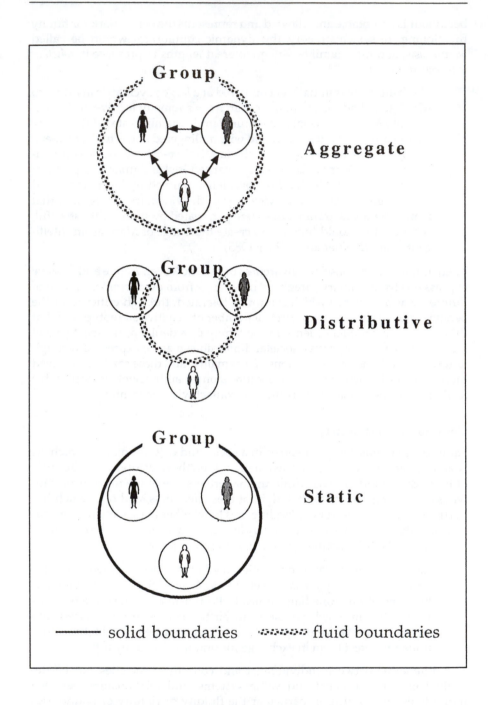

Figure 1.4 Examples of individualism (Adapted from Kim 1994)

stress on the *I* versus *you* distinction and on having an explicit and firm boundary between self and others, take an *independent* view of the self. Individualist societies have three main forms which Kim (1994) calls *aggregate*, *distributive* and *static* (Fig 1.4). In *aggregate* mode distinct and independent individuals are emphasised, who need to detach themselves from family, community and other ascribed relationships, and who are bound together by normative and ethical principles, rules and norms. There is 'a belief that each of us is an entity separate from every other and from the group' (Spence 1985, p.1288), and our boundaries are defined by our 'own internal repertoire of thoughts, feelings and actions' (Markus and Kitayama 1991, p.226) rather than those of others. Thus, the values of freedom, independence, self-determination, personal control and uniqueness are stressed, and individuals base their interaction with others on principles such as an internalised concern for the welfare of others, a preparedness to take prosocial action, equality, competition, equity, noninterference and exchanges based on contracts. American culture is often viewed as being an example of the aggregate mode of individualism. In *distributive* mode, the group is defined by common interests and attributes, and arises in part because of this commonality. The group boundaries are therefore fluid, and the group persists as long as it satisfies the needs and interests of its members. The distributive mode stresses relationships based on contracts between providers and users of services, for example. Voluntary organisations and interest groups are examples of the distributive mode. Such groups can become dominant and develop their own subculture to such an extent that they are in direct conflict with the goals of other individuals and of society and cannot be easily challenged. The boundaries become less fluid, and the group may come to resemble the static mode. An example might be where a profession develops a complete monopoly on the services it provides. Services are developed in the interests of members of the profession at the expense of the service users' interests and the profession then becomes relatively resistant to change. In *static* mode, emphasis is placed on the individual's 'inalienable' rights and institutions which uphold these. The welfare of disadvantaged, defenceless and powerless people is protected by law, as is the individual's right to autonomy and the freedom to pursue their own goals. Individuals tend to be unrelated to each other in static mode and so may not always act in responsible, moral, sane or humanitarian ways (Hogan 1975). The laws and regulations in such societies are therefore established and enforced so that people do not infringe the agreed group boundaries and no one enjoys special privileges, though individuals and groups can challenge the boundaries of these societies if they are regarded as an violation of their rights.

Collective societies, in contrast, stress 'we' consciousness, collective identity, emotional dependence, group solidarity, sharing, duties and obligations, a need for stable and predetermined friendship, group decision and particularism (Hofstede 1991; Hui and Triandis 1986; Sinha and Verma 1987). They generally take an *interdependent* view of the self (Markus and Kitayama 1991), and are defined by specific and firm group boundaries which emphasise a *we* (the in-group) versus *they* (the out-group) distinction. Their emphasis on collective welfare, harmony and duties does not usually extend to out-groups.

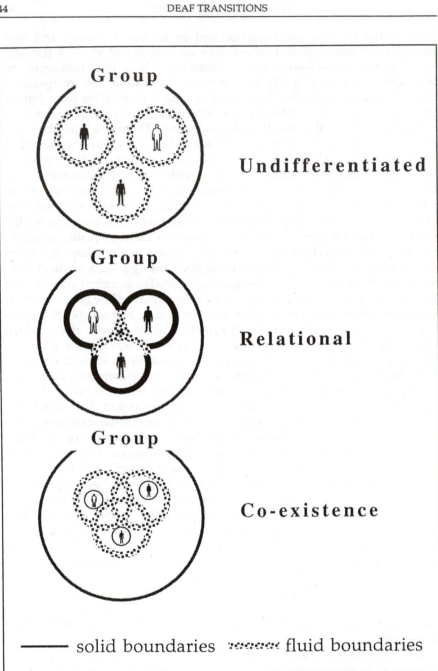

Figure 1.5 Examples of collectivism (adapted from Kim 1994)

There are three main ways of viewing a collectivist society which Kim (1994) describes as the *undifferentiated, relational* and *coexistence* forms (Fig. 1.5). In the undifferentiated form a person who has failed to achieve a measure of individuation and separation is defined by an 'enmeshed' identity, individuation being the state where an individual strikes a balance between enmeshment and absolute detachment from their societal or cultural group. Alternatively, this form is characterised by someone who has achieved individuation and separation but has chosen to give up their personal identity in order to immerse themselves completely in an in-group. The undifferentiated form may be observed in some religious cults or ideological groups, and, in extreme cases, a person may be governed *and defined by* an in-group (Triandis 1988). In the *relational* form, boundaries are fluid and thoughts, ideas and emotions pass freely through them. Relationships between in-group members are founded on common factors and these are transmitted to and shared by all people in the society. Children who grow up in such societies are expected to transfer appropriate social values of interdependency, identification and loyalty to all those they come into contact with in different contexts. The relational form has been observed within Korean (Choi, Kim and Choi 1993), Chinese (Yu and Yang 1994), Indian (Sinha and Tripathi 1994) and Turkish (Kagitcibasi 1994) cultures. The *co-existence* form of collectivism allows diverse, sometimes contradictory elements to coexist within a culture and within a person, and separates the private self from the public self, the public self having collectivist values and the private self maintaining individualist values of self-cultivation and personal quests (Sinha and Tripathi 1994). It is often a particular feature of Indian and Japanese cultures.

Each kind of society, like the family, will have its own patterns of communicating. For example, in the situation where a society moves from distributive to static mode to become a monopoly, which was described above, professionals might use particular styles of communication to reinforce the status quo. Alderson (1993) has argued that all decisions taken about surgical intervention in the Health Service are either reasoned with patients or forced on them, and that reason and force are at opposite ends of the spectrum, with persuasion in the centre. Within this scenario adults who did not feel children were competent to consent to surgery tended to dismiss professional coercion as necessary firmness, as if children's fear is irrational and therefore unimportant. It is this kind of mutual reinforcement in the 'powerful' elements of the vertical relationship which edges the child out of the picture as I have described elsewhere (Corker 1992, 1994). Alderson says that 'the most powerful way to justify coercion is to deny that children can reason, and to align reason with force; children's resistance is then seen as mindless "self-destruction", to be overriden by rational adults'. The resulting feelings of betrayal in the child can lead to a crisis over such issues as trust, which may regenerate the earlier psychosocial conflicts.

Belief and Value Systems and The Experience of Oppression – Expanding Erikson's Framework

Erikson's description of the life cycle makes reference to *age-related* stages and factors (Woolfe and Sugarman 1989), which have been deliberately omitted from Box 1.3. This is because it has been recognised that the proposed stages of psychosocial development can happen at different times for different people, and there are many factors which contribute to the resolution of conflicts which can drastically alter the timing of different stages. Some are obvious; for example, the period of generativity may last much longer today because people tend to be active to a more advanced age (Erikson and Hall 1987). Furthermore, Erikson's model is a male model and he stresses heterosexuality as the only valid expression of the ability to love (Erikson 1963, pp.261–6). Gilligan (1984) notes that for women, identity formation and intimacy occur simultaneously throughout the life span. The woman 'comes to know herself as she is known, through her relationship with others', while men are known and may learn to know themselves more in relation to the world of objects (p.12).

This reflects a general limitation in Erikson's framework in that it cannot easily explain and incorporate the cycles of identity development of those who are oppressed, nor can it embrace the developmental responses which oppressed people must make to the experience of:

- stigma
- competence expectations
- loss, both of social support and of society's image of 'the ideal self'

Brown (1986) says that if one's group is not positively evaluated by the larger culture and if:

- group boundaries are ill-defined
- movement in and out of the group is possible
- the social system in which the group is situated is perceived by the individual as legitimate and stable,

then the individual is more easily able to renounce group membership, exit from difficult relationships and continue their search for social identity. However, if one's group is not positively evaluated and the opposite conditions exist, it will be more difficult, sometimes impossible, for an individual to continue their identity search. They may have to 'pass', which will be described further below, or risk damage to their self-image. Clearly, the different forms of family, individualism and collectivism have very different implications for the way a person relates to their environment and for how individuals and groups are evaluated within the larger culture:

> Culture embodies those moral, ethical, and aesthetic values, the set of spiritual eyeglasses through which they come to view themselves and their place in the universe, Values are the basis of people's identity, their sense of particularity as members of the human race. (Ngugi Wa Thiong'o 1986, pp.14–15)

I would like, here, to explore this on a deeper level by exploring what we understand of identity development in two oppressed groups – gay and lesbian people and black and ethnic minorities.

In the humanistic sense, most individuals are *driven* towards patterns of being and belonging which preserve self-esteem. It follows, then, that the marginalised development of oppressed groups is often *reactive* – a backlash against attempts to impose a false reality which becomes a part of the process of identity development. Identity development must build in a way of creating new meanings, which can result in a commitment to a different socio-cultural structure of meaning which preserves and supports a different, more comfortable and more authentic way of being. However, there may be hidden costs for individuals. For example, a result of this backlash is that sometimes the family of origin is rejected in favour of a 'family' or community of choice because the family of origin represents and behaves true to the oppressive aspects of the majority culture. But this may mean that the experience of loss is amplified. Another possible pitfall can occur if the new meaning is a collective meaning which does not allow for individual freedom of expression and for individual interpretations:

> Paradoxes are inherent in all labelling and stereotyping in that they both aid and destroy identity simultaneously. They serve the forces of domination and control by restricting and limiting experience while stimulating radical innovation and creative strategies for accomplishment and eventual triumph. Derogatory labels are use by the victims as well as the victimisers and while self ridicule may reduce the pain and reinforce group identity it also serves to erode self-esteem. (Bernard 1992, pp.31–32)

Because of difficult social experiences, some people may internalise hatred and ambivalence and experience alienation from the self and others. These problems must also be resolved as part of the development and emergence of identity. For a person who is oppressed, one of the key tasks of identity formation then involves 'coming out' as different and integrating a sense of that difference into a healthy self-concept, which may, itself, be stigmatised by the majority society. This is what divides oppressed people from the oppressive majority in the way in which identity develops. For example, Lee (1992, p.10) says of gay and lesbian identity formation:

> A sense of gay and lesbian identity is individual-unique for each person, often in conflict with the perceptions and expectations of the straight world. Hence , it requires extra tasks at synthesis, and interaction with people who are positive about gayness...Arising out of human relatedness, it is often felt as disruptive in relationships of basic importance – especially family, and friendship – as they struggle with accepting a gay member. A task of gay people in synthesising identity is, where possible, to help heal those disruptions in external systems and the self...Like all minority identities, it often fails to find support in the wider environment. It therefore needs to develop its nurturing and support systems and to be politically active, when able, to effect change.'

Erikson's stages indicate competence as being a successful resolution of the industry-inferiority conflict. Grace (1992) suggests that the concept of competence or competence motivation is characterised by self-direction, selectivity and persistence and embraces an urge for achievement. This urge is satisfied both by overt accomplishment of the goals we have set for ourselves and through a general feeling of self-efficacy in our lives:

The person or group who interacts with an environment sensitive to his competence needs enjoys a high probability of achieving competence, skill, and, most important for stage development considerations, a positive sense of himself as a competent human being. 'A positive sense of competence' is considered to be the primary condition for establishing readiness for movement to higher stages of social-emotional development and potential achievement of self-awareness.' (White 1959)

However, not all cultures or subcultures within a particular society have identical values in relation to competence. Different groups of people will have vastly different views about what can be achieved or what is worth achieving which define their expectations of competence in others. This can result in underexpectation in respect of minority groups within these cultures who do not conform to the cultural norm and who subsequently manifest low expectations of themselves and a distorted view of their own self-efficacy. Both the experience of stigma and unrealistic or unfair expectations of competence can exacerbate the individual's sense of difference and this may result in a conflict between their self and the view the world has of them. This awareness, that they are not the same as everyone else, particularly if significant others show a lack of understanding or acceptance of difference, can result in individuals going through the stages of grieving for the 'lost self' – the socially acceptable self – and mourning the losses associated with this, to managing a socially stigmatised identity. The process of grieving through affirming was first described by Kubler-Ross (1969) and Bowlby (1979), and has more recently been refined in relation to stigma by Lee (1992) and Densham (1995). It involves some or all of the following stages depending on the individuals themselves and the way in which the environment responds to them:

- denial of stigmatised identity, and defensive withdrawal and avoidance of others and of situations which are uncomfortable
- anger, which may be direct or disguised and repressed
- bargaining and 'passing' behaviour
- depression as the reality of having a stigmatised identity emerges
- positive acceptance or acknowledgement of difference.

The developmental tasks frequently centre on resolving the conflict between isolation through internalising society's negative views, and living in fear of being stigmatised and rejected on the one hand, and a deep commitment to other similarly stigmatised individuals which may result in alienation from the majority society (including, sometimes, the individual's significant others) on the other. Grace (1992, p.37) points to the serious consequences which arise from the chronic sense of threat experienced throughout the individual's attempts at conflict resolution:

First, increasing amounts of time and energy must be devoted to survival and defence rather than to intimacy and growth. Second, people may develop a generalised view of the world as threatening and develop a sophisticated 'negativity radar' that can generate self-fulfilling prophecies of danger everywhere. Third, public self may become a form of disguise and armour, with private self consequently becoming increasingly alienated from the rest of the world. Finally, this growing isolation may foster a sense of shame about one's core identity and basic needs.

Kaufman (1980) describes shame as feeling exposed and painfully diminished, to such an extent that individuals have a fundamental sense of themselves as defective, deficient or lacking in competence or worth. Though shame originates through early interactions between people, at some point it becomes internalised and self-generating to such an extent that the individual may become their own worst enemy. They may then create any number of shame-based defences in order to protect themselves against additional shame, and to contain internalised shame to prevent it from being reactivated by interaction with others. This may be because shame subverts their competence motivation to such an extent that they become what Grace (1992) describes as 'competent frauds' who, because they cannot engage in authentic self-disclosure, make survival the primary task rather than growth, and 'competently build walls rather than bridges' (p.40). It may also be because shame becomes bound to any or all of the individual's inner and relationship experiences. For example, Grace (1992, p.39) continues with the following example of this destructive binding in the area of feelings:

> Anger contaminated with shame can boil over into rage and violence or freeze into resentment, cynicism and contempt. Sadness may become dammed up by shame to create a sea of despair or chronic melancholy and self-pity. Fear may escalate into acute panics, chronic suspiciousness, and lingering dread. Joy may be quashed by shame entirely, disqualified by a concurrent sense of unworthiness, or amplified into over-idealization of self or others, grandiosity and an irrational sense of entitlement. And guilt may be corrupted by shame into unfair and unrelenting self-criticism, acts of self-punishment, depression and suicide.

However, it is only after this process has happened, and any shame and guilt dealt with, that the stigmatised individual can move towards affirming a positive identity and attend to identity management issues. This discussion shows the importance of making a distinction between *chronological* and *developmental* ages in the development of identity in groups of people who are subject to any of the barriers described. Any factors which prevent the parts of a healthy identity converging to become a whole will result in *developmental lag* or *delay*. It has, for example, been shown that when identity is not completely foreclosed, developmental lag may slow the process of gay or lesbian psychological maturation (Grace 1992) and the growth of ethnic and racial identity (Phinney 1990; Phinney and Rosenthal 1992). If a gay or lesbian's chronological adolescence was a time of hiding, or what Goffman (1963) describes as 'passing' as heterosexual in order to gain the acceptance of others, *developmental* adolescence may not begin until early or even middle adulthood. If shameful feelings about their different sexuality have been internalised, this may cause gays and lesbians to react to the 'younger' parts of themselves and others with contempt and self-abuse, creating an additional source of developmental delay, identity diffusion, and continuing self-aliena- tion. If gay men or lesbian women do not have compassionate explanations for developmental lag, they will take on homophobic stereotypes that rein- force all the narrow-minded and negative attitudes of the heterosexual com- munity, and turn these stereotypes against themselves in a way which is ultimately destructive.

Within black and ethnic minorities, the development of identity includes making a commitment to a particular *ethnic* or *racial identity* through different patterns of identification, and integrating this into their personal and social identities. Much of the developmental activity is concentrated on identifica- tions with others and social identity and here, too, it is possible to distinguish different stages. There is first rejection of the majority culture's negative evaluation and then construction of an identity which includes ethnicity as a positive and desired aspect of the self (Ward 1990), and includes some or all of the following aspects (Phinney and Rosenthal 1992):

- self-identification as a member of a group
- feelings of belonging and commitment to a group
- positive (or negative) attitudes towards a group
- a sense of shared attitudes and values
- learning of specific ethnic traditions and practices, such as language, customs and behaviours.

This brings with it three additional developmental tasks, which Phinney (1990) calls *unexamined ethnic identity, ethnic identity search* and resolution of conflicts and contradictions which result in the *achievement of ethnic identity*. Additional developmental tasks tend to occur within the psychosocial conflict *identity-role confusion*, when group loyalties are being decided, and, as such, they are added to those experienced by individuals who are coming to terms with managing a stigmatised identity within an oppressive family or commu- nity environment. Phinney points out, however, that the final task in the search for ethnic identity is not always an easy process because not all people will choose their own ethnic group's patterns and values wholeheartedly, nor will they be prepared to limit their access to the larger culture. A chosen ethnic identity may therefore bring with it an adverse reaction from the groups or cultures that have been rejected, as has been observed in the call of John Small (1986, p.91), a leading black social worker, for the abandonment of the term 'mixed race' because it can lead to the belief that:

> such children are racially distinct from blacks...Many black people find the term derogatory and racist because they feel it is a conscious and hypocritical way of denying the reality of a child's blackness. Certainly mixed race children are regarded as black by society and eventually the majority of such children will identify with blacks, except in instances where reality and self-image have not merged.

However, Tizard and Phoenix (1993, p.159), in a study looking at, among other things, the racial identity of people from mixed parentage families, found that:

Just under half of our mixed parentage sample thought of people of mixed parentage, including themselves as black. Even fewer – 30 per cent – of the young people with two black parents, and only 16 per cent of the white young people did so. The rest of the young people of mixed parentage thought of themselves as 'brown', 'mixed' or 'coloured'…Of those in the mixed parentage sample who did not think of themselves as black, some seemed not to have heard of the view that they should do so, whilst others had made a deliberate decision not to, often because to do so seemed to involve a denial of their white parent.

Studies of racial and ethnic groups suggest that those who encounter more visible prejudice will have a different route to identity formation developmentally than those who may be more easily integrated into the dominant culture. Those whose own ethnic culture supports beliefs and values that are close to those of the dominant culture will have less difficulty in resolving the contradictions than will those whose family culture is at greater variance with the majority. Young people from ethnic minority families have also been found to reflect Marcia's four identity statuses (1994). Some, who wish to try to compete in and succeed in the dominant culture, may experience ostracism from friends of the same background who accuse them of 'acting white' and betraying their blackness. Some resolve this by distancing themselves from their own ethnic group; others deal with it by creating two or more identities which they assume in different circumstances. Many resolve the dilemma by wholeheartedly choosing their own ethnic group's patterns and values, even though it may limit their access to the larger culture. There is some evidence that in adolescents from ethnic minorities, the proportion of foreclosed identities is relatively large (Spencer and Markstrom-Adams 1990). This difference in identity status may reflect socioeconomic differences, but Hoffman *et al.* (1994) suggest that it may also be the result of living in a group that encourages adherence to subcultural norms. When social and ideological roles have been clearly defined by the community, foreclosure may actually provide a sense of well-being.

There are many ways in which the search for authenticity of black and ethnic minorities and gays and lesbians parallel each other. It has been suggested, for example, that the additional developmental tasks cited by Phinney above in respect of racial and ethnic identity can be observed in the development of the sexual identity of gays and lesbians (Lee 1992). However, there are also a number of ways in which the development of an ethnic or racial identity might be different from the development of gay and lesbian identity. These differences relate to variations in the mechanisms of racism and homophobia, and to the availability and visibility of support in the environment at particular stages in the developmental life cycle. Phinney and Rosenthal (1992) stress that ethnic or racial identity is set apart from most aspects of ego identity because there is no choice about it, only about how it is integrated. Children from black and ethnic minority families are generally exposed to positive and visible racial and ethnic images from their parents and communities *alongside* stigmatising racist images from the majority culture from a very early age, which contribute to and reinforce a broader picture of what is possible, and the commitments which can be made. (I use 'visible' here in the sense that race and ethnicity are not hidden.) Thus ethnic and racial identity can develop in a supportive environment which enables racism to be countered through collective strength, and there is less emphasis on the difference between the self and others *within* one's community than on the difference between the pride in one's community and the oppression of majority society. The experience of being apart does not usually come from shame unless this reflects how significant others feel about their identity in relation to the majority society.

With gay or lesbian young people, homophobia is insidious and reinforced by the belief and value systems, language *and laws* of many cultures. Most people have heard of the term 'racism', but many do not recognise the term 'homophobia', nor understand what it means. This gives a sense of gay and lesbian identities which are driven more deeply underground and hidden; indeed, this is perhaps why the phrase 'coming out of the closet' is more usually applied to this group when it can be relevant to the lives of other oppressed groups. Homophobia reinforces shame in the individual in two ways. Heterosexual assumptions about homosexuality are still consistent with *homosexual taboo*, and the social system in which gays and lesbians exist is, from their perspective, unsafe and unstable. There are many reasons for the attribution of taboo status, but predominant ones are the tendency to confuse homosexual *acts* with homosexual *identity* and also to confuse terms such as gender identity, gender role, sexual object choice and sexual orientation (Bernard 1992). We saw above that gender and sexuality are key elements of the ego identity and so it might be expected that any disruption to their integration, for whatever reason, may result in developmental delay. Bernard suggests that the presumption of an equation between activity and identity 'ain't necessarily so' and that 'similar acts may imply different identities for different people and similar identities eventuate in different behaviours. There is no absolute fit or congruency between doing, thinking or feeling.' (pp. 24–25). Although conscious awareness of homosexuality may not occur until early adolescence, a unnerving sense of difference may occur much earlier than that as each of the earlier developmental tasks come into focus. Ambivalence and complication can therefore arise not only in accepting a gay or lesbian identity but also in how to evaluate this identity positively when there is a potential risk of rejection by both the family of origin and the family of choice, and stigma may be in evidence *throughout* the process of identity development. This requires developmental tasks which are over and above the search for a social identity and, generally, must be resolved *before* that search can commence, which in turn means that gays and lesbians 'find their community' at a much later stage in the developmental cycle.

Thus the distinction between the stereotyping of an individual as socially unacceptable, shameful and taboo, and the stereotyping and marginalisation of an established group yield different pictures of identity development. This is summarised in Figure 1.6. The deaf community includes individuals who are stereotyped as socially unacceptable *and* an established group of people who are marginalised and stigmatised on account of their language and way of being. However, when deaf people embrace a further sense of difference – for example, if they are also black, from an ethnic minority or gay or lesbian

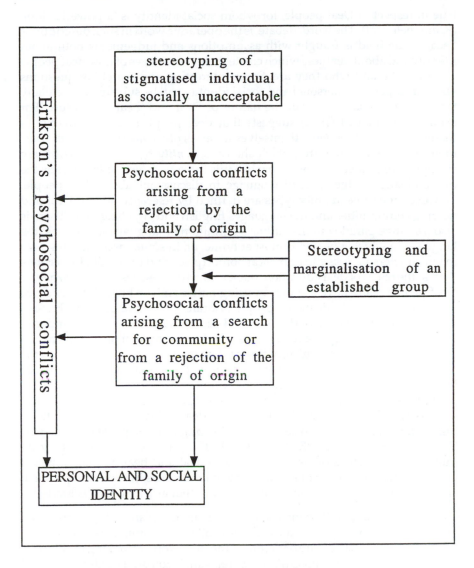

Figure 1.6 Psychosocial conflicts, stigma and stereotyping

–the process of identity development is more complicated and may be fraught with the tensions of multiple and simultaneous oppressions. In theory, it seems as if the number of alternative choices could be greater, but so too can be the experience of shame and taboo. The individual may face multiple rejections before a commitment can be made. It therefore becomes important to understand how deafness may be integrated into identity in different ways.

Exploring Notions of Deaf Identity

Much of the debate around 'deaf identity' has focused on social or cultural identity and identification as opposed to personal identity. This is particularly true in respect of Deaf people, for whom social identity is 'a powerful tool' (Kannapell 1994). The word 'debate' is the operative word in such descriptions because the field is fraught with assumptions and judgements both about identity and about deafness which create their own images of how deaf people 'ought' to be and who they are. Some interesting and searching questions about deaf people's personal and social identity can be subsumed in equally fascinating discussions about the nature of Deaf and 'hearing' culture. For example, Kannapell (1994) suggests that deaf people's *cultural* identity is made up of how they view themselves in terms of *language* identity, *personal* identity and *social* identity (which she calls *identity types*), all of which are strongly interrelated. The need to make this three-way distinction reflects the predominance of the issue of language in discussions about deaf people. However, the three identity types are defined by reference only to Deaf and hearing communities and the languages English and sign language. There is also a strange paradox in the author's definition of language identity as 'the language in which a person is most at home, or, in some cases, the language in which a person *chooses* to be most at home' (p.46), and the parallel assertions that, in the realm of deaf education 'there is much more question as to whether Deaf people really have a choice in using either ASL or English to reinforce their identity', and '...deafened people or oralists who prefer to use English with each other'. These assertions are in keeping with the common tendency to regard potential sign language users as having little choice and English users as having a choice which, at times when mainstream education is on the increase and the degree of 'teacher approval' associated with particular languages is still something of a hot potato, are unhelpful. Issues such as these are reflected in the widespread use of stereotyped descriptors of deafness in discussions about identity. Words such as 'deaf', 'deafened', 'hard-of-hearing', 'hearing-impaired', 'hearing loss' 'hearing', and signs such as DEAF, STRONG-DEAF, ORAL, ORALIST, HIGH-SIGN, HEARING, though they are intended as signifiers of *identifications* with deaf and hearing people which make up the individual's identity, can be of limited use in exploring personal structures of meaning, in much the same way that any language is limited:

> When you identify something, say a plant or an animal, you give it an identity. To say 'That's a weed' or 'That's a wild animal' is not to detect some essential feature or nature of the thing you are looking at. 'Flower' versus 'weed' is a dimension only relevant if you are a gardener. 'Edible' versus 'inedible' might be the (albeit not articulable) dimension used by sheep and cows, and 'wild' versus 'tame' is a distinction that surely only has meaning for humans (since 'tame' implies an encounter and relationship with human beings). The point is that it is you that is doing the identifying, and the identity you confer has more to do with your purposes that the 'nature' of the thing itself. The same applies to the things that make up human identities, such as masculinity/femininity, hetero-/homosexual, sane/insane, black/white, working-/middle-class and so on – these may be seen as socially bestowed identities rather than essences of the person. (Burr 1995, p.30)

Without an understanding of this and because of the tendency to stereotype, it is not always easy nor is it necessarily desirable to compare different people's descriptions of identity in terms of deaf-related labels. For example, Carty (1994, p.40, italics added) says:

> Identity is a very complicated concept, and most sign languages have signs for different aspects of it. For example, the sign for 'identifying with a group' is often an emphasised form of JOIN. Many of the terms Deaf people in Australia use to describe themselves and others *are about identity rather than about hearing level*.

In the same volume, Stone and Stirling (1994, p.50, italics added) look at the development and definition of identity in deaf children of deaf parents and of hearing parents:

> Deaf people may define deafness in a different way from those outside of the sociocultural group, who tend to define deafness in oral/aural terms. We expected that as a result of their home and school experiences, the distinctions between deaf, hard of hearing, hearing impaired and hearing might be viewed differently by deaf children of deaf parents and deaf children of hearing parents... The children were first asked to define the word 'deaf'. 68% of the deaf children of deaf parents and 44% of those with hearing parents responded that 'deaf' meant 'cannot hear'. Almost all of the children with deaf parents were able to define the term, but six of the twenty nine children with hearing parents could not... *50% of the deaf children with deaf parents mentioned degree of hearing loss as the basis for their choice of identity label*... Deaf children of hearing parents appeared to have less understanding of the terms 'deaf', 'hard of hearing', 'hearing impaired' and 'hearing' than those with deaf parents. *Neither group was familiar with the term 'hearing impaired' however*.

Kannapell (1994, p.46, italics added) adds another perspective:

> In recent years, however, *more and more young deaf people have been identifying themselves as hearing impaired*. Deaf people did not use this term ten years ago. Why is it accepted and used today? Even though the term has been imposed on deaf people by hearing people who apparently wish to define them by a characteristic they lack – hearing – rather than be one they have – deafness – many young deaf people seem to regard it as an acceptable term to describe their identity.

whereas Gregory *et al.* (1995, p.222), in a British study, says that:

> At the beginning we suggested that people might be concerned with identification with the hearing world or with the deaf world. In fact these strong identifications have emerged rarely. Most of the deaf young people lived in both and took a moderate position on this. While most accepted they were deaf and many saw it as an integral part of their identity, few talked about being proud to be deaf and strongly identifying with the Deaf community, although a significant number spent most of their social life with deaf people.

The above accounts together show a great deal of contradiction which may arise from differences in the groups studied, different usages of particular terms and, possibly variation in research method with some studies using preconceived categories of deafness and others taking a more open-ended and flexible approach. I feel particularly concerned about the affect of this on deaf people who are in the process of becoming or who are outsiders (Higgins 1980) and are caught between two or more worlds because they struggle for an identity which reflects accurately who they are. They are often marginalised or treated as an anomaly when they don't fit easily into a given category or have composite identities, when in fact this is true of most people, particularly when we consider personal identity. Often outsiders are the most 'competent frauds' and they build veritable strongholds around themselves in order to protect themselves from further hurt. When I worked with one such deaf client, I asked them to describe what this wall around them was made of. Their response was complex and sobering.

Kannapell's (1994) discussion on personal identity is disappointingly confined to the *deaf-related* terms that have been used to describe deaf people, and this appears to make the assumption that deaf people always regard deafness as a dominant aspect of their personal identity. I have no doubt that deafness is important, but my experience in counselling deaf people is that the degree of importance or dominance of 'deaf identity' is often socially constructed and may vary at different stages in the developmental cycle and under the influence of different environmental stressors. Parallels are often drawn between the experience of Deaf people and that of Black people (Taylor and Meherali 1991) or women (Nowell 1989), but in the latter two groups it is generally accepted that ethnicity and gender at the level of personal identity are integrated and evaluated by the individual in different ways and to different degrees. Because deafness works directly at the interface between self and others in its influence on communication, intimacy, social affiliation, and social acceptance, the psychosocial conflicts involved in its integration into personal and social identity are of crucial importance. Their resolution will depend on how the individual manages personal and socio-cultural stressors. In this context, scant or implicit reference is made to the belief and value systems underpinning Deaf or hearing culture[2] or those of other cultures and subcultures of the Deaf community itself. As a result, research shows limited awareness of the use of deaf-related terms as labels and stereotypes which 'both aid and destroy identity simultaneously' (Bernard 1992).

If we look at the functions of language – self-exploration, self-expression, social interaction with others and a conveyor of information about the environment, it seems that language must act *as a bridge between* personal and social identity rather than exist as a distinct identity type. Generally, within the deaf community, language is seen as inextricably linked to social identity as the

---

2   Woodford (1993) suggests that little attempt has been made to identify how deaf
     and hearing culture are different in relation to thought patterns, and asks whether
     we really understand how much of hearing culture depends on hearing and on
     language being in word form? Until the answers to these questions are known it is
     difficult to place the word 'hearing' in front of culture and understand what it
     means.

language or languages that deaf people are able to use or feel comfortable using will often determine the dominant social affiliations that they make. Language is also bound up with demonstrating group loyalty. If we view language as an identity type, we are in effect saying that it is possible, at least in theory, for someone to be Deaf and oral. Though there may well be individuals who would choose to exist in this state of personal identity, it may represent a conflict between their personal identity and their social identifications. They often exist in isolation because they are seen as socially unacceptable. This situation is, perhaps, similar to the confusion between homosexual acts and homosexual identity, with language being the 'act' that expresses our orientation towards Deafness or hearingness.

Some of our recent understanding of the development of 'deaf identity' parallels more closely what we know of identity development in other minority groups, and it is encouraging to see a more flexible and judgement-free view emerging. For example, David Moorhead (1995, p.85), in his sensitive analysis of the experience of deafness, suggests that identity development is organised around two dominant themes, which he calls *struggle* and *challenge*:

> Running through the accounts of deaf people and professionals are stories of their struggle to find and hang on to their sense of who they are, and to be free to retain that sense through the various circumstances in which they move at different times of their lives. This liberty, and the struggle to attain it, derives from people's wish to control the circumstances of their lives, and their continual challenge to the people, institutions, understandings and attitudes that restrict their ability to do this... It seems clear that people who are deaf – and those who work with them or share their lives – struggle continually against the meanings that others impose on their experience, and the way that this separates them from others. They struggle for acknowledgement of the way they see their lives and wish to live them, and aspire to connection with other people, to share and belong.

It is not clear whether struggle and challenge are two parts of what Marcia would call 'exploration', or whether they correspond to Erikson's original psychosocial conflicts (the developmental challenge) and the struggles to resolve these conflicts. Moorhead's analysis is supported by Carty (1994) in her discussions with Australian Deaf adults about the stages of identity development. She proposes a framework for the development of Deaf identity which in many ways parallels that in Figure 1.6 and includes elements of both Lee's framework for coming to terms with stigma and loss and Phinney and Rosenthal's ethnic identity search. Carty suggests that the following transitions form the developmental process:

- *confusion* arising from an awareness that we are not the same as everyone else
- *frustration, anger and blame* because of lack of understanding or acceptance of difference, particularly on the part of significant others
- *exploration* following a decision to explore self-identity options within deaf and hearing communities

- *identifications and rejections* as a consequence of further tentative exploration by trial and error
- *ambivalence,* as a result of experiencing negative characteristics of the group we have chosen to identify with
- *acceptance* of who we are and the reactions we may get from the in-group and others

Although Carty puts this forward as a framework for the development of Deaf identity, it might equally be a valid framework for integrating deafness into personal and social identity in other ways which do not result in becoming Deaf. It is clear that the key stages are the second and the third stages. Deaf children from deaf families may not experience the second stage in the early years, and may become aware of their difference only when they engage in sustained contacts with hearing people either individually or as part of a group of deaf people. They will be in a completely different situation to deaf people from hearing families or families of different ethnic origin who may be made aware of their deafness as a source of difference right from the start, albeit implicitly. Deaf people who live predominantly within the hearing community *and* who have been cut off from information about Deaf culture, sign language and Deaf history or have experienced stigma in relation to their deafness may face more limited self-identity choices at the exploration stage. Indeed, Moss (1987) found that deaf children attending mainstream schools were less accepted by their hearing peer group as they progressed through school, and Markides (1989) found that 51 per cent of deaf children considered another deaf child and 27 per cent a hearing child to be their best friend, whereas only 3 per cent of hearing children considered a deaf child to be their best friend.

Gregory and Bishop (1989) cite one of the goals of integration as the fostering of social integration, and this is clearly not being achieved from the point of view of the horizontal relationships that deaf children make. Densham (1995) reports that teachers of the deaf were the only professional group questioned who considered 'deafness to be worse than blindness' or were noncommittal. She also suggests that hearing parents of deaf children may 'shy away from manual methods of communication' (p.69) because they fear a 'cultural split in the family' if their child joins the Deaf community, and it, in effect, becomes their family of choice. This, as described earlier, would have possible implications for the vertical relationships formed by deaf children, and the outcome of their search for social identity and a comfortable language. Deaf people from ethnic minorities, whilst ostensibly having increased self-identity choices, may experience a huge conflict between their family of origin and their family of choice when they begin to explore the integration of ethnic identity and deaf identity. The effect of this may be to throw them back to the first stage because both choices are very compelling for different reasons and this may result in an identity ambivalence or confusion. Another important point, which is a direct result of membership of Deaf and hearing communities being conditional, is that self-identity options may demand an element of 'passing' behaviour in order to gain social acceptance and counteract stigma. Passing behaviour has been described in deaf people who become accepted by the hearing community by attempting to pass as hearing. But it has been only implicitly referred to in deaf people, such as those who have grown up in the hearing community and have found it wanting, and who then attempt to join the Deaf community (Jones 1995) in order to be socially accepted as a member of a supportive group. They may try to 'pass' as Deaf, and adopt sign language as their primary means of communication. However, if they have any inner, unconscious discomfort with elements of being Deaf, this will inevitably show itself, and may be misinterpreted by Deaf people as being a 'bad attitude' or a lack of commitment. If 'passing' is not an option, and it often is a very difficult option because joining the Deaf community is not easy (Ladd 1995), then the individual's self-image (personal and social identity) may be further stigmatised, spoiled and discredited (Goffman 1963). Higgins (1980, pp.82–83) says that 'the judgement and standards of those whom we identify with, whom we feel we are like or want to be like, most affect our self-feelings.' Rejection by the Deaf community as a 'heafie', when the community is seen as the family of choice and that choice has frequently been made following a painful rejection of the family of origin, has profound effects on self-esteem.

The boundaries between the different subcultures within the deaf community are not clear – certainly not as clear as the boundaries between different racial, cultural or religious groups or those between people with different disabilities, for example, and the deaf community itself does not present a 'united front':

> If the deaf community is to have political power, members must present a united, consistent front. Broad recruitment of deaf individuals into an identification with the deaf community poses problems. In deaf culture, there are criteria for membership, such as attendance at a residential school for the deaf, use of sign language, attitude about one's deafness, and so forth. The separation of the culturally deaf group members from members who are deaf but do not identify with deaf culture (e.g. oral and/or mainstreamed deaf and hard-of-hearing persons) creates subgroups within the general deaf population. (Rose and Kiger 1995, p.526)

Having a political identity is one way in which stigmatised individuals and groups resolve the remaining psychosocial conflicts after the identity-role confusion crisis has passed, as it is part of how they establish group loyalties and exercise generativity. At present, however,

- the sharply defined group boundaries of the Deaf community and the limitations to movement between Deaf and hearing communities,
- the lack of availability of a cohesive existential view of deafness, hearingness and the Deaf and hearing communities,
- the fact that 'deaf' and 'hearing' are both terms which tend to be ascribed by others and are not always self-ascribed by deaf and hearing people themselves, and
- the conditions placed on membership of both Deaf and hearing communities as the two extremes between which many deaf people move *in relation to their deafness,*

imply that many deaf people fail to make a clear commitment. They have no option but to adopt a self-constructed identity which, as we saw earlier, will probably not be their final identity because it has not been conferred on them. Their search for personal and social meaning may be long and tortuous.

Identity Development – Creating the Ideal Environment

It is perhaps important to remain mindful of our potential to cause psychological damage and trauma, and to be aware of deaf identity in the context of identity as a whole:

> It seems apparent that people construct their sense of who they are from a range of different experiences, and not just from being deaf. People's identities and self-images are formed by their racial, cultural and gender experiences, from the experiences in their families, and how they understand these, and from what happens to them in their day-to-day existence, and their understanding of why it does. Indeed people's accounts seem to challenge our notions of 'being deaf' and 'becoming deaf', especially when we place these in the context of their other experiences. (Moorhead 1995, p.86)

The goal of each stage of development is not to eliminate the characteristics of unsuccessful outcomes but to create alternatives so that the balance is shifted towards more healthy choices and decisions. This in many ways parallels what we might expect from the counselling relationship. Conversely, relationships which stigmatise, judge, stereotype, lack empathy with individual ways of being, or which are concerned only with the maintenance of a particular rigid set of beliefs and values without recognition that many individuals do not want to or are unable to live up to these expectations will not contribute to or maintain that individual's sense of self-esteem. Individuals may experience developmental lag or delay because the environment is at odds with what they really want for themselves and who they really want to be, and does not provide them with sufficient choices or options to feel strong in who they are. Because the family and social context of most stigmatised individuals is so often found to be deficient, it is sometimes necessary for the environment created by the counselling relationship to provide what is needed to enable growth. In other words, the counselling relationship must provide the characteristics of an ideal, pro-competence social environment which allows for and aims towards:

- positive evaluation of identity and identification
- the integration of all the parts necessary for healthy identity formation
- the resolution of psychosocial conflicts
- safety, legitimacy and stability without judgement
- sensitivity towards developmental lag and delay

In such an environment, an honest sense of *personal identity* results in a congruent, satisfying and competence-based *social identity* to share and to enjoy with others, and this can be translated into relationships in the real world. Early identity confusion can be tolerated, examined and eventually resolved from an inner locus of decision-making that values honesty over conformity. This environment also has a number of implicit functions which are firmly within the domain of the personal qualities that the counsellor brings to an empowering counselling relationship. These might include the following:

- the emergence of a different sense of self and a need to identify with other people who embrace the same difference is tolerated;
- acknowledgement of different behaviour and feelings is supported by respectful attitudes towards people who are different and their need to form relationships with whom they wish;
- finding community can be a public exploration of visible, diverse and easily accessible resources;
- relationships can occur in a context of positive sanction and recognition of their importance and value;
- self-definition and reintegration can be a time where individuals who are different would simply address the same existential questions faced by the majority of people, thus removing the additional tasks which they currently face;
- a flexible notion of identity is held, which implies that it is:

> ...ordered along a dimension that ranges from inner to outer. Some definitions (like those positing an inner core) focus on the interior of the person's being as the source of sameness and perhaps even the person's identifiability over time. At the other end of the dimension, cultural and social-psychological conceptions of identity focus instead on the cultural and social structures and conventions that constrain who we appear to be to others and ourselves. Somewhere in the middle are conceptualisations that are more interactive, examining the interplay between the psychological interior and the sociocultural context. (Grotevant *et al.* 1994, p.12)

As I learn more about deaf people through their own eyes, I can see how the social constructionist emphasis on the processes of 'identification' and the development of 'social identity' can act as a barrier to self-understanding and the achievement of personal identity in exactly the same way that a pathological view of deafness can, because the direction that these processes takes may be at odds with the person's structure of meaning. But there is a second view of society or community as a place where we, as individual deaf people, feel comfortable and 'at home' with ourselves and which to a large extent reflects who we are and embraces our fundamental values. In such a community we are more able establish a *mutuality* between ourself and our world (Erikson 1959). For some, the counselling relationship must be a temporary 'home' for mutuality, both a place of safety which marginalises labels, stereotypes and stigma by embodying a preparedness to accept the existence of and explore some of the more unsavoury aspects of the social and cultural milieu, and a place in which individual deaf people can gain recognition, acceptance and affirmation of deafness, without assumptions about 'deaf identity' as the main driving force in their lives.

As we turn to the narratives themselves, some readers may wonder why I have felt it necessary to devote so many pages to what may be loosely described as overlapping theories in a book which is focused on practice and process. I have not done this in order to put theory before practice or to imply that theory is more important that practice. This chapter has aimed to provide a context for the ensuing narratives which attempts to anticipate the kind of readers this book may attract. Like rules, theories and frameworks are not etched in stone – they contribute to the social and cultural construction of knowledge, beliefs and values of clients, of counsellors, and of those who have never experienced counselling from either perspective. In some ways I hope that the structure of the second part of this book will show the usefulness of this process of construction. But, in other ways, I hope that the difficulties of attempting to impose any structure on unpredictable, of-the-moment experiences of individual human beings will be exposed. As I implied in the Preface, I am aware of my own shortcomings as a commentator and interpreter of the experience of others, and I do not see my own expression of these roles as conclusive or finite. But when that experience is unknown or causes discomfort I am also aware that it helps to compartmentalise it in order that its existence can somehow be justified. In other words, for myself, I am happy to let experience be what it is – individual and timeless; but I know that view will not be shared by all who engage themselves in the narratives. The leap we take now is, after all, a leap into the 'boundless and measureless' ocean which has currents and cross-currents for all concerned.

Part 2

The Narratives

CHAPTER TWO

The Bubble and the Coal Hole

I have all the symptoms of *fright*... It really seems like I'm cut loose and very vulnerable... Still, I have a feeling of *strength*... I'm feeling it internally now, a sort of surging up, or force...something really big and strong. And yet at first it was almost a physical feeling of just being out alone, and sort of cut off from a support I have been carrying around... (Rogers 1961)

Introduction

Most of us have expectations about how parents and other primary caregivers develop relationships with children. There is sometimes a big gap between our idea of a 'model parent' and the one we end up with, and that is something which affects parents as much as it does children. The 'model parent' is probably as much of a myth as the 'model child' and both, in being ideals, represent a set of goals which most families are under pressure to conform to, but generally do not attain *in full*. As a deaf parent of hearing children myself, I would describe my experience as one where the goal posts are constantly being moved and I seem to be perpetually in midfield. I know my children also experienced negative pressure from outside the family to see me as 'their deaf mother' rather than just their mother – this meaning that the outside world had low expectations of my competence as a mother. I initially envisaged my 'mothering' role as providing my children with safety and security, wrapping them in a cocoon to protect them from a cruel world until such time as it was safe to allow them to explore that world on their own. Even when they began to explore, I wanted to provide them with a bubble which they could see through and enjoy its swirling rainbow colours, but which would, at the same time, provide them with a safety barrier, their own little microcosm which preserved an atmosphere of the values I wanted to transmit to them and continued to nurture them with knowledge and learning. There was, however, often a gap between what I wanted to do and what I actually managed to do – I inadvertently burst the bubble many times, because like bubbles, safety is fragile, and what is safe for one individual is not so safe for another. This is especially so when the family unit is founded on a particular difference which means that all the wisdom of other families' experiences is in danger of being obsolete or inaccessible, all the family rules have to be renegotiated, and all the best laid plans go out the window. The best outcome was compromise, and that did not stop dreams for a better one. This thing called 'deafness' threatened to take over on many occasions. So the bubble is the first image with which we begin this chapter, an image of what most parents are encouraged to hope for when they have children, and how fragile it is. The second image is one of what can happen for the deaf child when the family acquires a new member called 'deaf', who seeks to control every aspect of family life and vies with the child for their parent's affections.

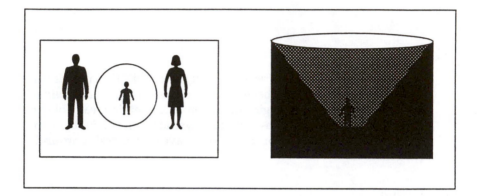

Figure 2.1 The bubble and the coal hole

These two images represent a broad spectrum from the point of view of parent/child relationships, and it is impossible to predict where a particular family will lie on this spectrum. 'Deaf' can bring out both the best and the worst of family life, and this is his power. In some families, 'deaf' has been a long-standing family member and the family has learnt from their heritage to develop lifestyles and patterns of relating which place him at the centre of the family constellation. It is appropriate, therefore, that the narratives in this chapter begin with that of Caroline. Families where both parents and children, and sometimes many members of the extended family, are deaf are in the minority, but they are the closest we can get to the 'pure' deaf experience. Such families generally have hallowed status in the Deaf community, which inevitably means that they attract a mixture of awe and envy. The evidence suggests that life in such families closely parallels life in any family until the world of others intrudes.

Caroline

My first memory was at a hearing nursery. I remember there, I felt...not frustrated...but sad, really really sad, looking up at all those hearing adults talking to each other, controlling the children, and it was all going over the top of my head. When my mother came, I could feel my face light up and I just latched on to her, the feeling of bonding was so strong. I was so pleased to see her. Outwardly I remember the toys and the faces of the adults there, but inside, I was sad because there was no information getting through. I have a photograph of myself when I was at the nursery, and I look sad in that. It really brings back memories, black feelings, I feel like I just want to cut it off, leave it behind. How did that change? How I turned from a sad, maybe angry child into one who was happier, I don't know? When I think of the upbringing I had, I remember that my mother was very clear about social rules, for example. I felt so sure about where I stood. We knew that it was OK to sign with each other when we were in the house, but when we were out, in the hearing world, we were taught to SIGN SMALL; we were taught that that was the way to behave in the hearing world. And I think we had family signs as well. Like we used to sign AWFUL FATHER IRRITATE. It mean that my father was going to or had been to the barber's for a haircut and he was grumbling because he wasn't satisfied with it or whatever. So if he came home from work and we knew that he'd had a haircut, we signed that and we all knew what it meant. My mother said that it was also because I was always determined, but cheerful, always smiling as well – I think I did that because it all seemed so stupid, these hearing people trying to make me smile, and I'm thinking to myself, 'Why are you grinning at me, trying to make me smile? I'm not stupid!' Maybe I was looking at them through Deaf eyes even then? At other times, I remember photos of me with my cousin. I was really fed up because they were always comparing me with my cousin – when I was seven or eight, they gave me a ball, and I thought 'Why are they giving me a ball? Is it to make me smile again?' And so something in me just said 'No!' But in the end I just took the ball because I was so angry and I laughed at them when they weren't looking. I don't know whether it was linked to this feeling inside that when I looked at hearing people trying to make me smile and thinking they are so wonderful, and I am thinking, 'Huh! what's so wonderful about being hearing – hearing?' I wanted to be different from them.

I remember I preferred the holidays with my mother's family. My mum worked and my brother and I needed looking after, so we were sent to stay with other people in the family. Her sister is hearing, but can sign, and my brother would go to my father's family who were hearing and couldn't. Inside I used to shudder at the thought of going there as well. I didn't want to go there because of the stress, lack of communication. My brother had good speech so it felt as if it was right for him to go there, but I resisted it. I always preferred to go to my aunt's because of the communication. My mother was often angry with me because every time we were meant to visit my father's family, something always went wrong with me – I was ill or something like that. But I actually think I was scared of going because I knew what it would be like, that I would be frustrated because of all this talking in the air with no regard for me. My father relied on fingerspelling only, but I found it so difficult and frustrating because it felt like the talking was very short and the fingerspelling was very long – they didn't match. The access was limited, and communication was not spontaneous. With my mother's family, it was so different, they signed fast and fluently and I knew what was going on; there was never anything missing. Sometimes, however, I had to go to my father's family because my brother and I would swap over – I really don't know how I got through it without giving up.

It was a beautiful place, with plenty to do, but all I could think about was getting back to the place that I knew. But I had to spend four weeks there and I think I got very bored – no communication, nothing. Eventually mum and dad realised that they couldn't send me there because my Deaf identity was battered there.

The Deaf roots are so strong that even hearing children born to Deaf families become immersed in the Deaf way of life. However, as the following narrative suggests, the contacts that hearing children have with the outside world can mean that the early years are a time when a gradual separation from one's parents can be accompanied by a growing awareness of difference which is not always easy to articulate.

Fiona

When I was very young, I don't remember feeling very different from my family. There was no obvious difference, at least none that I could describe easily. It was certainly nothing as conscious as saying my parents are Deaf and I'm hearing and that means I am different from them. I had a Deaf cousin, and there was nothing obviously different about her family dynamics and the dynamics of my family life. We both came from large working-class families and in that sense we were very similar. However, I do remember that there were things that happened to my cousin which did not happen to me, and perhaps that started to give me a sense of being different. But, again, it wasn't clear. For example, she went to a Deaf school and I didn't. She had hearing aids, and I didn't. I remember asking myself why she went to a Deaf school and had hearing aids because every other aspect of the family dynamics seemed to be the same. I also remember wondering if I had been a bad girl, and that is why these 'privileges' had been withheld. I felt accepted as Deaf by both Deaf and hearing parts of the family. There was no stigma, no difference; my behaviour was seen as 'normal'. Part of that may have been that we were such a large family that we were like a small closely-knit community and so we were accepted. The neighbours would fingerspell to us, even they seemed to accept us, not perhaps in the Martha's Vineyard sense, but they tried. Outside of the family and the immediate community, though, there was no empathy. I always felt as if I was the outsider looking in. When it was in the Deaf setting I was in there, a full part of it and I never though twice about it.

Sam's situation is the reverse of Fiona's. He is Deaf and born to hearing parents.

Sam

I remember well when I was a child of about one or two I was watching my father and brother talk and but I couldn't understand what they were saying. I was puzzled and upset I think, because they wouldn't look at me. At the same time I was confused because they were speaking to each other and the language went over my head. Then they both looked across the room at my mother – I saw the direction of their eyes and body change – and spoke to her. I wondered how they knew they had to look in her direction. I was curious and confused. I didn't know who I was then. I thought my birth had been 'normal' the same as any child. I remember when I was growing up in the very early years – up to the age of two and a half – I would go out the back door and walk out onto the farm land. I could see cows and sheep in the distance, which belonged to a neighbour. I was just amazed by the sight, interested in it, naturally curious. Although I had some of the unsureness of a child, I felt safe because my father always seemed to be there watching for me. I remembered the image of that. Things began to go wrong when on one occasion my father came out into the yard and picked me up – I wasn't sure why – he picked me up and took me back into the house and said 'Watch, watch, Sam, watch...' pointing at something. I saw he was angry. That's the first time I had seen him angry. Before, he was warm and loving, he cuddled me. Now he was angry, so I looked at what he wanted me to look at. I didn't know because my attention was distracted, but my mother had come into the room. She shouted and shouted at me, shouted and shouted...and I just didn't respond. I was then very upset and confused at my father's reaction to me looking where he had told me to look. I know now that my mother was testing to see if I could hear, but I didn't know then. They realised that I wasn't responding even when they shouted at me. So they decided to take me to the doctor's. I remember his white coat – he looked strong and powerful. I was scared and I clung to my mother not understanding what was happening. He repeated the same kind of tests that my mother and father had tried and eventually announced that I was deaf. My parents were broken apart. My mother and father were crying – I'd never seen them do that before. A child of one or two usually makes their parents happy, but they were crying. I remember feeling that awful sinking feeling inside because I didn't know what I had done as I had just been playing with them while the 'tests' were done. I wanted to know what was going on – I didn't understand. I thought I was responsible for their tears and I was very worried. When we arrived home my father called a family meeting and told my brothers that I was deaf – that I couldn't hear anything. The family were shocked. My brother couldn't quite believe it because he thought he had seen me trying to talk. All of this I found out later, but at the time, I was just watching the shock on people's faces and feeling very unhappy.

When I was three years old, the worst experiences of my life began. I had been used to helping with the work on the farm even at that age, but one day my father came and got me and took me into the house, where he put my coat on. I saw that a suitcase had been packed with my clothes in it. I looked at my mother and she was crying. There were no kisses and hugs, only crying. Something was wrong, something was different. There was an atmosphere in the room which I will never forget. My father took me to his friend's car and we drove off. I remember looking out the

window watching the countryside flash by. To start with, the hills, fields
and the towns were familiar and, though I was still very confused about
what was happening, I took comfort from that. Then the landscape
changed. The towns were new, different, everything changed. I began to
feel a bit frightened and I started to cry. I started thinking about the
suitcase. It meant that I was going away from home. I pulled on my father's
coat sleeve and tried to get some reassurance from him. My father saw I
was crying so he gave me some money. It was like a present or a reward
so I stopped crying. But inside I still felt nervous and very confused.

We arrived at some sort of school – my father told me it was a school.
It was a large, very beautiful building. We walked up the steps to the door
and came face to face with this figure dressed in black and white who had
her arms folded across her chest and a cross hanging on her bosom. She
was smiling at me benevolently. I wasn't sure about this. I hid behind my
father because she frightened me. I'd never seen anyone like her before.
My father took me in the door and the first thing I saw was a large statue
of Jesus on the cross up on the wall. It was as if he was staring at me. I
didn't understand what the cross meant. I remembered that outside there
had been no children and thinking it was strange because my father had
said it was a school, but as the nun took us through the hall, I saw that
there were many children – all boys – and other nuns with them. I was still
clinging to my father's hand at this point. One of the children came up to
me and asked me to come and play. I felt tempted but looked uneasily at
my father. The boy's name, he told me, was Bill. The nun encouraged me
to go off with Bill. We talked and played a lot and I became quite excited
as I loved to play at that age. There was something about Bill that reassured
me. Maybe the nuns were frightening, but Bill – it felt as if I was able to
communicate with him easily. I think I felt an almost instant bond. I didn't
understand the words of course, but there was a lot of gesturing which hit
something deep inside me – it felt very familiar. Before that moment, for
the first three years of my life, there had been no communication. I tried
and tried but I was always uncertain, always confused, and felt as if I was
apart from my family in some way. So I felt happy with Bill.

Then I suddenly realised that my father wasn't there any more. I went
into a complete panic, crying and screaming, trying to fight my way
through the children to find him. A nun held onto me and I remember
kicking her and screaming 'WHERE DADDY?! WHERE DADDY?!' My
father had just left me at the school. No goodbyes. He just left me and I
was screaming to myself 'Why me? Why me?' The other boys started to
tell me that their experience had been the same. Their mothers and fathers
had just dumped them. There was a lot of bitterness. But when I realised
that we were all the same, there was something about learning that which
made me put a lid on my feelings – clamp them down – so that I couldn't
talk any more. I wanted to talk more, but I couldn't, I couldn't take any
more explanation. I had so much feeling of shock, loss. I thought I would
never see my family again, and that it was the end of our relationship. I
had this vision of growing up, getting older and never seeing them again.

I was just so confused because I was happy with my family. I was frustrated by the communication difficulties, yes, but my brothers just let me get on with my life, they left me alone, and I was happy being that way. Why was I now separated from them?

At the time when Sam was a child, it was common for deaf children to be sent to residential schools at a very young age, and there is no doubt that the enforced and, what must have seemed from the child's isolated perspective, cruel separation from the only people in their lives who were familiar resulted in extreme trauma for these children. This is especially so when no one was able to explain to children like Sam why the separation was 'necessary' or reassure them that it wasn't permanent, and the only reinforcement comes from other children whose experience has been similar. Peter's situation is different. He remained within the family home in the early years, and though throughout his narrative there is a pervasive claustrophobic, slightly suffocating atmosphere punctuated with episodes which are a curious mixture of tenderness and trauma, one gets the feeling that there is a tenuous relationship between Peter and his family which is struggling to be acknowledged.

Peter

My first home was a basement flat in an old terraced house, where the windows were below eye level. I have memories of looking up to the light as a child in more ways than one. As you went in the front door there was a sort of coal-hole with a lid which had been taken off, so I could look up. Sometimes I would hide in there, I would disappear, and I had this fantasy about being locked in, though I am sure that never happened. When I was in the coal-hole, it was dark… I think I used to have a brush which I would sweep the coal dust up with and I used to look up to the light above, a circle of light – just gaze at it. I don't know what it meant. I felt I could just disappear in the dark, feel small, like nothing. And then my mother would come and find me and tell me off for hiding in there and for playing with the coal. On the wall of my bedroom, there was a picture of some Jewish figure from history which seemed to move as you looked at it from different angles. It looked as if his head was moving, and I used to spend hours and hours looking at him. The curtains were blue with swirling patterns and quite thin. In the summer the light used to shine through the material. And I lay in bed with my bedding up to my neck and watch the patterns of the light moving, like faces of animals, changing and moving – it was almost as if there were animals in the room with me. Sometimes my father would come in to talk to me, but he was always silhouetted against the light of the window and I could never understand what he was saying. He tried to encourage me to practise with whistling sounds, wanting me to mimic him whistling. When I finally got it right – when I managed to whistle, the thumbs would go up. I still wish I had had more information when I was young. I needed more understanding. I always felt my hearing brother had more attention. But he was much younger, and I was jealous of him, I think.

When I was about four and I went to hospital because I had tonsillitis. If they were sore it was usual in those days that they were cut out, especially at that age. One evening, my parents said I had to go somewhere with them, so off we went – in the car, I think – to the hospital. I remember the hospital…being taken up these long winding steps, and looking around in a puzzled kind of way. I was taken first to a nurses' room and they told me I had to take my clothes off – I didn't like that, I wanted to resist. I looked around and remember seeing the white scales over in the corner with things in it, but when they saw me looking I was told to stop. Next I was taken to a ward with rows of beds down each side. All the beds had safety rails around them. I was put in bed there. At the end of the ward, again, there was a picture – it was very large, but not like the one at home in my bedroom. It didn't move like that one and was very far away. I looked around me at the other beds – all the patients were hearing of course. I was four years old and I didn't know why I was there. My mother and father said they would stay at the hospital, that they wouldn't be very far away, that they would come soon to see me. The next morning, after the operation my throat was very sore – so I stayed for two more days I think, and then my mother fetched me. I feel sure that if it had been my brother, there would have been more information and I would have understood what was happening to me.

Because of the dynamics of the relationships in the family when I was younger, I was always trying to make my mother laugh, because if I was successful in doing that, I knew she was happy with me – she loved me dearly. I now feel sad and upset about the memory of that. I remember one day when my brother was about two or three, I was in my bedroom and my mother came in and sat on the corner of my bed, which was on the floor, and she was brushing my hair and crying, crying. I got a feeling that my mother and father had had a big row, a terrible row – I don't know what it was about. My father went out all day and when he came back at the end of the day, I still didn't know what was happening. If you're hearing, you hear the row, you get the information. It was frightening seeing my mother cry and not knowing why. My mother's brother lived above us and I used to spend a lot of time with him. I used to get into bed with him for comfort, just comfort. He made these wonderful soups and he played cards with me. We always went on holiday together. His wife died when my mother was quite young, and he never married again. I sometimes wish he was still here. He was Polish and had a carpentry workshop. There was a horse there and I used to ride the horse a lot around the yard. It was wonderful. It feels strange really, trying to make sense of my world as it was then – all the images flashing by.

For Joseph, socioeconomic circumstances within his family meant that he experienced the repeated absence of his mother who had to work to support the family. Though he felt isolated from his family by the lack of a common language, it is interesting that he seems more preoccupied with what this meant for his understanding of his cultural roots as a Black person.

Joseph

When I was a young child, I felt cut off from my family and other people because my family couldn't use sign language. The problem was that my mother used to work round the clock to support the family because we did not have a father and so she didn't have enough time to spend with me. I didn't blame her. Also, I felt cut off from the kind of information that hearing children picked up about Black culture and other cultures, and from 'hearing' information generally. For example before the early eighties, there were no subtitles on television, and so I watched television, even enjoyed it without being aware of my own needs. It was like living in a very primitive age. I felt denied of this information and it stopped me from understand everything I needed to know about myself and my roots. It prevented me from forming a Black identity, because I didn't have the information I could explore it with. I became very conscious of my deafness because my family couldn't communicate with me very easily – there was a stigma – but I was not aware of my Black identity, and in our community that was taken for granted. Actually, I didn't like the Afro-Caribbean food that my mother cooked because it was too hot and peppery for me to eat. I preferred British food such as fish, chips and mince pie. I think that was partially because I went to a Deaf school that was predominantly white and that caused a lot of internalised oppression in relation to my Blackness and my culture.

Joseph describes a Black identity as being 'taken for granted' in his community, and this, coupled with his lack of access to information, gives a feeling of something intangible, though clearly important. The reference to food is a good example of how he first became aware that his culture was different. For Krishna, an Asian deaf woman, culture was full of contradictions when she was first diagnosed as deaf, contradictions which she now recognises as being partly to do with gender issues and expectations within her extended family and partly to do with the influence of authority figures on the structure of the family. The latter also dictated the family's reaction to the diagnosis.

Krishna

My childhood memories are not very clear, and what knowledge I have is based on what other people told me, in particular my mother. For example, I remember she told me that she had noticed that I wasn't hearing very well. Many times she took me to the doctor. The doctor said there was nothing wrong with me but my mother continued to be very worried. I can't remember not hearing. There was very much a sense of shock and numbness in my family to learn that I was deaf. I remember very clearly that when my paternal grandfather, who was living with us at the time, and my father found out I was deaf, I was totally rejected by them. My grandfather called me a name that I knew wasn't my name. He called me a very horrible word in our home language, Punjabi, which is unrepeatable. There's no English equivalent of that word, but it is worse than the use of the English word 'dumb'. That was the name he often called me and when I saw the reaction of other people to that word, that's how I knew it had such negative connotations. I remember my mother getting angry with my grandfather and telling him not to call me that. But when I found out what it meant I got angry myself and rejected my grandfather.

My father's side of the family had rigid views of the roles of women; they saw a woman's place as being in the home, bringing up the children and being submissive. These views were not of 'cultural' origin and were unacceptable to my sister and myself. My mother's side of the family consisted of very forward-thinking women. For example, my grandmother, now aged 94, was a teacher when she was 18 years old and practised as such until she married. In those days, very few women were educated in India. My great great grandfather on my mother's side valued women and insisted that all his four daughters were educated. So I don't feel what I experienced was cultural in the sense of one culture, but more I get a sense of a lot of different views operating in one culture. My paternal grandfather behaved in a very oppressive way towards the women, treating my brothers favourably. They were always given first place at meal times, served first, and we were expected to serve them. My mother, maternal uncles and grandmother have been and continue to be an enormous influence on me. But my mother's relatives did not mean so much to me in the early years as this was before I met them. Before that my sense of self was very weak, and often confused. My mother was supportive and caring. She was very oppressed although she always tried to make the best of all situations – she was a survivor. She deferred to people in positions of authority who knew what was best for me – she had little choice but to rely on their goodwill. There was never any real questioning that perhaps they might be wrong about what was best for me.

At home, it was all English language. I never learnt Punjabi at home or at school. My family were instructed to speak English with me, which was difficult to achieve. Punjabi was our home language but when people spoke to me it was always English. I liked it when they spoke to me in English, probably because it was the only language I knew, but it was like English with an Indian accent. I couldn't always understand it because I was so behind with language development generally. However, they spoke distinctly, clearly and slowly and I knew they were speaking to me like that because I was deaf, and that they only spoke to me like that. I didn't feel bad about it, because I was conscious that it reflected their effort to include me. However, when the family resumed their conversation in Punjabi, I would try to interrupt as I didn't want to be left out. I wanted to know what they were saying and would plead with them to tell me; but I would be fobbed off with the usual excuse 'We will tell you later.' I didn't like the family's treatment of me in this respect. I felt frustrated, isolated and often angry with them for not being understanding of my needs. As time went on, I became more resentful of my mum in particular. For about seven years I held these resentful feelings towards my mother but I suppressed them as I didn't feel I could say what was hurting me – non-acceptance of my deafness, over-protectiveness and lack of education. When I started school I was the only Asian child...there were no others in sight. I knew I was different from the other children, but how I was different, I didn't know. I didn't know it was colour – I couldn't call it colour yet because I didn't have the vocabulary. I didn't know at the time that my home was different from the other children's. No words or language to say how I was different, I just knew I was different. I do remember very clearly these massive headphones and them saying I was deaf, boxes here and boxes there and all these wires, going back and forth, back and forth. I felt like an object. Deafness was not valued and deaf people were not seen as being capable of independence. I was aware that, as a consequence, I was being over-protected, even hidden in some ways – the fact that I was deaf was being hidden in very subtle ways. I recall my hairstyle, for example, the way it signified changes in relation to my mother's attitude towards my deafness. I had long plaits to start with when my hearing aids were the old-fashioned kind – basically boxes held in a harness attached to the ears by wires – and every day, diligently, my mother used to do the plaits, first one and then the other. And then at some point, when my hearing aids were changed to a behind-the-ear model, she changed the hairstyle so that it was shorter and framed my face. She also used to tell others: 'My daughter's not deaf! She's fine, she can speak really well.' This continued for a long time. And I remember the other children teasing me about my hearing aids. I do remember I was very isolated before those first clear memories of hearing aids, but I can't put language to it, can't put words to it. I can remember the atmosphere and a sense of all this information just wafting over me and meaning nothing. I remember the very sweet face – of the peripatetic teacher who came to visit me, I didn't know who she was at the time…and sitting with her and feeling very warm and comfortable. We used to look at books; she just turned over the pages and I saw the pictures – nothing else, just the pictures – Peter and Jane, Peter and Jane…

Karen's narrative comes to us from a different perspective. She was born hearing to hearing parents and can recall difficult family relationships before she became deaf, which resulted in feelings of isolation. There is a sense that her deafness simply added to a set of family dynamics which were already around, but this did not in any any way diminish its impact, as it became a channel for the expression of some of the resentful, angry feelings she had been harbouring.

Karen

I can remember feeling left out in the family before I became deaf and so it is very difficult to recognise now how that relates to the experience of being deaf now. I mean I knew the feeling of being left out long before I knew I was deaf. I always felt in the middle, especially when my younger sister was born. I had a lot of feelings about that – feelings of competition between us. I remember when she was she was two and I was four, she was very ill. My brothers were very naughty, so it felt that a lot of attention was being focused on them or on her because she was ill and I had to be 'the good one'. It felt as if I didn't get enough attention because I was good, and because I didn't make any demands on the family. There were a few childhood experiences that keep coming back to me. For example, when I was young, I used to wet the bed regularly. I felt so ashamed of it for a long time, but part of it was...part of it was because of how my family responded, ridiculing me. Maybe I needed to get rid of feelings like anger and pain, which couldn't be expressed directly, and that was the only way I could express them at the time. It's something I have wanted to ask my parents about, but haven't yet. There were good things I had forgotten as well but they became so mixed up with the bad that they got lost. Another incident that sticks in my mind – something about my sister – I must have been four and our relationship was really competitive, and I remember having a doll for Christmas and swapping it for hers because I thought hers was better than mine. I felt really guilty because I did that. Another time, I became so jealous that I called my sister a pig, or something, and then I ran off, and again I felt really guilty. My brother ran after me and dragged me back home and I can remember very clearly my feelings of shame. I always felt my parents loved my sister more than they loved me, but as soon as I felt jealous, I began to feel that was wrong and shameful.

When my deafness was diagnosed my family couldn't cope. There was no information, no advice when they realised I was deaf. I was just given a hearing aid and that's it! I was about 17 at that time and I was given this box with wires, and I was the only one that had a hearing aid, and – well, you can imagine, at that age – I couldn't bear it and I refused to wear it. Later I was given behind-the-ear aids. I just had to struggle through, really. At home, my family used to sit down round the table to talk – that was a nice part of being in a family – but I couldn't be a part of that, and I could feel my emotions churning up and then I would just explode: 'What are you taking about? What about me? You never think about me!' And they would apologise and try for five minutes and then they forgot again. I realise that I also expected myself to be perfect and not have these negative feelings. These kinds of situations affected my feelings about my identity very much. I often felt as if I was not there. For a time I would try making demands and continually ask what they were saying, but then I started to feel I didn't want to be a part of those situations because I seemed to be making all the effort. Added to the diagnosis, there was the confusion caused by lack of information. No one ever told me what would happen in the future. Would I be completely deaf? From about 17 to 22, every time I had a cold, my hearing would go and it would send me into a panic. I had to get to the doctor to get antibiotics, finish them and then it would start all over again. I think that damaged me a lot and I just gave up. I also had to go to ENT appointments and they would give me these tablets and I had to take about 18 of these every day. Maybe the doctors felt better giving me them, but I got so fed up with it that I started to say what's the point, and I stopped going. But my mother still tried to collude with the doctor and got the ENT hospitals to keep sending me more appointments – I think that was for her benefit, not for mine.

Unravelling Narratives

The first and second stages in Erikson's framework for the development of identity are centred around the psychosocial conflicts of *basic trust versus mistrust* and *autonomy versus shame or doubt*, with particular emphasis on how trust and autonomy are established through the security of the attachment made between the child and his or her primary caregivers. Bowlby (1969, 1973, 1980, 1988a, 1988b) had possibly the strongest influence on the development of theories about attachment. He believed that all children have an inborn tendency to create strong emotional bonds with their primary caregivers, in particular the mother. On the surface level, these relationships have survival value because the child who bonds with the caregiver is then nurtured by them. But at a deeper level they are maintained by clear patterns of behaviour and communication which are designed to perpetuate the closeness between child and caregiver. One important distinction is whether a relationship is founded on an *affectional bond*, which places emphasis on the irreplaceable nature of a particular individual, or on an *attachment* where a person's sense of security is bound up in the relationship and they use the other individual as a home to which they can always safely retreat or return from exploring the world outside the relationship. Thus the child's relationship with the parent is an example of an attachment whereas the parents's relationship with the child is not, though their relationship with their partner or spouse may be.

The pattern of *attachment behaviours* underpinning these kinds of relationships give us a great deal of information about the strength or the quality of the affectional bond or the attachment. The quality of the bond developed will depend upon the opportunity that parent and child have to develop a mutual, interlocking pattern of attachment behaviours. Usually, bonding is both robust and effective, but both parents and children must have the necessary signals and skills to enable bonding to happen. If either child or parent is lacking in one of these areas, the relationship will lack synchrony and the bond is invariably weakened or fails altogether. Interestingly, Fraiberg (1974, 1975) found that the behaviour of blind babies, who smile less than sighted babies and do not show mutual gaze, led their parents to believe that they were being rejected by the baby or that the baby was depressed. Parents who feel depressed, incompetent or powerless, on the other hand, may be slower to respond to their child's signals and more negative or distant, sometimes hostile, towards their children. One possible outcome of the failure to develop a strong affectional bond is child abuse and neglect, and this is even more likely to happen when current life situations are very stressful (Bee 1994). Ainsworth *et al.* (1978) developed a classification system for describing the attachment behaviours of one-year-old children when placed in 'strange situations' and Main and her colleagues (Main and Solomon 1985; Main and Cassidy 1988) found a high degree of correlation between the security of attachment achieved at 18 months and that at six years of age. Four categories of attachment behaviours have been identified, which are shown in Box 2.1.

A useful way of unravelling the narratives which make up this chapter may be to consider the quality of affectional bonds and attachments formed in each family, and what factors influence this. When a counsellor first enters

---

Box 2.1 Attachment behaviours

Type of attachment	Behaviours observed
secure	Child shows preference for main caregiver (usually the mother), knows how to get their attention and does not avoid or resist contact when it is initiated. Child will generally be pleased to see them after a separation and can be calmed if upset.
detached/avoidant	Child does not make a distinction between primary caregiver and a stranger. He/she will not resist contact if initiated by them but is generally reluctant to seek contact and avoids contact with mother when there has been a separation.
resistant/ambivalent	Child is extremely upset when separated from caregiver and will often show anger towards them on their return, refusing to be comforted by them or by a stranger. The child will often resist contact with a stranger as well.
disorganised/ disorientated	The child seems completely detached and expresses emotion in a way which seems unconnected to other people who are present. The child seems confused and apprehensive, and demonstrates conflicting behaviour such as showing strong avoidance after seeking contact.

---

a relationship with a client, one or more of the early sessions may be devoted to listening to client stories. One way of demonstrating that they have listened and understood, and a measure of how empathy is developing, is the skill with which the counsellor is able to *pinpoint* issues that seem important for the client or issues which the counsellor feels are in need of further clarification. One of my deaf students referred to this as being similar to when we read something and use a highlighter pen to draw attention to or remind ourselves of significant or striking aspects of the text, and I have found this a very useful and visual analogy. Sometimes, pinpointing results in the client making further internal connections with things that may be subconscious or even unconscious. For example, when I interviewed Peter, there were two situations where this happened. The first was when he made reference to the coal-hole, and as he was describing this I noticed that his body language and facial expression conveyed a great deal of feeling. I commented that it was a very powerful image and that I could almost imagine being in the coal-hole with him at that moment. It was that comment that provoked his later reference to having 'a fantasy about being locked in'. On another occasion when he was talking about his uncle, a look of great affection came over his face and his eyes momentarily misted over. I suggested that he seemed to have great affection for his uncle, which he confirmed saying that he really 'missed him', but interestingly, for reasons that will become clear later, he emphasised that he got into bed with his uncle 'for comfort'.

At other times, pinpointing results in the counsellor identifying and summarising themes as connections are made between the highlighted points, and, as suggested in the introductory chapter, not only do we make connections for the individual, but in doing so, we can make connections between individuals. The above narratives contain a number of common themes and a predominance of particular feelings which reflect on the quality of the relationship that each of these people had with their parents and other significant adults in their lives when they were very young, which I will now go through with reference to examples from the narratives.

The first theme concerns the fundamental nature of the relationship between child and parents, the basis of affectional bonds and the child's trust in their parents to provide security and nurturance. There were some examples of a clear and positive bond. For example, Caroline says that 'When my mother came, I could feel my face light up and I just latched on to her, the feeling of bonding was so strong. I was so pleased to see her', Sam that 'I felt safe because my father always seemed to be there watching for me. I remembered the image of that', and Fiona doesn't remember feeling any different from her family, which implies acceptance. In some cases conditions were attached to the bond from the start. Peter says that 'I was always trying to make my mother laugh, because if I was successful in doing that, I knew she was happy with me', whereas Karen felt that she 'didn't get enough attention because I was good, and because I didn't make any demands on the family'. There is a sense of both wanting to please their parents and feeling responsible for their parent's feelings. In the case of Sam, however, conditions became a part of the relationship later resulting in a feeling of trust being betrayed: 'My father saw I was crying so he gave me some money. It was like a present or a reward so I stopped crying.'

A second, related theme seems to be concerned with whether the child's experiences were confirmed or denied by the relationships, both horizontal and vertical, that they made. Karen and Peter, for example, both felt a degree of sibling rivalry, suggesting that their hearing sibling was loved more or received more attention than they did, and both struggled with negative feelings of shame at the jealousy they felt: 'I can remember very clearly my feelings of shame. I always felt my parents loved my sister more than they loved me, but as soon as I felt jealous, I began to feel that was wrong and shameful' (Karen); 'I still wish I had had more information when I was young. I needed more understanding. I always felt my hearing brother had more attention. But he was much younger, and I was jealous of him, I think' (Peter). In contrast, Fiona experienced some ambivalence in relation to her Deaf cousin, which marked the beginning of a niggling feeling of being different: 'I remember asking myself why she went to a Deaf school and had hearing aids because every other aspect of the family dynamics seemed to be the same. I also remember wondering if I had been a bad girl, and that is why these "privileges" had been withheld.' Caroline received a great deal of positive affirmation for her Deaf self and was extremely aware of herself as a Deaf person: 'Maybe I was looking at them through Deaf eyes even then?...what's so wonderful about being hearing – hearing?' I wanted to be different from them', accompanied by a sense of where she and others belonged: 'My brother had good speech so it felt as if it was right for him to go there...all I could think about was getting back to the place that I knew...my Deaf identity was battered there.' Fiona also has her Deafness affirmed through a mixture of positive and negative experiences: 'There was no obvious difference, at least none that I could describe easily... When I was in the Deaf setting I was in there, a full part of it and I never though twice about it.' Any ambivalence that she experiences results from an awareness that others in the extended family were treated differently to her. For Sam, however, the affirmation of his 'normality' came from his horizontal relationships: 'I was curious and confused. I didn't know who I was then. I thought my birth had been "normal" the same as any child... There was something about Bill that reassured me. Maybe the nuns were frightening, but Bill – it felt as if I was able to communicate with him easily. I think I felt an almost instant bond. I didn't understand the words of course, but there was a lot of gesturing which hit something deep inside me – it felt very familiar.' Krishna's contact with others outside of the home marked the beginning of a sense of confusion rather than affirmation. She experienced feelings of difference in her first school, but was unable to put a name to them: 'I knew I was different from the other children, but how I was different, I didn't know. I didn't know it was colour – I couldn't call it colour yet because I didn't have the vocabulary. I didn't know at the time that my home was different from the other children's. No words or language to say how I was different, I just knew I was different...my sense of self was very weak, and often confused.'

There are a number of very strong statements about the need to depend on atmosphere and feeling-responses without explicit language to confirm or deny what was being conveyed, and the damaged communication that was experienced within the family or through contacts with hearing adults. Peter found it difficult to make the connections: 'I was four years old and I didn't know why I was there... It was frightening seeing my mother cry and not knowing why... It feels strange really, trying to make sense of my world as it was then – all the images flashing by.' Caroline was frustrated by the attitudes of adults she met outside the home: 'I would be frustrated because of all this talking in the air with no regard for me', whereas, for Karen, it was the attitudes of her family: 'Part of it was because of how my family responded, ridiculing me... My family used to sit down round the table to talk – that was a nice part of being in a family – but I couldn't be a part of that, and I could feel my emotions churning up and then I would just explode: "What are you taking about? What about me? You never think about me!"' There is, however, some sensitivity to behaviour, mood and atmosphere. Krishna says: 'I can remember the atmosphere and a sense of all this information just wafting over me and meaning nothing.' This sensitivity enabled her, for example, to understand that she was being insulted and rejected: 'When I saw the reaction of other people to that word, that's how I knew it had such negative connotations', and when she was being supported, but this was also mixed up with feelings about being alienated from her Asian self as a result of the stigma associated with her deafness: 'they spoke distinctly, clearly and slowly and I knew they were speaking to me like that because I was deaf, and that they only spoke to me like that. I didn't feel bad about it, because I was conscious that it reflected their effort to include me. However, when the family resumed their conversation in Punjabi, I would try to interrupt as I didn't want to be left out. I wanted to know what they were saying and would plead with them to tell me; but I would be fobbed off with the usual excuse "We will tell you later." I didn't like the family's treatment of me in this respect.'

In some of the narratives, the stigma associated with deafness within the family is very invasive. Sam describes the harrowing changes in his parents when it was discovered that Sam was deaf, and how he blamed himself for the change: 'That's the first time I had seen him angry. Before, he was warm and loving, he cuddled me… My parents were broken apart. My mother and father were crying – I'd never seen them do that before. A child of one or two usually makes their parents happy, but they were crying. I remember feeling that awful sinking feeling inside because I didn't know what I had done as I had just been playing with them while the "tests" were done. I wanted to know what was going on – I didn't understand. I thought I was responsible for their tears.' For Krishna, the sense of shock was also very much in evidence, though there was some division in the family: 'Many times she took me to the doctor. The doctor said there was nothing wrong with me but my mother continued to be very worried. I can't remember not hearing. There was very much a sense of shock and numbness in my family to learn that I was deaf. I remember very clearly that when my paternal grandfather, who was living with us at the time, and my father found out I was deaf, I was totally rejected by them…maternal uncles and grandmother have been and continue to be an enormous influence on me.' In other narratives, there are repeated references to feelings of invisibility and the objectification of deafness. Peter says: 'I felt I could just disappear in the dark, feel small, like nothing', and Karen that she 'often felt as if I was not there', whereas Krishna felt that both she and her deafness were being consciously hidden: 'I felt like an object. Deafness was not valued and deaf people were not seen as being capable of independence. I was aware that, as a consequence, I was being overprotected, even hidden in some ways – the fact that I was deaf was being hidden in very subtle ways.' Karen describes the objectification through the focus on hearing aids with some bitterness: 'I was given this box with wires, and I was the only one that had a hearing aid, and – well, you can imagine, at that age – I couldn't bear it and I refused to wear it.'

For Sam, the harsh reality of being physically separated from his parents resulted in acute feelings of loss and separation, the numbness of which was associated with blocked-off feelings: 'My father had just left me at the school. No goodbyes. he just left me and I was screaming to myself "Why me? Why me?"… But when I realised that we were all the same, there was something about learning that which made me put a lid on my feelings – clamp them down – so that I couldn't talk any more. I wanted to talk more, but I couldn't, I couldn't take any more explanation. I had so much feeling of shock, loss.' He felt a complete inability to understand why he had to be separated from them when he had felt happy with them: 'I was just so confused because I was happy with my family. I was frustrated by the communication difficulties, yes, but my brothers just let me get on with my life, they left me alone, and I was happy being that way. Why was I now separated from them? Karen also described how positive feelings became submerged in negative ones: 'There were good things I had forgotten as well but they became so mixed up with the bad that they got lost.'

A final theme is related to a growing awareness in some of the narratives that the stigma associated with deafness impinged upon other aspects of an emerging identity. Joseph, for example, felt that he was prevented from forming a Black identity both by the lack of accessible information and the fact that blackness is not something which is talked about, it just is: 'I felt cut off from the kind of information that hearing children picked up about Black culture and other cultures, and from 'hearing' information generally... It was like living in a very primitive age. I felt denied of this information and it stopped me from understand everything I needed to know about myself and my roots. It prevented me from forming a Black identity, because I didn't have the information I could explore it with. I became very conscious of my deafness because my family couldn't communicate with me very easily – there was a stigma – but I was not aware of my Black identity, and in our community that was taken for granted.' Krishna links it to role expectations of women and the relationships between women and authority figures within and outside the family: 'My paternal grandfather behaved in a very oppressive way towards the women, treating my brothers favourably... She deferred to people in positions of authority who knew what was best for me – she had little choice but to rely on their good-will. There was never any real questioning that perhaps they might be wrong about what was best for me.' Sam also refers to authority figures associated with religion, whereas Caroline felt 'sad, really really sad, looking up at all those hearing adults talking to each other, controlling the children.'

There is clearly a great deal of diversity in the dynamics of these families, as perceived by the deaf family member, but generally the narratives support the view that the quality of affectional bonds created between deaf children and their parents in the early years is critically dependent on how parents relate to 'deaf'. If their attitude is one of acceptance and their behaviour confirms this, the child is more able to positively affirm who they are and carry this into their relationships with others. But, as we saw, they do not always receive further affirmation in their contacts outside the family. For those who appear secure in their early attachments, the values they learn from these are taken with them outside and can be a source of strength. For those who are not accepted, the result is confusion and sometimes anger as they feel under pressure to become invisible. As the counselling relationship develops, some themes and issues repeat themselves over and over again in many different contexts. It is then that both counsellor and client are able to establish their primacy in the client's life. The issues of control and power raised in the final comment by Caroline feature very strongly in the following chapters.

CHAPTER THREE

Windows and Toast on Beans

Crucial to this sense of industry is the 'positive identification with those who know things and know how to do things'. One special teacher in the lives of many gifted individuals has often been credited as the spark which ignited outstanding later achievements. (Kroger 1996, quoting Erikson 1968)

The arts of power and its minions are the same in all countries and in all ages. It marks a victim; denounces it; and excites the public odium and the public hatred, to conceal its own abuses and encroachments. (Henry Clay 1834)

Introduction

The following two chapters are concerned with the emergence of personality and the growing awareness of a sense of social self both in relation to the first direct contacts with adults outside the family and in relation to peers. As children reach the stage in the development cycle where the psychosocial conflicts *initiative versus guilt* and *industry versus inferiority* come to the fore, these relationships become increasingly important in the extent to which they conflict with, confuse or reinforce the messages gained from the core relationship between the child and their primary caregiver. Parallel to these conflicts most children are also developing a *gender concept* and a growing *awareness of sex roles*. If the child has not been able to resolve previous conflicts centred upon the core relationship, or has resolved them in an unhelpful way, they may carry over some of the resulting uncertainty into new challenges. As we saw in the previous chapter, parents may lack confidence in their own competence or echo the confusion experienced by their deaf children when 'deaf' joins the family. This means that another adult, who offers 'expert' knowledge and experience of how to deal with 'deaf' can become a personification of a troubled parent's rescue fantasies. Because such a person may be seen as powerful or as 'having all the answers', in much the same way that the client may view the counsellor when meeting them for the first time, parents may not look beyond the authority or question whether what is being offered is right for their child. Krishna highlighted this point in chapter two, and other narrators alluded to it. Unlike a counsellor, however, other adults may not be aware of the power that they have, or skilled in creating safe environments. Without this awareness and skill, and especially when there is some doubt about whether home is a 'safe base' as might happen when the child's sense of basic trust in their caregivers has been damaged by their parent's lack of skill in providing protection and security for the child, or when the psychosocial conflict of autonomy versus shame or doubt has resulted in uncertainty about competence, further damage may be caused. We saw this in the previous chapter in that the distress experienced by Sam and Peter when they were separated from their parents was, in part, an outcome of not knowing what was happening and not having shared in the planning because of communication difficulties. But, *as children*, their instinctive response was to mistrust their parent's ability to protect them because the separation was *painful*, and to be angry at the threat to their autonomy. In such situations, the ability of the child to apply their own internal model of attachment to new relationships may therefore already be more limited, and substitute caregivers typically represent more challenges for the child in this position because they are 'strangers'. Nevertheless, the kinds of role models they are and the kinds of reinforcement they provide the child with, particularly in respect of the child's competence, are critical to the child's global sense of self-esteem – one of the most important expected outcomes of the pre-adolescent years.

Power, itself, as we saw in *Counselling – The Deaf Challenge*, may be ordered along a dimension which ranges from the abuse of power, through authoritarianism, control and enabling, to empowerment. From the child's perspective, an adult's abuse of power may be associated with fear and compliance, whereas empowerment might be perceived in the positive reinforcement of his/her own beliefs, values and ways of being within the context of the social and cultural environment. The images which convey these perceptions of power are shown in Figure 3.1 and are drawn directly from two of the narratives given below. Some of these issues were raised in the previous

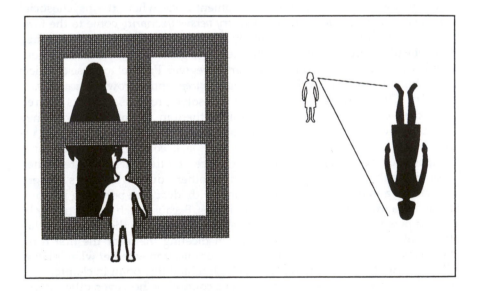

Figure 3.1 Windows and toast on beans

chapter, but there the focus was more on the core relationship. This chapter is concerned primarily with first school experiences where the narrator is separated on a day or residential basis from their home environment, the vertical relationships formed with 'professionals', and the developing awareness of a social self through early peer relationships. In addition, Caroline gives her perspective both as a child and, later, as a parent as she attempts to bring up and achieve an education of her Deaf children.

Krishna

I stayed in the mainstream school until I was eleven years old, then was sent to a Deaf school. My mother didn't really want me to go. But because they were saying that I was a very 'slow learner', my mother felt there was a possibility of an improved education so she allowed me to go and I stayed there for about two and a half years. Those years were some of the best years of my life because they brought me out of my shell. My personality, everything about me changed in a big way. It was interesting because just before I went to the deaf school my cousin from India came here to get married. She lived with us for a considerable length of time. She observed me before and after life at the Deaf school. Before I went to the Deaf school, she felt I was always a good child, very obedient, very quiet, and although I was physically there, I didn't follow what was going on, didn't seem to be an active participant in family life. But when I went to the Deaf school and began to come home at weekends, I was making demands at home, saying what I wanted, asking for things. I was really as I say coming out of my shell, I felt more animated, I was saying I want that, I want that, I want to learn, I want to become a teacher like my grandmother. It was like I had a new confidence. *That* was what was different. This meant that I didn't want to take part in household tasks any more, I just wanted to study and study, and I'd never never done that before. I became very outspoken too. So the main difference was that before Deaf school, I was very withdrawn and apart from everything, but as a result of going there I developed self-confidence and learned more language because I had access to both BSL and English, and began to express things that the family had never heard from me before.

Joseph

The poor quality of education and the lack of resources about Black culture and history left me feeling humiliated and intimidated – like a second class citizen – because I couldn't make good progress with our schoolwork. The teachers had such low expectations and the lack of understanding about what it means to be Black and Deaf. Many white deaf people have a similar experience in education, but it's not the same as that of Black Deaf people because we have the added experience of oppression. For example, *The Voice* started about 12 years ago to cater for the information and cultural needs of Black people, and it was very difficult for a lot of us to read this paper because all the stories and articles about racism and racial discrimination were written in English. This meant that information was not shared with Black Deaf people and also that we got cut off from each other and from our cultures. When I was young, I couldn't go to youth clubs where there were hearing Black young people because of the language problem. The youth club was supposed to be part of community education that would encourage and promote Black Deaf people's personal and social development. Most teachers of the deaf never discussed race, let alone Deaf issues, and would often dismiss these issues with 'It's too difficult for you to understand because it's complicated.' That sounded very patronising, and it meant also that we were discriminated against in school because white Deaf children picked up those attitudes.

Sam

School was so different. They had rules which were enforced rigidly. On my first day, in the evening, I saw the boys queuing up in several queues and Bill called me over to join his queue. He was very good to me, tried to educate me about the rules. We walked off and I looked behind and realised the other queues had gone. We walked into the dining room which had long tables and chairs with places set out for us to eat. I sat down and suddenly someone smacked my hand. I was shocked – it was so sudden, and looked up at one of the nuns. I looked around me and saw that all the boys were standing up still with their heads bowed, praying, though I didn't know it was praying. I just saw them standing with their hands together in front of them – it wasn't clear. At home, when it was meal time we just sat down and started eating. My mother and father never hit me. I started looking around again in confusion because I didn't understand what it all meant and made eye contact with one of the nuns. She had a very stern face and jabbed a finger in my direction. I started to shake, feeling the power emanating from her, then bowed my head, the same as all the other boys. I watched all the boys eating in silence and kept feeling inside that I wanted to go home, but I was so scared of this nun that I didn't dare say anything.

When food was finished, we were allowed a play time, then we were in queues again and marched off to the bedroom. I was surprised at the size of it. It was full of rows of beds. I looked at my watch and realised it was only six o'clock in the evening and yet we were being made to go to bed. At home, I went to bed much later because I was helping on the farm. I started to take my clothes off and saw the other boys looking at me in horror and pointing at me. Then I saw Bill get into bed first and wriggle out of his clothes under the bed covers. At home my mother and father were easy about undressing and I just copied them, it was natural. But here, it wasn't allowed. The effect of this experience on me became obvious later. For example, one thing I remember hating was that every Thursday night, we went into the bathroom. There was a woman in there, not a nun but someone who was employed to do domestic work, who had responsibility making sure we washed properly. By that time, I had moved from being a very happy-go-lucky child, very easy about my body, to being very shy and unsure of myself physically. I didn't like being watched undressing – I didn't want anyone to see me so exposed. This place changed me.

It felt as if my mind was being narrowed, making me feel very exposed. I felt very small and unhappy, worried about what this woman might do to me if I broke the unspoken rules again. It was almost like living in fear.

On that first night I got into bed and looked up. There were large windows with curtains all around. I pulled the covers up, my brain going over and over what was happening to me. Then I turned over and cried quietly, thinking about all the rules, the different things I had to do and the shock I felt about all of it. I looked out through the windows later when it was dark and saw the moon. I imagined it was smiling at me and that lifted my spirit a little. But I couldn't sleep that night, tossing and turning, sweating and crying. I was so upset in the end that I wet myself. In the morning, the nuns came and lifted the covers off all of us. When they saw I was wet, there was a lot of head-shaking and then they made me take all my nightclothes off. The older boys from a different dormitory – they were five year olds – were walking past and they laughed at me, pointed at me and called me 'baby' because I wet myself. I could only think about their language – new language for me. Bill comforted me, but I felt very churned up inside. I mean this was my first day and already I was being laughed at by older boys.

I went and washed and brushed my teeth, and once more we had to form queues and marched to breakfast. Again the routine was the same. We had to pray before we were allowed to eat. This time I looked around more carefully. There were a lot of windows, rather like the dormitories upstairs. But this was different. There was a kind of balcony outside these windows and the nuns could walk up to the balcony on the outside of the building and stand there watching us. It made me feel frightened, being watched all the time. After breakfast, we were allowed to play for half an hour and then we were all summoned to go to the toilet. Again we queued up at the door of each of the toilets. I was beginning to get a bad feeling again. I saw Bill in a different queue and asked him what was happening. He said when I went into the toilet, I must pull my pants down and 'go', but I mustn't flush the toilet. The nun would come in and check whether I had done anything or not and then she would flush the toilet if it was satisfactory. Again there was this shock. My mother and father never *made me* go to the toilet. I went when I wanted to, I had a choice. Here I wasn't allowed to choose. When it was my turn. I went in and closed the door. I tried desperately to make myself 'go', but I couldn't. The nun kept checking on me and made me stay in the cubicle. I kept trying but I couldn't. The boys who were behind me in the queue were starting to get angry because they *did* want to go, and they *could* go. Eventually the nun took me out of the cubicle by the ear and hit me on the back of the head in disgust. We went off to play again and Bill was very concerned. Later on we went into the classroom for writing lessons. One hour later I began to feel that I needed the toilet. I put my hand up and asked the nun if I could go. She refused to allow me and said that I had to go in the morning after breakfast – that was the rule and if I didn't that was it. My need to relieve myself got worse and worse. I was absolutely desperate to go. Bill could see that I was in trouble. I stood up again to attract the nun's attention and she slapped me down. Eventually I just burst. I couldn't hold it in. The nun looked disgusted. She opened the window and told me to get out. That was a really bad experience for me because again all the other boys laughed at my accident.

Three days later, someone came to test my hearing. I was made to put on these large headphones and indicate when I heard anything. Then they forced my head into a very uncomfortable position and made me keep it absolutely still, while they tried to get me to make speech sounds, 'p' and 'b' sounds getting them just right so that I made a feather move. I was really frightened. There was something about that experience that knocked my sense of myself sideways. I could almost feel this massive change happen inside. It caught me completely off guard. When I had a new teacher, whose job it was to teach speech, a small group of us had to sit around a table which was equipped with microphones and ear pieces. We were made to speak into the microphones to monitor our voices. But we had to have the volume up to maximum and that meant that the sound was so loud that it hurt our ears. This teacher used to walk around the room checking on each of us to make sure that we were getting it right. When she was looking at another boy I noticed that some of the boys quickly turned the volume knobs down when they knew she wasn't looking. I thought maybe it would be a good idea if I tried the same thing because my ears were becoming painful. I watched the teacher walk around the table and when she walked behind me, I lost sight of her so I thought it was safe. I reached out slowly and warily and turned the volume knob down. I felt someone grab me by the hair and wrench me out of my seat. I was told off for breaking the rules and made to apologise. She then turned the knob up again and I had to endure the pain to a point where I went completely white and felt ill. The teacher eventually noticed and made me go into another room, where I was violently sick. She made me clean it up myself and again all these images flashed by of the nun in black and white, strict, severe, the cross, the windows, and I remembered home and being happy. It didn't fit with my father giving me money and assuring me it would be all right. I wasn't happy in this place and I longed to return home. I felt I had no freedom to be who I was at that school – the nuns were so powerful.

Peter

For me, my identity, or should I say identities, is something about fitting. I have many parts to me which have been important at different times in my life and as I have gone through that life, meeting people, I have gained insight into what these different parts mean to me. For example, I am Deaf, gay and Jewish, and these three aspects of myself are very difficult to merge. I think I first realised that I was gay when I was at school, though because there was no information – no one told me what *gay* meant and I'd never heard of the name or the word. But I was interfered with when I was very young at school; I remember being touched in the toilet. It was a deaf school for boys – we were queuing up for the toilets as we were made to do then, and I was at the back so I couldn't see what was happening at the front. The toilets were outside with no roof and when you got inside the toilet there were brick walls all around and the seats were large and flat, square, made of wood and there was a hole in the middle. And all the boys had to stand up inside – I know that because I was told – and when it was my turn the other boys were looking at me. I was standing up feeling a bit scared and stupid and I was made to pull my trousers and pants down. They all laughed and I didn't know what it meant. I remember I was given a small rubber bung while they looked at me and it just didn't connect. It became like a symbol of some sort – I didn't know what it meant but it stayed in my mind. Why did I remember that in particular? Because it meant information and communication were at a very basic level. It was more visual, but the meaning wasn't always clear – you didn't always know what was meant. So that rubber bung became a symbol of my early life when no one explained anything. Whether it's connected to the fact that as I am from the Jewish religion I was circumcised – I don't know. The meaning wasn't clear at the time.

My first deaf school was a day school and all the children were from working-class families and backgrounds. I think there was a big access problem, and certainly not enough information available to understand our environment and what was going on. The language level of many of the children was very low, and access to language was poor. Although I cannot remember being aware of being Jewish, I think I must have been aware of some difference because I didn't like eating the meat at school. Maybe I knew that, when we were at home, we only ate meat that was cooked the Jewish way so I had very mixed feelings about eating meat at school. But which came first? Jewish, Deaf or gay? I can't answer that, and I'm not sure I want to. But I think there was evidence of them all in different ways even when I was very young. I was definitely aware of two different cultures because I can remember that when I was at home in the family, my mother used to light the candles on the Menorah and I knew that it was a special Friday and the next day would be the Sabbath and my father would go to the synagogue. These customs were not evident in the lives of the other children I knew. I remember feeling different from them, but it's hard to remember *how*.

What I do know is that there were expectations on me to conform, in particular to be straight. Being gay is not generally acceptable in the Jewish faith. As I went through life, my father always said to me that I would marry some nice, rich Jewish girl, and would place a lot of emphasis on that. I can remember at the second school I went to that I got into trouble because one of the older boys bothered me sexually and I felt upset by it; I told my mother, and both my mother and my father were very upset and angry – there was a lot of confusion. But the next day when I arrived at the school, I saw my father waiting outside the school and I went into a panic. I was really worried and wondering what was going on. He was there to see the head teacher and the next thing I knew was that the boy had been expelled. But I felt unhappy, I felt guilty in some strange way because I knew that I *liked* boys somehow, but I wasn't clear about what that feeling meant to me. I later justified it by saying to myself that this boy was trouble and that I didn't like him anyway because he was a bully. But I still feel as if my head was in the clouds, and that I didn't understand a lot of things that were going on in my youth.

I remember one school holiday. I was on my own a lot, because my brother was much younger than me and so we couldn't easily play together. He went to a hearing school. I remember I went to a park on my own and there were a group of children playing on a see-saw and swings, and a girl came to me. She started talking to me and I talked back to her with my voice (I didn't have good speech when I was young). She kept asking 'Where do you come from?' and I said that I lived on the moon because that was my way of explaining why I had a strange voice and strange speech. That was all I could think of, and I remember all of them looking at me in a very puzzled and very strange way, trying to make sense of why I said that I came from the moon – something that they knew couldn't be true – and trying to work it out. All I was conscious of was wanting some link, some communication, but how? It was difficult. My parents always said that I had to talk. My mother always helped me to read and practice my speech, to repeat words over and over again. It went on and on and on. I got a lot of attention in *that* way but I also made my mother angry because I often didn't get it right. As a result, I was often frustrated even though I knew that it was the family's way of caring.

My first conscious awareness of being gay was when I went to boarding school. I started to become more aware that some boys played with other boys. What was interesting for me was that for them, it was just something to do, to have fun with, and although I never analysed it, I think it might have been different for me. I never had sex counselling or education to help me to confirm or deny it. There was no one in the school at all, no counsellor, no advisor or anything who could help me understand what was happening to me. I always felt guilty and secretive – I had to pretend that it never happened in many ways. Also, at boarding school there were only three or four Jewish children and I think there was anti-Semitic behaviour from the other children and the teachers. I felt that there were one or two teachers who didn't like the Jewish children. Comments were made, but it was very subtle, just a feeling with no name that could be attached to it. For my Bar Mitzvah, I had to learn Hebrew with one of the Elders. I didn't know what it meant really; he would translate but it still meant very little to me. I had to read the Torah at the Synagogue in front of my family and I remember I had this terrible earache, a pounding in my ear which was really painful. I didn't want to go through with it but I had to. There were these noises in my ear and I had to read and I hated that time. I hated it. And, at the age of ten, I had to wear shorts, which looked stupid on me. All the other boys, even ten- and eleven-year-olds, wore long trousers, but I had to wear shorts until I was 13, which was when I had my Bar Mitzvah. But I went to deaf boarding school before that, and the regulation uniform was long trousers so I could wear them there. That was a great relief, but again, it was like school and home were different cultures.

Fiona

When I went to my local school, I knew things were different because people asked me questions in English and I signed back. I then couldn't understand why they didn't understand my responses. When I was at playgroup, before I started school, no one ever played with me – I was always alone. At primary school, I then became the 'dummy' and knew somehow that it was linked to 'privileges' given to hearing children which were withheld. For example, I wasn't allowed to play the piano because the staff believed there was no point since my parents were 'deaf and dumb'. In some activities, other children would beat me when I tried to join in because I didn't fit. I know all of these things made me different, but I didn't understand why. I never had any awareness or concept of the fact that it was because my parents were Deaf and I wasn't. I didn't understand that there was a difference between being hearing and Deaf.

Even hearing children didn't try to deny my Deaf experience. They just treated me as the 'dummy' because I was very quiet when I was with them – they never knew I was there. With them, I couldn't feel that I had my own personality. There was a lot of teasing, but I would never respond, never. I couldn't tell my parents that this happened at school. I would say nothing happened and that I have got lots of homework, but I would never tell them about the difficulties with peer relationships. I do remember trying to educate the younger members of the family when they went to school. I became like the second mother – the 'hearing mother'. I told them that if anyone said anything to them in school they must respond that they have the same nose, the same eyes, the same ears – they can hear and speak. They were to make it clear that they could sign but that was something the hearing children with hearing parents couldn't do! I told them to do it but I could never make myself as assertive as that! So what I am saying really is that it was, in a way, as if hearing children were denigrating my experience as a negative one by associating me with a 'dummy'. They were putting a label on me which carried a negative association with deafness, and perhaps that meant I was more like a Deaf child in a sense. Yes, a Deaf child that could hear which is a very peculiar way to feel, thinking back. How we managed I don't know. I always remember feeling they talked about my family as if they were somehow 'bad', and questioning myself inside FATHER MY THICK? NO! because I understood my father and I knew they couldn't. When I eventually asked my father how to deal with it he was just so fair and consistent, he never said they were stupid, he just said that they don't understand and it is not their fault. So that's the way I learnt to treat situations like this.

Caroline

How I turned from a sad, maybe angry child into one who was happier, I don't know? Perhaps it was when I went to deaf school, because that was a completely different environment. I went to a deaf school as a day pupil. I loved school, had many friends. In the classroom it was oral, but outside, in the playground, when we were with each other we were allowed to sign. I hated learning speech – hated it – I felt so stupid having to repeat the s, s, s... Every time I got it wrong, I had to do it all over again and I was asking myself 'Why do I have to keep going over and over it, I don't understand what it all means!' I never understood why I had to say that and not that, or say that in that way and not that way. It was just so stupid, a waste of time when I could have been learning more important things. Anything to do with speech – headphones, hearing tests, I hated that. I always had this frustration inside me wanting to burst about the emphasis on that. They played these tones and sometimes I would say I heard and they said no, no, you can't have done. I never got it right. I realise now looking back that I must have had tinnitus and I thought I was hearing something through the headphones when it was the noises in my head. Sometimes I was deliberately naughty and said things that I knew were wrong; but they made me feel so guilty, blamed me all the time because I couldn't speak properly and they were always telling me off. Almost in the same breath, they would then tell me I was doing fine, my speech was really good, and that was particularly cruel because when I left school and I talked to hearing people, I realised they couldn't understand my speech. It was so inconsistent and it backfired on me because I had been led to believe my speech was good. I felt they had lied to me. Even on the last day they said now don't forget your t's and your s's and I thought, 'I'm leaving school and the only things I have to remember are my t's and s's!!' And in the back of my head I was thinking 'Why?' I didn't understand. I remember working very hard up to the time I took an entrance exam to another school and I failed. I didn't know why I failed. A lot of other Deaf children seemed to know that they had failed because they had said something wrong or something like that, but I never knew until later – it was the oral test! There was just all this emphasis at the time on speech.

I liked maths best, but I was always frustrated with English because I kept making the same mistakes, I realise now because sign language was interfering in exactly the same way that French might interfere with an English accent. For example, I always said 'toast on beans' and they said 'No, that's wrong, it's "beans on toast"' and I would argue with them because my mum always signed TOAST-ON-BEANS and that meant that 'toast on beans' must be right. But they would still say 'beans on toast' was right. It's so ridiculous, I mean you have toast, what's on it? Beans! So it must be 'beans on toast'. You don't have a pile of beans with toast on top! It's crazy! [laughs] I can't remember what my mum told me about the education system, but I am conscious that school and home were quite separate – school was school, when I finished there at the end of the day, that was it! Home was home – separate, quite different. I think knowing I had that home helped me. I remember once that I was doing an exam with one teacher and two other people came in to supervise the teaching. It was a new subject and he was really cross because I knew the answers! Afterwards, he said 'How did you know?' I was clear it was because of my mum and dad, I learnt to pick up things from them. And I realised that nobody really understood that. No hearing person really knew the extent of what I knew or how I felt because of my parents. They assumed that Deaf people knew nothing. But I also learnt to use my common sense, through reading for the meaning of the messages and mulling over them, thinking about things and discovering what they meant. I didn't have to be taught, couldn't be taught, I just wanted to know so I found my own way of learning.

My mum started school at nine and my dad, I think at 12. It was just picking up extra information from them. My father told me stories about the time when he was sent to school. His father was out walking one day – my father was at home – and he saw two deaf boys playing football so he went over to talk to them. He told them about his son (my father) and took them home to meet him to share experiences and I think that was when my father started fingerspelling. My father explained that he would go to a particular school. These two boys were shocked and said it was a terrible school, so my father was eventually sent to a different school which was an oral school where they taught fingerspelling. He had to fingerspell full English, but when my father left school he fingerspelt BSL, not English – that's interesting. My father learnt late and my mum, though she started a bit earlier, missed a lot of school because of illness. Both parents have sign, but their written English has BSL structure, same as mine. So really with writing, I never asked them for help because it would always be picked up as mistakes. I think at that time I knew sign had a language connection but I didn't know it was a real language. You know English is a language and you should learn English...but sign language? Its not full, not complete in the same way, it's a bit limited, so you don't learn it in the same way.

That reminds me of the time when Richard was born and I realised he was deaf and I thought instinctively, he must learn English. He will have sign yes, but it's important he learns English. That was because I didn't think sign language was a language – my language – then. English was almost like God! So with Richard, I signed, but also taught him English from the word go. That's why now, he's more SSE (Sign Supported English). Now, with Elizabeth, I felt really fed up with the peripatetic teachers by then, fed up with their interfering. I felt that *they* had brought Richard up, that I was losing my power as a mother, that my views were not respected as my children's mother, just ignored because I was a Deaf mother. *I* didn't bring my children up, *they* brought them up; *they* told me what I should do. For example, I remember taking the children to a farm, and Richard was really naughty – it was hell! – I was grabbing him and saying 'You are *not* going on the tractor, you've got to behave first or something will happen if you do.' The peripatetic teacher came up and said in a really patronising way, 'Oh no, no, no, let him go on the tractor.' I insisted, 'No. He's got to stop being naughty', and she argued with me, 'Oh let him, the ride will be so nice, good for him.' And he was watching all of this! Maybe being forced to take sides. I think that sometimes, parents are frightened to say 'No' to a child when he's deaf because they don't want the tantrums, and the peripatetic teachers collude with that fear. But I felt it wasn't always appropriate to let him have what he wanted and it was certainly nothing to do with his being Deaf anyway. He was a *child*, and like any other child who is naughty, parents must deal with that.

So when Elizabeth was born I thought I'm not going to let *them* interfere. I'd had enough of them bringing up my children. I stopped them coming. When Elizabeth was six months old, she was babbling away really nicely, so the peripatetic teacher said she must have hearing aids, and I said 'But why?' I was told it was because her voice was awful and she must have hearing aids to improve her voice. I remember saying 'She's not your child, she's my daughter, so we will leave the hearing aids!' and she kept on at me, 'But you'll damage her!', and I said 'If she's damaged then it's my fault, I'll take responsibility for that, it's *my* problem, not yours.' So Elizabeth didn't have hearing aids until she was two years old, and she seemed fine. But I was still thinking of the importance of English, I think because of the strong views of the peripatetic teacher and the way they invaded me. So when Paul was born, I started to look and link it with the teaching. I started work in a school for physically handicapped children, because there was a deaf child there, and I started to realise the link with teaching in a group. I realised that sign was a natural language, it was being used naturally. So I researched it more at university, and discovered it *was* a language. I was really angry because no one had told me, but at the same time I realised there was very limited research in my parent's lifetime and I was angry for myself because it felt as if all those years had been wasted – I didn't understand or learn my language fully. So I was determined not to do the same with my children. We developed 'family signs' in exactly the same way as I had done when I was a child, and this use of sign language really did give us a feeling of coming together as a family. For example, Elizabeth developed a different sign DINNER, which was touching the index finger to the nose. It was a really nice description because it was like children following their noses to the smell of dinner cooking. So we made that a family sign – it was only used at home. As the children got older it changed back to the traditional sign, but I think it was a shame really! There was another – GRANNY BAG. At the nursery when it was used the teachers used to get really upset because they thought the children were signing that Granny was an old bag! But it didn't mean that at all. My grandmother used to bring a bag of sweets when she came to visit, and so she became GRANNY BAG.

With Sally, the peripatetic teacher had plenty of other children to deal with and I think because she had been with me with the other children, she decided she could trust me to be alone with Sally. Oh, that was a marvellous feeling – no peripatetic teachers, sheer freedom! So with Sally, I concentrated on sign with no influence from English. When the peripatetic teacher did come to observe – they can't bring themselves to stay away completely [!] – she was horrified and said I must teach through English, and I refused. I still feel I was right, because in the end all the children had the same level of language. I mean Sally was bright. She learnt to read and write English in school – the teachers were good so she learnt, and she had sign at home. The outcomes were the same, not different. When the child is first diagnosed the peripatetic teacher just comes – straight away – and I remember that with Sally in particular I was really fed up because with the other children if you said you didn't want to see them, they kept on knocking and knocking on the door – like door-to-door salespeople! I know it's not the same in all areas – at least I hope it's not – but with all their insisting that the deaf child *must* have hearing aids and *must* go for hearing tests and so on, there's no allowance for the child to be a child. They teach and teach and teach without leaving the child alone to learn for themselves, without allowing them to grow up in their own way and learn for themselves. All this insistence on quick quick quick, must act quickly or you'll damage their voice, I think it's really misguided, because they don't watch the child carefully, they don't see what's really happening with the child. Sally had tinnitus when she was two, I think because they kept on crowding her with headphones and loud noises to test her hearing. And even when she was crying – with pain or frustration, I don't know – and I was begging them to stop, they said 'Oh no! just five more minutes. We *have* to finish the test.' I felt so upset and angry, because they just carried on and I knew my child was hurting. I realised that they forgot to test her for recruitment, and they should have done, because Elizabeth and Richard both had it, so I think she was literally hurting with the pain of recruitment. That's why I didn't want the hearing aids because really they should have a special adjustment to stop the pain of loud noise. I think *they* actually damaged her.

Fortunately, now Sally seems fine. But they don't give up. When she started a Deaf school I got a phone call asking if they could take her to the ENT hospital, and they wanted to give her some tablets for 'the problem' and I said that was fine but she was taking some other tablets for something else and she had to finish those first. Later they phoned back and said the tablets weren't helping and that Sally's hearing had gone in one ear. I said 'What do mean her hearing's gone – she's deaf! She's DEAF! What you trying to do? There's no tablets that can make Sally hearing!' At Christmas, I got a letter saying they were very sorry that Sally's hearing had gone, and they felt she could take one hearing aid off. I was still thinking how ridiculous the whole thing was – they agreed she could take her hearing aid off! Then I got another letter from the school asking me to consider a cochlear implant because it was unlikely that Sally's hearing would come back. They just *don't* give up. Anyway, I discussed it with my partner and he said that we should sit down with Sally and ask her how she felt about it. It wasn't right for us to make a decision ourselves. So, we said to her 'You know your hearing's gone now?' and she said 'Oh, I can sign, it's all right!' When we asked her about a cochlear implant her response was a very strong and positive one mixed with shock at the thought of it: 'No way. NO WAY!' She was 12 at the time. News travelled in the family quickly, and the feeling from her brothers and sisters was the same. No one wanted her to have a cochlear implant. Then about two months later, her hearing went in the other ear, so she took out her other aid as well. She seems fine, but I think she's also a bit frustrated at school now because she is more aware of people talking over her head and a lot of information passing her by. So we shall just have to wait and see what happens. All the time this professional bullying was going on, particularly with Sally. I felt so churned up inside, trying not to loose my temper, to release all those bottled feelings of a mother's rage at her child being hurt and at the same time wanting to tell them what I thought of them. Sometimes I was crying with frustration along with Sally. I felt I had no power. In part I felt alone with no support from the professionals – the people who should know how to provide it. There was no back-up to help us through. I couldn't talk to anyone. I just felt the house was taken over. I had no control. I feel *she* controlled all the deaf children in her care – no, it wasn't care – the children she was responsible for; she controlled my life.

Unravelling Narratives

By the time a child reaches school age, the core relationship usually would have provided them with an environment in which they learnt that they could trust the adults around them who were acceptable to their caregivers and that they could exercise a degree of free choice tempered by an element of control. The first school experiences therefore become a time where increased autonomy means that they can begin to explore a new environment without the fear that their caregivers will abandon them, and that they are able to be more assertive or aggressive in exercising choice and getting what they want. They are moving from the inward thinking 'I' to the more outward thinking 'I in relation to others', and become much more goal-orientated as they learn new practical skills and cultural skills and norms. During this process, the child's own experiences are particularly important, as they provide a second building block to self-esteem. Their own competence or acceptability is shaped by their direct experience of success and failure, the labels and judgements they receive from others, and the approach to relating used by the adults around them. We saw in chapter one, for example, that adults who are authoritarian, permissive or neglectful are more likely to view children as partially competent or incompetent. Similarly, children who are overly aggressive, do not show a healthy balance between compliance and defiance, and lack what is called pro-social or altruistic behaviour are unlikely to develop reciprocal trust, equal social power and endurance in their friendships, with serious consequences for their sense of self-esteem. We might then consider what kind of environment would encourage children's healthy development at this time and compare this with the environments described by our narrators in this chapter. I have adapted Eisenberg's (1992) view of an environment for helpful and altruistic children to include some of the specific factors referred to above. This is summarised in Box 3.1.

Box 3.1 An environment for building self-esteem

The environment:

- creates a loving and warm 'family' climate
- explains why and gives rules
- encourages children to do helpful things
- encourages children's skills in self-assertion and empathy
- encourages children to respect, understand and be sensitive to the beliefs, values and ways of life of others (altruism)
- acknowledges and affirms children's altruistic thought and action as theirs
- is pro-competence
- provides adult models of thoughtful and generous behaviour
- provides adult models of authoritative behaviour

The following discussion will centre on the contents of Box 3.1, though it must be clear that the school environments experienced by the narrators fall far short of the ideal, and in some cases completely contradict it. Given this, the first theme I identified was related to what the narrators have inherited from their core relationships and, in particular, their feelings about home as a place of safety. Caroline, in the part of her narrative which is written from a parent's perspective, gives some indication of the kind of qualities which might enable the home to become a safe base: 'parents are often frightened to say "No" to a child when he's deaf because they don't want the tantrums, and the peripatetic teachers collude with that fear... I felt it wasn't always appropriate to let him have what he wanted and it was certainly nothing to do with his being Deaf anyway. He was a child, and like any other child who is naughty, parents must deal with that...we should sit down with Sally and ask her how she felt about it. It wasn't right for us to make a decision ourselves...allowing the child to grow up in their own way and learn for themselves.' Caroline clearly received these kinds of attitudes from her own family as a child. For her, home was a place where she felt her sense of herself being positively affirmed: 'I think knowing I had that home helped me... I learnt to pick up things from them [her parents]. And I realised that nobody really understood that. No hearing person really knew the extent of what I knew or how I felt because of my parents. They assumed that Deaf people knew nothing.' Because of the strong affectional bonds she had formed with her parents, she was able to assert herself even when her experience of the world was challenged and her parents were also subject to low expectations: 'I always said "toast on beans" and they said "No that's wrong it's 'beans on toast'" and I would argue with them because my mum always signed TOAST-ON-BEANS and that meant that "toast on beans" must be right. But they would still say "beans on toast" was right. It's so ridiculous.' It is interesting that there is no question of doubt in her mind about which experience tallies with her own and this fits with the view that once a self-scheme model is created it tends to persist because the individual will seek out environments that support it and challenge those environments that do not. What was probably interpreted by Caroline's teachers as 'defiance' is in fact healthy refusal and self-assertion.

Fiona had a similar experience, but her questioning was implicit rather than overtly expressed: 'I always remember feeling they talked about my family as if they were somehow "bad", and questioning myself inside FA-THER MY THICK? NO! because I understood my father and I knew they couldn't. When I eventually asked my father how to deal with it he was just so fair and consistent, he never said they were stupid, he just said that they don't understand and it is not their fault. So that's the way I learnt to treat situations like this.'

Sam, however, though he knew that home wasn't perfect, saw it as an escape from the fear and the atmosphere of menace that he encountered at school. He gives clear indications that he had learnt about choice and control at home, indicating a degree of autonomy: 'At home, when it was meal time we just sat down and started eating. My mother and father never hit me... Again there was this shock. My mother and father never made me go to the toilet. I went when I wanted to, I had a choice. Here I wasn't allowed to choose.' But what he encountered at school was *rigidly enforced* rules and control: 'Then they forced my head into a very uncomfortable position and made me keep it absolutely still, while they tried to get me to make speech sounds, "p" and "b" sounds getting them just right so that I made a feather move', which made him fearful, compliant and withdrawn: 'I was so scared of this nun that I didn't dare say anything... I felt very small and unhappy... It was almost like living in fear... It made me feel frightened, being watched all the time.'

Krishna, on the other hand, though there is a sense that her home environment meant a lot to her, gives an indication that she was compliant and that this was not changed by her early school experiences. She was 'always a good child, very obedient, very quiet, and although I was physically there, I didn't follow what was going on, didn't seem to be an active participant in family life'. She describes her later move to a Deaf school as a wholly positive experience where she 'felt more animated... It was like I had a new confidence. Those years were some of the best years of my life because they brought me out of my shell.'

Sometimes, the safe base was recreated or discovered in peer relationships experienced in school. For example, Caroline says that 'I loved school, had many friends. In the classroom it was oral, but outside, in the playground, when we were with each other we were allowed to sign.' Even Sam acknowledges that he was able to find friendships based on reciprocal trust, mutual 'comfort', and empathy which endured through all the pain he experienced. However, Sam also encountered negative labelling by peers and a hierarchy of dominance where the bullies were more powerful: 'The older boys from a different dormitory – they were five-year-olds – were walking past and they laughed at me, pointed at me and called me "baby" because I wet myself.' This experience was echoed by Peter, though for him the ruptures became connected with anti-Semitism: 'They all laughed and I didn't know what it meant. I remember I was given a small rubber bung while they looked at me and it just didn't connect. It became like a symbol of some sort – I didn't know what it meant but it stayed in my mind', and a general difficulty with forging communicative links: 'I said that I lived on the moon because that was my way of explaining why I had a strange voice and strange speech. That was all I could think of... All I was conscious of was wanting some link, some communication, but how?' Joseph also experienced this in a different context: 'I couldn't go to youth clubs where there were hearing Black young people because of the language problem.' For Fiona, the teasing from her peers produced her first questions about her Deaf identity: 'With them, I couldn't feel that I had my own personality. There was a lot of teasing, but I would never respond, never... They were putting a label on me which carried a negative association with deafness, and perhaps that meant I was more like a Deaf child in a sense. Yes a Deaf child that could hear which is a very peculiar way to feel thinking back.'

Most of the narrators had very negative and unsettling experiences of their relationships with professionals, and some clearly felt that these adults acted as bad role models for other children, encouraging children to develop behaviours which were not altruistic. Joseph felt that teacher attitudes were racist: 'Most teachers of the deaf never discussed race, let alone Deaf issues, and would often dismiss these issues with "It's too difficult for you to understand because it's complicated." That sounded very patronising, and it meant also that we were discriminated against in school because white Deaf children picked up those attitudes.' The associated low expectations held by teachers left him 'feeling humiliated and intimidated – like a second class citizen – because I couldn't make good progress with schoolwork, and cut off from other children and my culture'. In Fiona's case, the low expectations of Deaf people were also extended to her: 'At primary school, I then became the "dummy" and knew somehow that it was linked to "privileges" given to hearing children which were withheld from me. For example, I wasn't allowed to play the piano because the staff believed there was no point since my parents were "deaf and dumb".' For Peter, negative attitudes were in part linked to anti-Semitism: 'I think there was anti-Semitic behaviour from the other children and the teachers. I felt that there were one or two teachers who didn't like the Jewish children. Comments were made, but it was very subtle, just a feeling with no name that could be attached to it.' Caroline could not see the point of being made to learn something which was alien to her experience: 'I hated learning speech – hated it – I felt so stupid having to repeat the s, s, s... Every time I got it wrong, I had to do it all over again and I was asking myself "Why do I have to keep going over and over it, I don't understand what it all means!"'... a waste of time when I could have been learning more important things.' Her frustration was increased because there was no consistency in acknowledging success and failure: 'I would say I heard and they said no, no, you can't have done... Almost in the same breath, they would then tell me I was doing fine.' From a parent's perspective, however, Caroline remembers how invasive professionals were and intrusive of her privacy, which again was linked to their perceptions of Deaf people: 'I felt that they had brought Richard up, that I was losing my power as a mother, that my views were not respected as my children's mother, just ignored because I was a Deaf mother. I didn't bring my children up, they brought them up; they told me what I should do…they kept on knocking and knocking on the door – like door to door salespeople' and their insistence that their way was right, even at the expense of the child's well-being: 'And even when she was crying – with pain or frustration, I don't know – and I was begging them to stop, they said "Oh no! just five more minutes. We have to finish the test." I felt so upset and angry, because they just carried on and I knew my child was hurting.'

The alien environment created by professionals is particularly evident in the emphasis on control in order to force compliance, the lack of information and explanation given and the general lack of empathy with children's worries and fears. Peter reports starting to become aware that he had a different sex role to his peers but he was unable to get the understanding he needed: 'there was no information – no one told me what *gay* meant and I'd never heard of the name or the word'. He had to resort to symbols which were ambiguous in their meaning: 'that rubber bung became a symbol of my early life when no one explained anything. Whether it's connected to the fact that as I am from the Jewish religion I was circumcised – I don't know. The meaning wasn't clear at the time… Comments were made, but it was very subtle, just a feeling with no name could be attached to it.' He developed an awareness of the difference between home and school cultures only because he was alert to the fact that some things happened at home which did not happen at school and vice versa: 'I cannot remember being aware of being Jewish, I think I must have been aware of some difference because I didn't like eating the meat at school… I was definitely aware of two different cultures because I can remember that when I was at home in the family, my mother used to light the candles on the Menorah and I knew that it was a special Friday and the next day would be the Sabbath and my father would go to the synagogue. These customs were not evident in the lives of the other children I knew. I remember feeling different from them, but it's hard to remember how…it was like school and home were different cultures.'

For some of the narrators, the effect of the school environment was profound psychological and emotional damage, resulting in a complete loss of self-esteem. Sam remembers the change he underwent well: 'There was something about that experience that knocked my sense of myself sideways. I could almost feel this massive change happen inside. It caught me completely off guard… I had moved from being a very happy-go-lucky child, very easy about my body, to being very shy and unsure of myself physically', and also the way in which it caused him to start asking questions about religion and his parent's role in his experience of pain: 'All these images flashed by of the nun in black and white, strict, severe, the cross, the windows, and I remembered home and being happy. It didn't fit with my father giving me money and assuring me it would be all right.' Sam's comfort came only from his friendship with Bill and his imagination of things better: 'I imagined the moon was smiling at me and that lifted my spirit a little.' Peter found it increasingly difficult to deal with the different parts of himself that were emerging, in part because of the climate of conditions he was surrounded with and the pressures on him to hide his sexual orientation: 'What I do know is that there were expectations on me to conform, in particular to be straight. Being gay is not generally acceptable in the Jewish faith. I felt unhappy, I felt guilty in some strange way because I knew that I liked boys somehow, but I wasn't clear about what that feeling meant to me. I later justified it by saying to myself that this boy was trouble and that I didn't like him anyway because he was a bully…it was just something to do, to have fun with, and although I never analysed it, I think it might have been different for me… I always felt guilty and secretive – I had to pretend that it never happened in many ways.' It is somewhat ironic also that one of the most important events in a Jewish boy's life – his Bar Mitzvah – became associated with excruciating pain: 'I had to read the Torah at the Synagogue in front of my family and I remember I had this terrible earache, a pounding in my ear which was really painful. I didn't want to go through with it but I had to', followed by relief that after it, he was able to join the culture of the school fully by wearing long trousers. Fiona's experiences in the school environment eventually became associated with a change in role in respect of the younger members of the family, which reawakened awareness of the contradictions of her emerging self: 'I do remember trying to educate the younger members of the family when they went to school. I became like the second mother – the "hearing mother".'

Thinking back to the earlier part of this discussion, I am left with a strong sense of children diminished by and withdrawing from the menacing atmosphere of power created by professionals and often handed down by them to other children. It is almost as if power and control themselves become part of the culture of the school, and mitigate against any altruism that may potentially exist. It is quite remarkable that children growing up in such circumstances can develop friendships with each other at all, but these narratives are testimony to their resilience and will to survive. It is notable, however, that only Caroline truly asserts herself when faced with conflict –'I just wanted to know so I found my own way of learning' – but even she is unable to be totally successful in ridding herself of the menace as an adult: 'All the time this professional bullying was going on, particularly with Sally, I felt so churned up inside, trying not to loose my temper, to release all those bottled feelings of a mother's rage at her child being hurt and at the same time wanting to tell them what I thought of them. Sometimes I was crying with frustration along with Sally. I felt I had no power. In part I felt alone with no support from the professionals – the people who should know how to provide it. There was no back-up to help us through. I couldn't talk to anyone. I just felt the house was taken over. I had no control. I feel she controlled all the deaf children in her care – no, it wasn't care – the children she was responsible for; she controlled my life.' As we will see in the following chapters, the quest for personal meaning from the springboard of an environment which drains one of competence and self-esteem often becomes mingled with a search for the children who become lost in the process.

CHAPTER FOUR

Boxes and the Bees' Hive

Whenever I look for myself, I find the group; whenever I look for the group, I find myself. (Bion 1961)

Wandering between two worlds, one dead,
The other powerless to be born,
With nowhere yet to rest my head,
Like these on earth I wait forlorn.

(Matthew Arnold, *Stanzas from the Grande Chartreuse* (1855))

Introduction

The first four stages of Erikson's developmental life cycle are taken up with exploring and absorbing from all the components which make up identity. Throughout these stages, the focus is still very much on 'I', but there is still no concrete answer to the questions 'Who am I?' and 'Where do I belong?' At the next stage of development some move must be made to answer these questions, and so the psychosocial conflict *identity versus role confusion* becomes the central task. This task cannot be faced before adolescence because all the parts which must be integrated are not present before then, but it may not happen until well into adulthood because an adaptive balance between positive and negative resolution has not been found in one or more of the earlier stages. The exploration that occurs during the first four stages of psychosocial development allows the individual to form identifications by trying out different roles, values and skills and establishing where he or she is like and unlike others. But at some stage, a choice must be made – some identifications must be accepted which are in accordance with the individual's beliefs, values, skills and interests, and others rejected. This what is called *identity formation*. Kroger (1996, p.18) describes identity formation as involving 'a synthesis of earlier identifications into a new configuration, which is based on, but different from the sum of its individual parts'. Sometimes, however, a decision will be made to reject all past identifications and begin the task of forming an identity which is completely different from its roots, and may not be socially acceptable if it is the result of defiance or diffidence. Erikson called this *negative identity resolution*. He pointed out that such a choice does not always answer the question 'Who am I?' and so the relief it brings may only be a temporary one:

> Such vindictive choices of a negative identity represent, of course, a desperate attempt at regaining some mastery in a situation in which the available positive identity elements cancel each other out. The history of such a choice reveals a set of conditions in which it is easier for the person to derive a sense of identity out of a total identification with that which he is least supposed to be than to struggle for a feeling of reality in acceptable roles which are unattainable with his inner means. (Erikson 1968, p.176)

Moreover, the first identity that is formed is not necessarily the only one or the final one (Marcia 1994). While identity choices are being made, we exist in a kind of impasse between childhood and adulthood, but the identity we subsequently become committed to must enable us to take our place among the many and varied roles of adult life. This is reflected in the self-concept. Harter and Monsour (1992) have shown that the self-concept becomes increasingly differentiated at the time of identity formation because we view ourselves differently in each of the roles we occupy. Usually our self-concept also becomes more flexible in that the categories are held less rigidly. Because there are so many roles, it is impossible to avoid confusion completely, and we may apparently lose our own identity through over-identifying temporarily with the heroes, or the villains, of cliques for example, to keep confusion at bay. Erikson (1980) emphasised that behaviour such as intolerance towards or the desire to exclude others who are different in some way is often a necessary and unavoidable *defence* against identity confusion. However, as we have stressed on a number of occasions now, the process of identity formation is not simply a question of deciding who we are. It is also very much about having this identity taken for granted in the relationships we make with

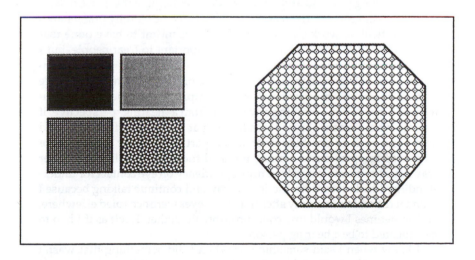

Figure 4.1 Boxes and the bees' hive

others. This in itself can be a source of confusion for those who are different or do not easily 'fit', and they, too, must develop defensive behaviours.

Two images emerge from the above descriptions, both of which are referred to in the following narratives. These are shown in Fig. 4.1. The first is one of boxes waiting to be opened and the contents redistributed and the second is of a bees' hive, also made up of compartments but compartments which are less rigidly divided and where there is free movement from one compartment to the next, giving a sense of integration. This chapter is about the struggles to integrate the parts of ourselves and the defences we develop in the face of confusion.

Fiona

I didn't understand that there was a difference between being hearing and Deaf even when I left school at 16. I just felt normal, there was no feeling of a split identity, just a tangible difference between me and other people in some situations which I didn't have the language to identify, let alone describe. Although I sometimes felt different outside of the family because I was treated differently, I felt a part of my Deaf family because I was never treated differently. However, it was only when I went away from my family where no one knew my background that problems started to arise over who I was. Once people got to know me, I was treated as a little bit strange because I had Deaf touching behaviour, or I couldn't understand them when they looked away because I needed the eye contact. I suppose this means that I wasn't seen as 'hearing'. It was only when I was 25 that I was told by my Deaf friend that although she knew I was hearing, I didn't behave in a way that was acceptable in hearing culture. When this friend met my family, she fitted in easily, but when I met her hearing family, I would touch her father's knee, for example, which felt as if it was a normal expression of warmth to me but was obviously not appreciated by her father. Nothing was said at the time, but it later became the cause of a lot of friction between my friend and myself which I didn't fully understand. It was difficult to work out exactly what I was meant to have done that was so offensive. I knew touch was very important to Deaf people, but I couldn't understand why it might be wrong with hearing people. Eventually, I had to learn that though it wasn't 'wrong' to touch hearing people in itself, there were times when it was appropriate and other times when it wasn't, but I wasn't learning any of this from a 'hearing' perspective, if you see what I mean. I knew I was hearing at that point – I knew I could *hear* – and because this behaviour was a part of my prior experience of what was acceptable and normal, it was difficult to view it in any other way. Another example involved my dependency on eye contact for understanding. I had to learn how to look away and continue talking because I found it difficult to focus my attention if my eyes were occupied elsewhere, and sometimes I would lose concentration altogether. It felt as if I had to be educated to be a hearing person.

I knew when I said something or when I did something that wasn't acceptable – I had a Deaf second sight. I am not sure if I have yet become fully aware of how different I am, but at some point the way I spoke or the way I behaved seemed to *become* acceptable to hearing people and their behaviour towards me changed. When I was communicating with Deaf people, on the other hand, nothing has ever been said that makes me feel I am out of place or 'wrong'. I am learning all the time and I *have* been changing and adapting. But I am *now* getting Deaf people saying that I am behaving like a hearing person, when before they would never say that, they would always say SAME DEAF. When I did start to change I feel sure it was the result of a conscious decision. I deliberately wanted to make those changes. Despite that, I feel as if I am viewed as a second-class hearing person really. I don't know what it means to *be* a hearing person. I can speak, I can listen to television, I can listen to the radio, and I enjoy watching and listening. But I don't know the modes of behaviour, or hearing ways of thinking. I don't know what that means. My views and my decisions all seem to be based on my Deaf upbringing and my perspectives and my feelings have come from my Deaf family. I look through *their* eyes – they taught me to look through their eyes. And I suppose from a hearing person's perspective, that is all very back to front and upside down – a completely different way of viewing and relating to things and people. I don't know what it is like to meet a Deaf person for the first time from a hearing person's perspective – I don't know what that feels like, so I can only guess. When I am watching TV and listening to the radio I can hear the words but I can't focus on the words themselves. I don't just look and listen to what is being said, I look at the body, at the eyes, because there is so much more information there and I ask myself about the real meaning of what is being said through the eyes. It's not that I am not interested in the words, it is just that I can't listen to them without watching. Before, I wasn't consciously aware that this was happening, but I am more aware of it now because of occasions when I have been asked, for example, what I think of someone whom I don't know well. I might look at them and their language tells me that they are hiding something – I don't know what specifically – but I sense something under the surface. If it is a Deaf person who asks, it feels like a test to check whether I am really in tune with the Deaf way, because invariably their perception will be similar to mine. But for me, it is just observation – the power of observation that has been gleaned from, naturally acquired from my family.

My experience has been broadened in one sense because growing up in a working-class community with Deaf parents there is a particular set of dynamics. When I left the family home, it changed – when I became that Deaf person apart from her 'base' and I was treated differently as a result. I started to ask myself if I would always be different, whether I would ever fit somewhere totally? Why am I always different? Why can't I be the same as anybody else? What else do I have to do? Lots of questions like that. I do feel now, and it may sound negative, that it doesn't matter what I do, there is nowhere for me to fit in, there is nowhere I can fit in exactly and feel a whole person. I have to go to hearing events if I want to feel hearing, to Deaf events if I want to feel Deaf and so on. If I am to feel Catholic I go to the Catholic church, and as a woman I have to go somewhere different again. None of them satisfy all the needs at the same time. It's as if I exist in different boxes and I think 'Which box is going to be opened today?' They are all separate and together, if you see what I mean, and I manage them like that – but this is all *me*. When I am with other people I usually make a decision about what is the most important thing I want to show them and what I want to keep back. More recently I have started to do that with the Deaf part, to hold that back. I haven't felt able to say that I have Deaf parents, for example, until I am sure it is safe. When I first left home I always talked about my background, sometimes as a way of justifying my 'strange' behaviour, so that other people could understand it from the perspective of my background rather than stick labels on me which said 'strange person'. I felt that if I was clear about my origins, it allowed other people to make a decision about whether they wanted to speak to me or not on the basis of what they knew.

When I talked about having these boxes and how I use them to cope – perhaps that makes me difficult to read because I have to be a different person in a different situation. It perhaps means I am not clear to other people and so they are always speculating about who I am. If that's the case…that seems quite important. Maybe it *is* about finding what my bottom line is? But that thought makes me feel really uncomfortable because I don't *know* what it is. When I am on my own I feel safe, and maybe that is when I am closest to knowing, because it is the fundamental me. I can only be that person when I am on my own, because my sense of who I am is so fragile that the minute I am with other people, it is easily shattered and pulled apart. I get to know myself better when I am alone, and perhaps I might might feel stronger in myself when I can relax enough. I worry so much about what other people think all the time, but then we have to be very strong *not* to worry. [laughs] It's just a little bit too much for me; I just think 'Oh grow up, let them think what they want to think and get on with your own life!' But that takes a lot of courage.

Peter

I don't see myself as Deaf-gay, not like some others, but I think that might be because I have a different background. Perhaps it's because I got used to being secretive, keeping my life in separate boxes all the time which I could control or cope with, but it felt like I lived a lie, I didn't tell the truth about myself. For so many years, I carried on like that, and so these traits stayed. Now I am more open, but it is not about standing up on a platform and making an announcement. I can't do that and that may have a lot to do with my personality. But I have this dream when I look at other Deaf people who are gay that I want to know what would have happened if I had left home, when I was younger, if I had been able to escape. The only time I got away was when I went to Israel for one year and lived on a Kibbutz, but again, it was a hearing environment. I thought I was going to Israel to learn what it was about. I remember when I went through the centre of town I saw two Deaf people signing at the centre of the town. I stood there watching them from a distance on the other side of the street, trying to understand what they were signing. I couldn't see very well and

I didn't want them to see me looking at them. I never went up to them, I *never went up to them*; and when I think about it now, it was a *missed* opportunity. But at the time, I could feel something in my brain saying, 'You're not allowed to sign. You can integrate with hearing people very well and communicate with them' – until they form a group and then I pull out, that is. I was acutely aware of looking at these Deaf people signing and feeling a pull towards them. And for many years I struggled with that voice in my head. I had a lot of problems for a long time about my Deaf identity which were very painful to deal with.

Andrew

Sometimes, when I look back at my life as a deafened person, there is a strong sense of *before* and *after*, but I am not sure where the physical deafening fits in all of that. I just know that somewhere deep within, the *before* exists as a memory which echoes through to the present and influences my life along the way. I get this very deep feeling that in a strange unidentifiable way the *before* is somehow linked to or responsible for the *after*, both in terms of what is happening inside of me and what happens between me and those I relate to. I feel that I want to see myself as being like a bees' hive, where every little cell in my body and every aspect of who I am is perfectly integrated into a whole which exists for the mutual good of all and that is how I was *before*. It is easy to think of my body like this, but my body is so solid – so *there*! It's not so easy with my thoughts and feelings. But I get a picture of myself in the *after* stage as being more like a chameleon. You know what I mean? A creature that changes colour to merge with its surroundings. For the chameleon it is a defence mechanism and it sets out to confuse – to protect it from predators and to hide it from its prey. That is what I do a lot of the time – I confuse, I disguise myself not because I am divided or ashamed of who I am, but because I need to protect myself against those who seek out my vulnerability. They seem to expect constancy and consistency, and would rather have me split apart or going all one way or the other because they want me to conform and they want me to be simple to know. But I am not a simple person. I don't think many people are – they just like to believe that they are! I don't think I take on this chameleonic image consciously. It's just that there have been many times when I have been aware of looking back at a particular situation and recognising that I behaved in a very defensive way. I think I actually need to have the bees' hive back, which is why I need to hang on to myself so fiercely, and why I am fed up with being challenged about that or viewed as 'deviant'. I don't want to live with inner conflicts – there are more than enough of those in the external world I am forced to live in. In that world, one part of me is treated as if it is a disease which somehow infects the other. But, at times, I am not sure which is the disease and which is being infected. On the one hand, I am told that I was 'normal' *before* and now, in the *after* phase, I am somehow 'deviant', and on the other I am told that my feelings about deviancy *before* were 'normal' and now, in the *after* stage because they are directed at me, they don't feel 'normal'. You see the contradiction?

I 'become' more Deaf when I am with Deaf people, and more hearing when I am with hearing people. Again this is not a conscious thing, it just happens, and it has nothing to do with wanting to please them – I've given up on that! I just want to be accepted as I am by people regardless of whether they are Deaf or hearing. Both Deaf and hearing people say that I am not one hundred per cent successful in filtering out the other part, and that must be because I am *not* one hundred per cent of either. For example, when I am with Deaf people, I often shift into more English-based sign when I relax and stop drilling myself inside that I *must* sign in BSL. It is natural and totally spontaneous. When I am with hearing people, my food gets cold very quickly because I have to watch them to pick up the conversation and I cannot deal with a plate of food without looking at it. I am always the last person to finish the meal. There *are* conflicts, of course, but they are certainly not the kinds of conflict that shatter my identity into pieces, perhaps because that was there *before*. But it doesn't stop people contradicting me and compromising who I feel I am, even trying to tell me I am somebody different. It's almost as if they want me to unlearn everything I learnt in the past and start again according to their model. For example, when with hearing people and in hearing mode, like most hearing people I have learned to drop eye contact when I am tired, disinterested or preoccupied with my own thoughts. As I am also deaf, I cannot engage in passive listening in the way that hearing people often do. I need to lipread to understand. Often hearing people interpret my apparent lack of attention as an indication of laziness, or being difficult or unappreciative of the efforts they are making *because they are so focused on the deaf part of me* and have adjusted their behaviour accordingly. They are often engaging in another kind of passive listening in this respect. When I am with Deaf people, I get a different kind of tiredness related to having to function in my second language which generates a lot of frustration for me. I feel Deaf people cannot get to know me because I cannot express myself fully, and actually I feel bad about that. Bad because they won't give me the benefit of the doubt and bad because I feel I have gone as far as I can without becoming alien to myself – someone completely false. I feel in my heart that I am Deaf – the emotional pull towards Deaf people is very strong even if, for the most part, I know I am rejected by them. Perhaps that is because in my head I am still 'hearing', whatever that means because I don't think that hearing people define themselves as hearing. It's only Deaf people that give them that label.

I can see how certain values become attached to one side and different values become attached to the other, but does that mean that these experiences *are* those respective sets of values? I have learnt enough to know that these values are not constant either, and that often they are attached by those who have no direct experience of a particular situation, and certainly not *my* particular experience of that situation. It's interesting too that when I try to explain what my experience is, it is always disputed, it is never good enough for the person who is on the receiving end of the explanation. I get very frustrated with being asked to justify my existence, or to leave the Deaf or hearing parts of my self out of different situations.

We never ask a hearing person not to be hearing and not to give a hearing view because the fact that they are hearing means that we take it for granted they will give a hearing view. But there is no stigma attached to being hearing unless you try to become Deaf. If you are hearing, you have no experience of being deaf and you can only imagine what it *may* be like, often only in *your* terms and in relation to *your* feelings about what it would be not to hear; and if you are Deaf and you have no experience of being hearing, you may have an equally limited view of what it is like to be able to hear or to be hearing. I think this also applies to the feelings themselves. I feel I *know* what it is to be both Deaf and hearing. This all makes it more difficult to understand the rejection of part of me who *sometimes* feels negative about being deaf or about any number of other things. I find that very difficult. I mean sometimes I *do* feel negative about being deaf – so what! I *sometimes* feel negative about other things too which have nothing to do with being deaf! My feelings change from day to day in intensity and colour, as most people's do. However, I don't feel negative about *everything* which is part of being deaf. Feeling negative about deafness carries a stigma, and that stigma is *reinforced* by hearing society because it is how they expect us to feel. In the same way, that stigma is *rejected* by Deaf people because that is how they expect us *not* to feel. So suddenly you become 'not really Deaf' or 'hard of hearing' in order to somehow justify those negative feelings. So where can 'home' be for someone like me outside of myself? That is certainly where I felt happiest for a long time.

Joseph

I want to treat both of my identities as whole, no matter which comes first at any moment in time. But sometimes I feel that my Black identity and my Deaf identity don't fit together easily or that it is difficult to integrate them because of values which become linked to Black and Deaf. Maybe it's because of different languages and cultures, different values, beliefs and lifestyles. For example, the West Indian language, Creole don't fit with English language because of structural and experiential differences. But, on the other hand, Creole and BSL have the same social history, as both of these languages have been oppressed. However, Creole is only used by older West Indians with limited education and many Deaf West Indians from the younger generations are only educated in English and sign language because of Western beliefs and values. In some situations, with Black Deaf people who are not aware of their racial identity because they are immersed in the British way of life and have never had the chance to seriously think or talk about issues affecting their lives, their sign language is used in Black ways. For example, if you use the second and third index fingers in a curved 'C' shape and then strike the front of the fingers on the wall or the table, it is way of signing YOU-ARE-HARD-ALL-RIGHT which means something to Black Deaf people. There are lots of other examples like that of Black signing which are difficult to describe in writing. It is easy to feel comfortable with all sections of the Deaf community because BSL brings us together, but only if attitudes and behaviour towards each other are liberally minded.

For me, the differences sometime make me feel as if I am living with a continuous identity crisis as a result of being a 'pig in the middle' between Black and Deaf. That means my identity is whole, but it's also in crisis a lot of the time. But if the crisis becomes too great, such as when I am oppressed as a Black or a Deaf person, or both, it also feels as if Black and Deaf are forced to be separate. It's the force and the lack of acceptance that make the crisis. But sometimes the crisis is more like a confusion and that stops me from feeling like a whole person. Sometimes I felt bitter about my deafness because I was born into a hearing family and I felt isolated from and rejected by them. But when I began to learn more about Black history and to get involved in Black festivals and celebrations, for example, I began to ask myself 'Who am I as a Black person?', but it felt as if the deafness had got in the way of learning about that. Maybe that's something about learning. It increases my deductive and thinking power, but it also makes me change my attitudes and perceptions of myself in relation to society 'at large', including the Deaf community. I worry sometimes that after many years of learning and studying it may become difficult to relate to Deaf people at the grass roots level because I have had opportunities to further my cognitive and intellectual development. So there is that disadvantage to learning, in that knowledge can make me feel more different in some situations.

Sam

When I was ten, I moved to a different school. The pain I experienced there really hit me hard – Wham! The first day, a small group of us arrived talking to each other as we had been taught to do and we became aware that we were being laughed at. *This* school was a signing school where speech was the subject of laughter. Watching the older boys, we saw them signing fluently without using their mouths at all. I was shocked and confused because we had been told we must speak at the old school and here, in a different school, the rules were different and this created even more confusion. Bill felt the same. Five of us had been transferred together and we just clung to each other and stuck together as if for security. This school was very tough. There were Christian brothers here. At first I was happy because I hated the nuns so much, but in the end I realised that the Christian brothers were different – and much worse.

Again we had dormitories, but they were smaller. In my dormitory there were many wardrobes. My bed just happened to be next to a wardrobe where a statue of Jesus stood on the top looking down at me. There was a light by my bed which shone upwards which illuminated the figure and it brought back memories of that first image of Jesus on the cross. We went to bed later in this school – half past nine – but when I lay in bed, the statue frightened me. I thought it was watching me, almost waiting for me to say something. I used to pull the covers up over my head so that I didn't have to look at it and feel the fear. Late at night I used to feel the footsteps of the Christian brothers coming into the dormitory, walking past the beds and checking on us. One night I was awake, though pretending to be asleep in case I got caught. I saw the Christian brother go back to same bed several times, pull back the sheet and touch up the boy who was in that bed. I was very shocked. My old school was bad, but nothing like this ever happened. Having seen the Christian brothers for what they really were, I began to worry because I realised that the boy in the other bed was one of the new boys, the same as me. Then my worst fears became a reality. He started to walk across the room and I realised he was coming to my bed. Because I knew what was going to happen, I tried to resist by crossing my legs over and turning away. But the Christian brother beat me until I cowered and cried. But I wouldn't let him touch me. Eventually he moved away leaving me like that clinging to my bed clothes. I thought perhaps he had hidden under the bed and I was petrified even to move. I had never thought he would beat me.

In the morning, another Christian brother came in and noticed a large bruise on the side of my face. He asked me what happened and I was very unsure and nervous about telling him in case he did the same thing. Eventually, he just dismissed me and told me to go and get washed. I talked to Bill about it later. We both felt it wasn't fair. We'd been placed in another school that was wrong, where more bad things would happen. After we'd had breakfast, we had time outside playing football, and suddenly someone kicked me really hard on the leg. while the others laughed. I realised that I was going to have to become tougher if I was to survive here. This school was a bad influence on me, but I had to change. Also, the power image of the Christian brothers was a very strong influence – a negative one. I remember also that some of the older boys, who were almost at the point of leaving the school, were given special responsibilities. They were part of this power game. There was one boy whom I hated. I was the only one who would challenge him and none of the other boys dared to support me. When we played football he would always kick or elbow me brutally and that went on throughout my time there. One day this boy concocted a plan with some others to trap me and get their own back. Off one of the corridors on the ground floor, there was a small bedroom with a toilet opposite. As I walked passed, the toilet door opened suddenly and as I was distracted by this, some boys grabbed me and dragged me into the bedroom. They beat me and then pulled my lower clothes off and felt my genitals, laughing and swearing, until I just gave up fighting. I tried to resist them but I couldn't – they were too strong. I felt really bitter, screaming inside again 'Fuck! Fuck! Why me? Why me?' When I recovered, I pulled my clothes back on, still feeling so angry and walked out of the room and down the corridor. I saw an adult and tried to attract their attention. They saw the state I was in and he said 'Oh you've been fighting again!' He said 'again' – I didn't want to remember the last time I got beaten. He could see that my clothes were torn and that I was hurt and he took me along to the staff room. The people in there just stared at me, then one of them asked me what happened and I said 'Nothing!' He hit me on the arm, and threatened me, told me something bad would happen if he caught me saying anything. It felt as if I had to say 'Nothing' and mean it.

At this school when football had finished we had to go to the shower rooms. The showers had curtains and we took our clothes off and went into the cubicles to wash. One of the Christian brothers used to come round and turn the showers off and look us up and down. I didn't feel comfortable with that, I felt angry at the invasion into my privacy. He would always tell me to turn around to face him and say that I hadn't soaped myself properly and he would make me go through the whole procedure of washing again while he watched. This happened every day for weeks and weeks.

The Christian brothers were responsible for waking us up every morning, getting us moving and for guiding us. I remember one time when I was about fourteen I was woken up and I got myself dressed. I noticed that one boy was still asleep so I went over and tapped him to wake him. There was no response. I grabbed his hand because I was worried that he would get into trouble, and it was cold – so cold. It somehow reminded me of when my father took me to my grandfather's funeral wake and he looked like that – the dead look like that – deadly cold. I was shocked – the boy felt the same as he had looked. I went up to the Christian brother and told him that I thought Michael was dead. The Christian brother realised that I was not joking, and quickly cleared all the boys out of the dormitory telling them that Michael was just asleep, there was no problem. He went over and on looking at Michael confirmed that he was dead. I was very shocked because Michael had been one of the boys who had suffered much abuse and beatings – in many ways worse than what I endured because he couldn't resist as he didn't like drawing attention to himself. This was the first time in my life that I had found a dead person. At breakfast the news went round and some of the boys were talking about it as if it were a fact of life, the same as animals dying on a farm for example. Really inside I wanted to cry and was very upset, but I just joined in with them and pretended that I didn't care. Next day the Father wanted to meet me, as the person who had found the body, so the Christian brothers came to find me. As we walked to meet the Father the Christian brothers would greet each other by crossing themselves and inside I was thinking what hypocrites they were, abusing boys and pretending to be such good men. I still wanted to cry inside when I came face to face with the Father. As he was shaking my hand, I could feel a lump in my throat rising up, but the Christian brothers noticed this and were nudging me reminding me to be respectful to the Father. I just smiled reverently at him, denying my friend's death. The pain in my throat was terrible as I watched him. After talking to me for a bit longer, whilst all the time I had a smile frozen on my face, he gave me ten pounds I think, which was a lot of money at the time, and I put it in my pocket without really taking it in. The Christian brother led me away and demanded that I gave him the money. I tried to protest, because the Father had given it to *me*, but I let him have it because I had no energy left. He said it was for the Christian brothers' records. We walked on a bit further and suddenly something snapped inside. The anger that had been welling up for so long just exploded to the surface and I ran off screaming, and crying down the stairs, anywhere to get away from him. Next day Michael's family arrived and I was told that I had to be a coffin bearer because Michael would have wanted me to be. There was talk about trading this duty for the ten pounds that was mine. In the end I agreed to be one of the people who bore the coffin down to Michael's parents. As I walked, I kissed the coffin, and Michael, goodbye, and tears began to trickle down my cheeks. I had never experienced so much pain. The Christian brothers had damaged me, and they had probably contributed to Michael's death. After Michael's family had left, one of the Christian brothers summoned me to the office and asked me to put out my hand, and thinking he was going to give me the money, I put it out whereupon he beat it repeatedly with a leather strap until I was crying and my hand came up in big red weals. Later, I just hid my hands from the other boys and said nothing.

The beatings continued. About one month after Michael's death I was in a class of about five, and we were told that we must know who made the world. The class was led by one of the Christian brothers and when he arrived, he took out the strap and placed it on the table where we could all see it. He had a list of our names and if we gave the wrong answers to his questions, he marked up the number of lashes we would get on the list. The whole class was like that. If we got it wrong, he pulled our trousers down, laid us across the table and beat us. I was still uncomfortable about being exposed like that. When that was finished he forced us to write about the class, made us work very hard, making us improve our writing. We had to do it because we were scared of being beaten again. I remember another night in the dormitory, one Christian brother told us that if we wanted to get up in the morning at seven o'clock to go to Mass, we had to tie a knot in our towel which hung by the side of the bed so that he would know whether to wake us or not. In the night, one of the boys crept out of bed and tied a knot in Bill's towel and went back to bed, unbeknown to Bill. In the morning, the Christian brother woke Bill up for Mass, and Bill, confused, said he didn't want to go to Mass. The Christian brother beat him and pointed to his towel. Bill realised he had been the butt of a joke and so he got up, dressed and went to Mass. Later I asked him if he wanted to talk because I could see he had been beaten, and when he explained, I was determined to find out who had done this cruel thing to him. I found the boy responsible, who thought the whole thing was funny, but hadn't realised that Bill would get beaten. I warned him that if he did that to Bill again, I would beat him! But later someone did the same thing *to me*, and I was beaten the same as Bill. I went down to Mass – I had no choice, but as I was watching, I was so tired that I fell asleep. The next thing I knew I was being punched from behind, shaken into paying attention. When Mass was over, I went to breakfast and looked around me, trying to work out who had played this joke on me. I don't know who it was, so again, I was left with my feelings of anger and 'Why me? Why me? It's not fair.' I never had any explanation of why these things were happening to me, no reasons were given why friends would suddenly become enemies and kick me when we were playing football for example.

At this stage my education was very 'oral'. I had a little sign which helped me communicate with the other boys secretly, but not really enough. I am sure, even then, that I felt more comfortable with signing.

The oral way always felt it was forced on me and carried so many painful memories with it that I never had confidence in myself communicating in this way. In my class there were other boys who were good speakers, but I never was. It felt as if that class was the wrong place for me – it was not suitable. Because many of the boys in the school had very similar experiences, we were able to share with each other and it helped us to develop communication and language. I actually thought my speech was perfect, but when eventually I did go home and try it out on my parents, they could never understand what I was saying. I wondered how the teachers could understand me and my parents couldn't. It created more confusion for me about who I was. If I wrote something down I could make myself understood, but not if I spoke it. I had hoped that if I learnt to speak well then I would be able to fit in with my family better, but I was still isolated from them. I had endured this terrible place and I was still isolated. I felt very disappointed.

When I returned to school, I had discussions with Bill about our time at home, and I realised how different our lives were. I told him about the farm and that I lived in the country in a house which was separate, where you couldn't see another house for miles. He was so surprised. He told me that he lived in a terraced house and went out to play football in the street and things like that, whilst I had to help with the work on the farm, helping to harvest, collecting the eggs and so on. I realised eventually from talking to other boys who came from farming backgrounds that we were all made to work. It was like a very strong cultural tradition in farming communities, but I had inside some anger about that. It meant for me that his mother and father gave him time to himself and cared for him, whereas my parents had no time for me. They were always too busy on the farm, and that came first. When Bill's mother and father came to visit, I felt as if I wanted to go back with them. I wanted a mother and father that would give me time and look after me. Bill misunderstood my reaction to his parents to start with, thinking that I didn't like them, and I had to explain to him about my feelings of resentment about my own parents and how the two sets of feelings had become very confused. Between September and Christmas, I never saw my family, and I only had five and a half weeks at home in any one year. The rest of the time was spent at school. But I was at school so much that when I went home, for the first two or three days I was excited and happy and then the gloom began to set in as I realised I still had all the communication frustrations and difficulties. I could communicate with the boys in my class at school but again all the feelings got mixed up because school was somewhere I hated and had communication which I loved and home was somewhere that I loved and needed to be, but had no communication I could follow or understand. That made me frustrated and angry.

I remember one parents' day, my mother and father came. I didn't know how to greet them or whether I was happy to see them or not. The Christian brothers were hovering around watching and seemed to be friendly towards my parents. I didn't understand that. I told my parents what the Christian brothers did to me at night; they went rigid. Then the

Christian brother started talking to my parents, soothing them and telling them that I was confused and was talking about washing myself. They of course believed him. They believed the Christian brother was a good man. I realised that my mother and father didn't believe me, and that marked a turning point in my relationship with them. They didn't believe me, and they believed this evil man. I did not know what to do. My father gave the Christian brother some money and I was thinking money, money, again, always money. Money for the nuns, money for the Christian brothers – and what do they give me?

The more I was beaten, raped and abused in other ways, the more confused I became, wondering what I had done to deserve this. All of this confusion was made worse because I wasn't sure whether I could tell my father or how I could explain because I knew that if the Christian brothers found out, I would just get beaten again. So fear was another dominant emotion – fear of the Christian brothers' power over me which left me feeling powerless. I didn't know how to respond to that power in a way that would clarify things for me. It was very difficult to provide proof of what was happening. It was like there was a split in me, half of me saying 'I want to tell… I want the pain to stop' and the other half saying 'No you can't tell or you will be hurt again.' That was the inner struggle, that was the confusion, and it split my identity in two.

Krishna

I really started thinking about myself when I was in my mid-twenties. When I left school, I started my working life in a factory, then moved on to a clerical job where I worked for about seven years. I recall feeling very dissatisfied in that job because they set limits on what I could achieve. I knew that when I was in that job I enjoyed meeting people, and I used to end up chatting to all of them. But I felt frustrated because of not being able to get promotion, which I later recognised was a consequence of discrimination on the grounds of race, gender and of disability. I didn't know what I wanted to do, but I just wanted to do something with people. We have a very good family friend, a woman, who was a social worker, and she has and continues to have a lot of influence over my life as a person whom I look up to. She encouraged me to think about doing social work, though I don't think I really knew what social work meant until I later commenced work as a social work assistant. I had this perception that social work was just about working with older people and disabled people, and that it would be easy. But I came face to face with the social work jargon and culture, and words like 'discrimination', 'power' and so on which I had never heard before. I had *experience* of discrimination but I didn't have the language to name it; it was just an *experience* of not being accepted. My language was just very basic office-worker English from the point of view of vocabulary. In this job I was exposed to words like 'racism', 'sexism', 'disablism', 'homophobia', and so on, and it was all new to me. I began to ask a lot of questions of myself that I hadn't been able to ask before. It was mind-blowing trying to make sense of it all, and in some ways I felt naive – still feel naive in some ways because I'm still learning, always learning. I remember one experience – a colleague, who was gay but I didn't know that at the time. He used to talk to me a lot and held my hand while he was talking. I saw him behave in a very similar way with everyone and so I thought and felt there was nothing wrong with it. One day another colleague came up to me and suggested that what this man was doing was wrong. When I asked why it was 'wrong' they told me this man was gay and that such mannerisms were typical of gay people. I was confused, puzzled, – I didn't understand what 'gay' meant. She sat down and explained to me what it meant and I was quite amazed by this new information – a whole portion of human life experience had been some-how missed. It was the same with terms like 'learning disability', 'ageism', 'autism' and so on. So suddenly, I was exposed to a whole range of things, experiences, language. When I began to really take all of this in, to absorb it, I began to question myself. 'Who am I then? They're so and so, they're so and so, but who am I?' I felt lost and so confused.

Karen

I also feel that becoming deaf had a very big impact on my identity. It was very difficult, as it happened when I was a teenager and still trying to find out who I was. I remember a time, not very long go actually, when I was with a group of hearing friends. We had met through sharing a house, we became friendly and one-to-one, that was fine – I had really good friend-ships one-to-one. But in a group situation, I was very withdrawn – like a different person almost – not very demanding, and I would get very fed up with it all. I remember there was a time when my personality felt nonexistent in this group, as if I couldn't express my personality, because everyone was talking around me. I just couldn't be spontaneous and express myself, and that's something about my identity which is linked to that, I need to express myself and be actively involved in conversations to feel a sense of my identity. I feel that my personality, my identity, became very much a function of my interaction with other people, so that when the interaction was not there, it was difficult to feel a sense of identity at all. When you become deaf, you can't so easily get the fullness and the spontaneity of the interaction with most hearing people any more. All the time, inside, you're struggling – there's a voice that goes 'What's she saying, what's he saying?' and you feel that you are being deprived of that information somehow. It takes the place of the natural give-and-take interaction. You're not *involved* any more. If you can't get answers to your questions, you can't be involved because you're always left behind won-dering what they are talking about and how to respond. I remember meeting someone at a party who had known me before, and we had this really difficult conversation – he was impossible to lipread. We started talking about when he first knew me and he used to catch me out when I didn't understand him. He would ask 'What did I say?' At that time, it had felt like a challenge because I had to admit that I hadn't heard him. And then he now says 'Oh I thought that was because you weren't listening!' and I thought 'Oh shit!... I really thought you understood that I was deaf' when all the time *that* was all he had been thinking. That hurt! All those years I'd carried a false impression of that person.

Even when I was 16 or 17, I was still very passive. If I went out with a boy it was always because *he* asked me or because *he* chose me. I didn't choose him, even though I was flattered if I was asked. I lacked confidence and couldn't say 'No', so I probably would have gone out with anyone. I couldn't feel they wanted *me*, or feel positive about that. And so, to feel good about myself, I just went with a lot of different men, maybe to the point where I was quite promiscuous. I got pregnant twice and had abortions on both occasions. The first time was when I was 17, that was by a more long-term boyfriend. I was very young at the time and hadn't asked at the health centre about the pill or anything. His mother arranged the abortion privately and I remember talking to the doctor and they were going on about it being one mistake and I thought that was rubbish. I didn't think about contraception. I just went along with things. I didn't know what I wanted. After that, I had many relationships – I just had no boundaries and at the same time it was as if I was living my life through them and that there was no me. I had no identity. I think especially of my time as a teenager. My confidence was very low and I was very passive. It's interesting because I've been told that deaf children have two main ways of responding to difficult situations – one is being very passive and the other is being very angry and acting it out. I was definitely passive, I think because of who I was before I became deaf – 'the good girl', who if she did one thing naughty it wasn't just childish naughtiness, it became as if she had committed a criminal act. It was that bad! If my brothers were naughty, fine. If I was naughty, it was much worse, perhaps because I learnt to bottle up all my negative emotions, and when they were expressed, they seemed that much more intense. It may also have been because my parents did not expect bad behaviour from me, and so, when it did happen, it seemed very uncharacteristic and so perhaps bothered them more.

Unravelling Narratives

When we left Caroline in the previous chapter, it seemed as if she had already become committed to a particular identity which she was prepared to give up with the greatest of reluctance, even when faced with extreme pressure to do so from the environment. She calls this her Deaf identity, and it does seem that being Deaf is both central to her life and a source of strength for the other aspects of herself – it is something that 'remains the same despite change'. This Deaf identity appears to be very much based on a subscription to Deaf family values because the views of Caroline's parents feature prominently in her decision to be who she is, and on relationships formed with other Deaf people. Her family does have Deaf and hearing parts, albeit hearing parts who have sustained contact with Deaf people, and her experience of being with hearing people is not generally a positive one, and tends to be avoided or shunned as much as possible. There does not appear to have been an extensive exploration process where she has made a commitment based on past identifications to accept Deaf and reject hearing. I feel, then, that her identity is a *foreclosed* identity, a result of the dominant experience of positive reinforcement from her Deaf family and a Deaf peer group, which enables her to deal with the negative attitudes of hearing people. Her Deaf identity is, however, foreclosed upon the Deaf context, and, *as long as it remains in this context*, it can be adaptive (Marcia 1994).

What is very clear from the narratives in this chapter – the factor that ultimately distinguishes them from Caroline's narrative – is that identity crisis and confusion are dominant themes, and the crisis is often associated with doubts about the nature of identity which results either in the need for further exploration, or in a psychological impasse, where splits in identity are the main preoccupation. It therefore becomes important to ask about the precise origins of confusion and/or crisis for each of the narrators and whether they provide us with any suggestions about the implications this has for their subsequent identity status.

If we take Fiona's narrative as a starting point, she feels that she 'didn't understand that there was a difference between being hearing and Deaf even when I left school at 16. I just felt normal, there was no feeling of a split identity, just a tangible difference between me and other people in some situations which I didn't have the language to identify, let alone describe.' This suggests that, like Caroline, Fiona had a *foreclosed* identity of which Deafness was a dominant characteristic. Up to this point in her life her family provide her with the base for forming her childhood identifications: 'My views and my decisions all seem to be based on my Deaf upbringing and my perspectives and my feelings have come from my Deaf family. I look through their eyes – they taught me to look through their eyes. And I suppose from a hearing person's perspective, that is all very back to front and upside down – a completely different way of viewing and relating to things and people.' There is a commitment, but to a large extent it seems to be determined by Deaf family values, rather than by Fiona herself as a consequence of the identifications she has formed in childhood outside of the family. I feel this is reinforced by the circumstances surrounding her subsequent identity crisis, which threw her into a *moratorium*. When she *leaves* the family home – the Deaf context she foreclosed on – she begins to explore different identifications, and this exploration makes her increasingly aware that her identity is split and managed in boxes: 'I started to ask myself if I would always be different, whether I would ever fit somewhere totally?...it doesn't matter what I do there is no where for me to fit in there is nowhere I can fit in exactly and feel a whole person... It's as if I exist in different boxes and I think "Which box is going to be opened today?"... They are all separate and together if you see what I mean, and I manage them like that – but this is all me.' Though she is aware that *she* existed in all of the boxes, she didn't know what 'her bottom line' was.

At this point in the narrative, I decided to use probing skills and asked Fiona what she felt about finding that 'bottom line'. Her response was that 'it seems quite important. Maybe it is about finding what my bottom line is? But that thought makes me feel really uncomfortable because I don't know what it is. When I am on my own I feel safe, and maybe that is when I am closest to knowing, because it is the fundamental me. I can only be that person when I am on my own, because my sense of who I am is so fragile that the minute I am with other people, it is easily shattered and pulled apart.' If we paraphrase this response, we could say that in the context of what she had said before, leaving the Deaf context confuses her and causes her to ask questions about her Deaf identity. We know that a conscious attempt to commit herself to a new identity was made, which is different from the unquestioning acceptance associated with her earlier foreclosed identity: 'When I did start to change I feel sure it was the result of a conscious decision. I deliberately wanted to make those changes.' This search involved her in trying to jettison some parts of her childhood experiences in order to affirm her status as a hearing person: 'I haven't felt able to say that I have Deaf parents, for example, until I am sure it is safe.' Yet she feels safe only when she is alone, and she is fearful of rejection.

Peter also talks about boxes, but the context is different: 'Perhaps it's because I got used to being secretive, keeping my life in separate boxes all the time which I could control or cope with, but it felt like I lived a lie, I didn't tell the truth about myself.' Peter's boxes have the function of self-management, but they also provide containment for secrets – aspects of himself, in particular his sexual orientation, that he wanted to hide. At this point in his life, he seems to border on a negative foreclosed identity, that is, an identity which is based on an unhelpful resolution of earlier conflicts, because when he comes close to making a clear commitment, voices from the past hold him back: 'I never went up to them; and when I think about it now, it was a missed opportunity. But at the time, I could feel something in my brain saying, "You're not allowed to sign. You can integrate with hearing people very well and communicate with them."' We will return to distant voices in chapter six.

Andrew's narrative is interesting and complex. My reading of it is that at some point he had achieved an identity which was affirmed by and socially acceptable to others and which he wants to retain: 'I feel that I want to see myself as being like a bees' hive, where every little cell in my body and every aspect of who I am is perfectly integrated into a whole which exists for the mutual good of all and that is how I was before. It is easy to think of my body like this, but my body is so solid – so there! It's not so easy with my thoughts and feelings.' Since becoming deaf, he has experienced confusion in the boundary between himself and others as a result of the pressure he feels he is under to form a negative identity: 'it doesn't stop people contradicting me and compromising who I feel I am, even trying to tell me I am somebody different. It's almost as if they want me to unlearn everything I learnt in the past and start again according to their model.' This has shaken his identity to its roots and has made him protective of himself: 'But I get a picture of myself in the after stage as being more like a chameleon... I want...to confuse, to disguise myself, not because I am divided or ashamed of who I am, but because I need to protect myself against those who seek out my vulnerability.' He is, however, very clear about who he is and the contradictions it involves: 'I am not one hundred per cent successful in filtering out the other part, and that must be because I am not one hundred per cent of either. On the one hand, I am told that I was "normal" *before* and now... I am somehow "deviant" and on the other I am told that my feelings about deviancy *before* were "normal" and now, in the *after* stage because they are directed at me, they don't feel "normal". You see the contradiction?' He is committed to this composite identity, and is extremely reluctant to abandon it, but he recognises that it is fragile because it is not accepted by others: 'I feel I have gone as far as I can without becoming alien to myself – someone completely false. I feel in my heart that I am Deaf – the emotional pull towards Deaf people is very strong even if, for the most part, I am rejected by them. Perhaps that is because in my head I am still "hearing", whatever that means, because I don't think that hearing people define themselves as hearing. It's only Deaf people that give them that label...when I try to explain what my experience is, it's always disputed, it is never good enough for the person who is on the receiving end of the explanation. I get very frustrated with being asked to justify my existence, or to leave the deaf or hearing parts of my self out of different situations.' There are many similarities between Andrew and Fiona, though they are coming from opposite ends of the spectrum. Neither feel they have a 'home' outside of themselves, something which we will return to in chapter six. Andrew's resolution appears to be the result of an extensive inner exploration of who he is in 'the *after* phase', followed by a commitment. He looks outwards, absorbs what he sees and interprets it for himself on both cognitive and emotional levels. He exists on the border between a new achieved status which allows him to make his own decisions based on internalised, self-constructed values whilst being sensitive to external demands, and a moratorium status where he 'vacillates between rebellion and conformity' (Marcia 1994, p.75), and which side of the border he comes down on depends very much on how severe the pressures are and how strong or how adaptive he can be at any one moment.

For Karen, becoming deaf had 'a very big impact on her identity', in part because it happened when she was a teenager coming to terms with who she was. However, what is striking, and what makes her different from Andrew, is that it results in her sense of self diminishing completely in some situations to the point where she 'was very withdrawn – like a different person almost – not very demanding... I need to express myself and be actively involved in conversations to feel a sense of my identity...[it] became very much a function of my interaction with other people, so that when the interaction was not there, it was difficult to feel a sense of identity at all...my personality felt non-existent.' Though she initially had 'really good friendships one-to-one', there comes a point where the feeling of confusion was so great that she lives her life through others, and, indeed, she feels that intimacy depended on her ability to do this. For this reason, I feel she had a *diffused* identity status: 'I just went along with things. I didn't know what I wanted... I just had no boundaries and at the same time it was as if I was living my life through them and that there was no me. I had no identity.' This results in a corresponding loss of self-esteem: 'If I went out with a boy it was always because *he* asked me or because *he* chose me. I didn't choose him, even though I was flattered if I was asked... I couldn't feel they wanted me, or feel positive about that.'

Joseph refers to external pressures to be different and how these result in a feeling of continuous identity crisis: 'For me, the differences sometimes make me feel as if I am living with a continuous identity crisis as a result of being a "pig in the middle" between Black and Deaf. That means my identity is whole, but it's also in crisis a lot of the time. But if the crisis becomes too great, such as when I am oppressed as a Black or a Deaf person, or both, it also feels as if Black and Deaf are forced to be separate. It's the force and the lack of acceptance that make the crisis. But sometimes the crisis is more like a confusion and that stops me from feeling like a whole person.' Like Andrew, he is clear that he wants 'to treat both of my identities as whole, no matter which comes first at any moment in time'. Joseph is also very perceptive of the relationship between himself and others, and makes an interesting observation about the role of knowledge and learning: 'Maybe that's something about learning. It increases my deductive and thinking power, but it also makes me change my attitudes and perceptions of myself in relation to society "at large", including the Deaf community. I worry sometimes that after many years of learning and studying it may become difficult to relate to Deaf people at the grass roots level because I have had opportunities to further my cognitive and intellectual development…knowledge can make me feel more different in some situations.' Some would say that knowledge is power, but for Joseph it clearly means that his difference is exacerbated, something I feel is also true for Krishna: 'I came face to face with the social work jargon and culture, and words like "discrimination", "power" and so on which I had never heard before. I had *experience* of discrimination but I didn't have the language to name it;…I was quite amazed by this new information – a whole portion of human life experience had been somehow missed.' Following the feeling of 'coming out of her shell' and the renewed confidence in herself that she gained as a result of going to Deaf school, this new experience precipitates confusion and causes her to question some of her earlier positions: 'When I began to really take all of this in, to absorb it, I began to question myself. "Who am I then? They're so and so, they're so and so, but who am I?" I felt lost and so confused.' Her *moratorium* continues.

Sam's sense of crisis and confusion continues during adolescence and is also compounded by features of the new environment he finds himself in. There are changes in respect of communication and rules: 'I was shocked and confused because we had been told we must speak at the old school and here, in a different school, the rules were different and this created even more confusion', and in the structure of peer relationships: 'I never had any explanation of why these things were happening to me, no reasons were given why friends would suddenly become enemies and kick me when we were playing football for example.' But Sam also enters a phase of inner questioning of childhood identifications and positions as exemplified in this statement: 'all the feelings got mixed up because school was somewhere I hated and had communication which I loved, and home was somewhere that I loved and needed to be, but had no communication I could follow or understand. That made me frustrated and angry.' Through sharing experiences with Bill, he learns that other parents had different priorities and he begins to realise the implications of this and to question his own upbringing: 'It meant for me that his mother and father gave him time to himself and cared for him, whereas my parents had no time for me. They were always too busy on the farm, and that came first. When Bill's mother and father came to visit, I felt as if I wanted to go back with them. I wanted a mother and father that would give me time and look after me.' This is without the sickening abuse he experiences which generates a psychological and emotional confusion of its own: 'It was like there was a split in me, half of me saying "I want to tell... I want the pain to stop" and the other half saying "No you can't tell or you will be hurt again." That was the inner struggle, that was the confusion, and it split my identity in two.' This highlights his growing disenchantment and anger with religion: 'inside I was thinking what hypocrites they were, abusing boys and pretending to be such good men'. Though the questioning is clearer, it is still inwardly focused because he continues to deny his feelings in outward expression, largely because of fear: 'I just smiled reverently at him, denying my friend's death.' I want to emphasise here that the numbness Sam described in chapter two – the putting the lid on feelings – was much in evidence as he continued with his narrative. I felt very strongly that he was back there in that school, at that time, reliving his abuse in great detail. But he seemed to me to be totally devoid of emotion, like a metronome ticking from one horrific experience to the next. This also describes in some ways how I felt as I listened. Counsellors who work with clients who have been abused describe how invasive of personal boundaries the experience can be:

> Although boundaries have been established in the early stages of therapy, it is not surprising that clients who have experienced such extensive invasion of their own boundaries should also challenge those that have been established in therapy. While boundaries exists to hold the client psychologically, and to provide predictable containment for their confusing experience, it is equally important to be aware of the appropriateness of moving or changing the boundary. (Walker 1992, p.163)

She talks about a client whom she feels jumps in too quickly, leaving her wishing that he would 'paddle around the edge', and this was my immediate internal response when I first listened to Sam's story. It made me acutely aware of one important issue – the difference between the use of counselling skills and the task of counselling. In this situation I was using counselling skills, I was *not* counselling, and as a consequence I had not been as careful about establishing boundaries as I might have been if Sam had been a client of mine. Sam's story sent me so deeply into a sense of shock, that it was some time before I realised that I was also feeling completely numb, completely sucked into the whirlpool created by his abuse and afraid that I might not see the light at the end of the tunnel. Walker (1992, p.197) would describe this as becoming an 'emotional sponge' and I feel this description is particularly apt. On the realisation that I was feeling like this, I then felt inadequate and powerless – almost wishing that I had not started the interview. When I later translated the tape of the interview, I was aware of bracing myself for a second onslaught, but by that time, I also felt an overpowering sense of rage at what had been done to Sam and I think that helped me to deal with my own feelings.

So, this chapter leaves us with a strong sense of unresolved crisis and struggle, which our narrators take with them as they move on to adulthood. In the following chapter, we will see that even the most stable identity configurations can be sternly challenged by unexpected change, and the most deeply entrenched sense of confusion or crisis can become clearer and more manageable.

CHAPTER FIVE

Swamps and Rivers

> The person-centred approach…depends upon the actualising tendency present in every living organism – the tendency to grow, to develop, to realise its full potential. This way of being trusts the constructive directional flow of the human being toward a more complex and complete development. It is this directional flow that we aim to release. (Rogers 1986, p.199)

> If I accept the other person as something fixed, already diagnosed and classified, already shaped by his past, then I am doing my part to confirm this limited hypothesis… If I see a relationship as only an opportunity to reinforce certain types of words or opinions in the other, then I tend to confirm him as an object – a basically mechanical, manipulable object. (Rogers 1958, p.15)

Introduction

Most people agree that without a clear and committed identity, it is difficult to establish intimate relationships in which we are strong enough to make sacrifices for another's welfare without losing ourselves in the other's identity. We saw in the previous chapter that one possible resolution of the identity/role confusion psychosocial conflict, the diffused identity status, can result in just such a merging of self and others. With the foreclosed identity status, there is a different kind of merging related to the context foreclosed upon, though the boundaries between self and others are clearer than for the diffused status. This form of resolution of the identity issue is adaptive as long as we remain in and make relationships in this context. The following psychosocial conflict, *intimacy versus isolation*, often becomes the first test of how adaptive is the identity configuration we have affirmed for ourselves. However, as Marcia (1994) and his colleagues have shown, identity formation and intimacy can co-develop – something which is quite common in women, for example – and sometimes commitment to a particular identity follows the resolution of the intimacy versus isolation psychosocial conflict. From the developmental perspective, intimacy has a broad meaning which includes intimacy from same- and opposite-sex friendships, in love, in sexual union, and even in relationship with oneself or one's life commitments (Evans 1967). An important aspect of intimacy is commitment or communion – a shift of developmental focus from 'I' to 'we' (Kroger 1996), going with the flow of the

commitments we have made and recognising and responding to the effects
that these commitments have on others:

> Growth of the self requires meetings between I and Thou, in which each
> person recognises the other as he is; each says what he means and means
> what he says; each values and contributes to the unfolding of the other
> without imposing or manipulating. And this always means some de-
> gree of distance or independence. It does not depend on one revealing
> to another everything that exists within, but requires only that the
> person be who he is, genuinely present. (Moustakas 1974, p.92)

The counterpart of intimacy is isolation, which tends to result if there is a
failure to commit ourselves to loving relationships because of competition or
fear, for example. We may only be able to relate on a stereotypical or formal
basis, or to seek intimacy with the most unlikely people which increases the
chance of our isolation through rejection. Within this conflict, then, there are
images of feeling stuck, being unable to branch outwards and a reluctance to
explore the boundaries between self and others and an outward flow of energy
merging with others (Figure 5.1).

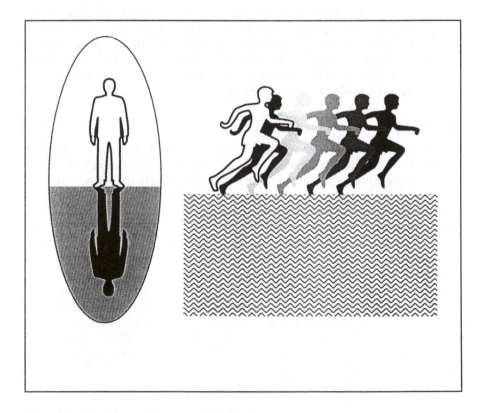

Figure 5.1 Swamps and rivers

As with all the psychosocial conflicts that we have explored thus far, there are different ways in which this one can be resolved, some of which involve an element of both intimacy and isolation. Interestingly, it is at this stage, as our narrators move into adulthood, that the narratives develop a pattern which divides this developmental stage into two parts one or other of which, or both of which, is chosen by them. The distinction between these two developmental routes is founded on the suggestion above that intimacy can be defined as a relationship with oneself or one's life commitments. On the one hand, energy may be focused on learning more about ourselves, and on the other hand, there may be some overlap with the next psychosocial conflict as we begin to adopt a generative attitude. On the one hand, growth may be directed inwards, for rivers can, after all, flow underground. This period of inner exploration may be perceived by others as withdrawal or isolation, but I would like to suggest that in the case of some of our narrators, it is a necessary developmental strategy, a 'taking stock' of past experiences, a psychological and emotional moratorium. This reflects Kroger's (1996, p.28) view that:

> It is the recognition of one's ultimate aloneness which gives intimacy its base, and it is one's capacity for security in that aloneness which makes genuine intimacy possible.

Because growth and self-understanding is clearly continuing, it is not a negative resolution of this stage and, as such, I felt that it merits separate discussion because of the way the interviews developed. Inner growth is therefore the focus of the following chapter, whereas this chapter looks at intimacy through relationships.

Peter

I started to feel at home with being deaf, really properly at home with it, when I started to try and gain a professional qualification. I decided that I would get involved with a summer play scheme with deaf children who signed, and I enjoyed myself. The more I got involved with the deaf children and organised activities for them, the more I felt a sense of belonging. I also became emotionally involved with a woman friend, a colleague, and this friendship felt very close. She was a daughter of Deaf parents herself and could sign fluently. There were a lot of deaf young people and I was always trying to help them sort out problems, in particular because there was one particular kid who was disruptive, always lying, and I was trying very hard to help them to see what they were doing. I was in my first gay relationship at this time and I remember going back to the house where I lived with the trauma provoked by that camping holiday. I was very spaced out by the experience. I phoned my mother to say I was back and I didn't really know how to talk to my hearing partner at first about what was happening in me. It felt like I had been visiting another planet, but it wasn't an alien planet, and then coming back to earth was a shock. My partner was a good signer, very quick to learn, but I still couldn't get it out. Anyway, I felt ill, and I went up to bed, and I started to cry – I howled and tore at the bed clothes. My partner came to try to comfort me, but I couldn't tell him – I was too wound up and upset.

I became very depressed and I think it was that experience which made me realise that I had to own being Deaf, I had to take it in me and welcome it. It happened because I had been through a 'Deaf time', being with and relating to deaf children and suddenly all the problems I had had before started to make sense. I began to understand what had happened to me before. It was a very deep experience.

Caroline

I think I realised more about the hearing world when I started work – I couldn't explain what was happening before that. The first two weeks weren't bad because everyone was very excited and trying to be helpful by writing down their names and things like that. Then that fizzled out – it never lasts, always too good to be true. I started trying to fit in their way, but that wasn't possible all the time because I was reliant on trying to lipread, and feeling a pull back in the direction of my sign, my natural place. I felt dragged in all sorts of different directions trying to pick up a half word here and there, but no real information. I think I realised then that it was impossible to fit with hearing people. I know I'm Deaf and I belong in the Deaf community. The only thing I looked forward to was the Deaf club on Wednesday night. I used to rush to finish work and get home, eager to get into *my* world, after six hours of no communication. I remember once my work colleagues asked me to go ice skating with them and I felt all churned up with indecision, but anyway I decide to go. It was a mistake, because I was trying to concentrate on skating and I couldn't concentrate on understanding their speech at the same time. So the next time they asked, I said 'No, I feel tempted, but no.' They thought maybe they should come with me to the Deaf club and that was hard for me too because I knew that my Deaf friends wouldn't understand or accept them. I almost felt caught in the middle, not sure what to do. But then I thought if they come with me to the Deaf club, they might be able to see what it was like for me being the only Deaf person in a hearing group, They did make the link – realised why the Deaf club was *my* world, and that was a positive experience in the end because after that, it worked better.

When I was pregnant with Jane, I thought that, because I already had four deaf children, she would be deaf. When she was born, I continued to think she must be deaf because she had no reaction to sound – nothing. But I remember that when I went to the toy library, the teacher there – a different peripatetic teacher, with a nicer personality [!] – played a sound like a *womb* sound and said that Jane liked the sound. Inside I was raging and upset; I thought, 'What do you mean, how could she like it, she's Deaf! What gives you the authority to try and test her hearing like that?' It felt as if it was the same old story again. Then I came home and felt a little depressed, started looking at Jane and questioning. 'Is she hearing?' But I still felt it was impossible. She couldn't be hearing. But I remember now, that Jane slept with no problem – I should have recognised that because the other children were so active, sensitive to any touch or any vibration, it was impossible to get them to sleep. But Jane always slept beautifully. So when I took her for this hearing test, and they said 'She's fine!', I said

'You mean she's Deaf?' 'Oh no, no, she's hearing…hearing'. And I thought *'Hearing*? But she can't be hearing.' So I asked to see the audiogram because I thought there must be something wrong with the machine. The audiologist said 'Your reaction is the same as a hearing mother who's just been told their baby is deaf!' Inside I wanted to say 'Oh come on, you're the professional! You should have known to break the news gently. You would have broken the news gently to a hearing mother if you'd found their baby was deaf. But me, you just throw it at me… Wham…without a thought. How do you think I feel?' But she just didn't realise. I looked at the audiogram and saw that her hearing was normal. I felt numb, as if a barrier had closed down around me and I was in the dark… I looked at Jane, my hearing baby, and I felt distant from her, that I didn't want her to be a *hearing* baby. I knew I had to get her home, and I kept looking at her thinking 'She's hearing?' When I'd got her into the car, I just sat there. I couldn't drive off. I think I was in shock, and I felt very alone. I looked at her and she was laughing, as if nothing had happened. So I just stared into space and thought about how I was gong to drive home. It just hit me…so…hard. [cries]

When I got home, Richard was there with my Mum – they looked at me and signed WHAT HAPPEN? I said, 'Well, it's bad news' They realised immediately that Jane was hearing, and their reaction was also one of disbelief. Mum cried. It was strange because looking back, when Richard was born, my sister had two children and when the first was born and found to be hearing, Mum was really proud, because it was her first grandchild and it was hearing. Then, it felt like it was normal to have a hearing child – it linked with the Deaf community attitudes at the time where the birth of a hearing child was celebrated and the birth of a Deaf child was seen to be something to be pitied. When Richard was born, the family couldn't accept he was Deaf. There were big arguments, questioning how he could be Deaf and I was alone again arguing with the family saying 'He's Deaf, and that's it! There's nothing we can do.' But with Jane, Mum cried because she felt it would have been much better if she had been Deaf, she could have accepted it if she had been Deaf. Richard was shocked, Mum was crying and I thought 'How am I going to tell the rest of the family?' I had to wait until the evening. We were watching TV, I saw it moving but it was like a blur – I wasn't really watching it. I felt there was no support, no information or understanding of what I'm going through. I didn't know how to begin. It's different for a hearing mother with a Deaf baby – there is someone there to support – even if they're not always very helpful. I didn't know what to do that was best for her, I had no one I could ask, I hadn't even begun to think about such a situation because, for me, hearing had always been 'out there' and not part of my family. I just didn't know what I was going to do with her – should I talk to her with my voice, however bad, or should I sign? They might tell a hearing mother that she must sign with her Deaf child, but Jane is hearing, her first language must be spoken English, so am I meant to talk to her? I just didn't know which way to go, where to turn. There was just this word going through my head all the time – it was like it was planted in my brain, sending out new shoots every day – *hearing*? At night I would toss and turn or lie awake thinking *hearing, hearing*. If I woke up suddenly, it was the first thing that came into my head – *hearing*. It was just so difficult to accept.

A few weeks later I went off on a course. I think I was starting to accept it, but inside I was still not with it, not myself. I was still very muddled and confused – very ambivalent. That course was about Deaf community, culture and identity and I could feel all those feelings starting to bubble up. Then one night I was in a crowd of people and I just broke down and cried. There were a lot of hearing adults who had Deaf parents there and there was so much support, so many stories about their past and relationships with their parents, what they wished their parents had done and what they didn't do. I was able to ask lots of questions about how to relate to a hearing baby, what to do, what's the best way. That helped. But also I had sign language, and my identity was strong as a Deaf person – I was sure about who I was, and when I looked at Jane with these new eyes, all I felt was that I wanted her to grow up not regretting that she had a Deaf family because I know that is something that can happen – we are talking about two different worlds.

Krishna

I then began to wonder about other areas in my life, particularly education. It became a priority to me to get some professional qualifications, a real education, as a kind of backlash against the fact that both deaf and hearing education had failed me. I was not able to complete my education because I was never allowed to try for exams, and they felt that working in a factory was all I was capable of (even though, at that time, the pressure to work was high as my father was unemployed and there wasn't much money around). It was so liberating to be able to make a decision to return to college to do an Access course and a professional degree which would qualify me for what I wanted to do and be a passport to other things as well. I recall when I took the step of doing a social work course, my mother was extremely worried and anxious as to whether I would be able to study at this level and succeed. It was as if all *her* fears from the past were informing her – the authority figures in education coming back and saying that I didn't have the potential – using her as a mouthpiece. She had many problems letting go of the doubts and reservations that had been planted. But I had become determined and single-minded in doing what I felt was right for me and I had to pursue this course despite her fears. Needless to say, I got unlimited support from her while studying – it was hard work, but worth it.

At the same time I had decided that I wanted to renew contact with deaf people, but where were they? I had lost contact with all the deaf people I knew at the Deaf school. From that time onwards I had never seen another deaf person. I actually felt at times as if I was the only one who was left deaf, that maybe they had all become hearing! Somewhere I knew I wasn't alone because there had been another girl who was Asian and deaf at the Deaf school. I went to a centre for deaf people and said that I wanted to be in contact with deaf people, particularly with other Asian deaf women to share our experiences of being Asian deaf women in society. It was clear from meeting with them on a regular basis that they felt triply disadvantaged in terms of their race, gender and deafness, particularly in respect of being labelled, having little or no sense of belonging, isolated, marginalised and a deep sense of powerlessness. When at college, I discussed this with my personal tutor and explained the feedback from the group and my feelings of being uncertain of how I could effect change on an organisational and political level. He implied that I would have to be a *pioneer* and I was frightened by that – the responsibility it entailed and the conflicts it brought. I wasn't sure I wanted that. The real meaning of social work hit me hard! The experiences I have had with working with groups of people have also made me aware of how difficult it can be to integrate all the parts of me, and have brought me face to face with the inner conflicts which society imposes on me. For example, in some of the groups I have been involved in, membership has been limited to one category. I have been part of a Black workers' group. As a Black, deaf female professional, this means that there is an important part of me – my deafness, disability and gender – that is being marginalised, unaddressed and subjected on occasions to appalling attitudes from Black, able-bodied, male professional attitudes. Similarly there are women's groups which I often find are white and able-bodied in their philosophy and ways of doing things. I struggle with that – I struggle a lot with it actually. So I do have conflicts, I know that, and I really have to think about whether I am being two-faced sometimes when I want to express what's here in *me*, I want to say what's in me, but I also feel I have to go along with the flow. But I will only do that as long as I know I'm not hurting people. If the flow is authoritarian and insensitive, or if I'm being forced to label or put people into boxes, it is very difficult to relate to it.

Sam

I feel very bitter because of how my childhood experiences influenced my adult life. I remember going on holiday once with my wife and son, and my son was crying. My wife asked me to go and tend to him and I can remember picking him up, holding him at arm's length and feeling so angry that he was crying. When I saw how tense the muscles on my arm were, I was shocked. It was like the past coming back to haunt me. I put my son down because I was frightened I would hurt him, and I started crying with confusion – it wasn't fair on my son, but I couldn't stop the feelings welling up. It wasn't his fault. I was frightened at that moment that because I had been abused at school I would end up abusing my son. That was when I realised I had a lot of problems inside, a lot of unresolved feelings because over the years I had held on to these awful feelings and they had now got out of control. So I felt very bitter. I suffered so much pain physically, and then emotional pain of the anticipation that the next day would bring yet another beating. My anxiety level was so acute that I could almost see it stretching out in front of me out of control. At the same time I couldn't face that future. I dreaded the next day, I remember hoping that it wouldn't come. I felt hopeless, like I was throwing a ball that always came back to me no matter how far I threw it. Every time it came back it was bigger, and as it got bigger it became more heavy, sinking deeper and deeper, a dead weight inside of me.

Fiona

All my confusions and doubts began with my first Deaf partner. He was Deaf from a hearing family and I am hearing from a Deaf family. There were a lot of clashes when I said things, and he disagreed, and I thought, well, he is Deaf and he should understand that I have the culture and expectations of Deaf people. The relationship seemed to be continuously about compromise, because of the deep emotional attachment to my roots, and it hurt. I started to get confused. The first year of the relationship was like a testing ground. He said you should behave like this, you should be thinking this, you should be doing that. *That* is the hearing way. But I could only respond, '*This* is me. If you don't like it, fine!' It felt as if I was constantly being pushed into making some choice, but even then I was not sure what the choices were and what they meant.

By the third year of the relationship I was so completely confused that my confidence in myself and in relating was lost. I didn't know who I was any more. When I was growing up there was this acceptance of who I was – that was the family's attitude. Looking back I think that perhaps my partner couldn't accept the fact that I was *more Deaf* than him. When we went out to Deaf clubs and Deaf events, people always said I was the Deaf person and he was the hearing person. The first few times it was funny, but I think it bothered him because it felt as if his claim to being Deaf was challenged in some way. As time went on, it bothered him so much that he started to become resentful of me, and felt that I was oppressing him because I was behaving in a Deaf way and he *was* Deaf. I accepted him as he was but I think he found it difficult to accept me. I think I began to feel a need to change the way I thought about myself because of all the pressure from him to change, and how it made me dwell on things so much more. If I had got out of the relationship earlier I wouldn't have felt so confused, but I think it would have taken longer to repair the damage. When the two of us finally split, I bought a big stereo system for the first time in my life. This was my present to myself – an attempt to affirm my status as a hearing person – and it became my symbol of being a hearing person; it was new, just like the new hearing person I had become. I had had a small stereo before which I put away in a cupboard because it wasn't an essential part of my life because I was still a person who could hear sound, but not really a 'hearing person' in the way that hearing people are. I hadn't reached that stage in the development of becoming hearing.

I remember the Australian film *Passport Without a Country*, about hearing children of Deaf adults. There are parts of me which say that expression – 'passport without a country' – is relevant, but there are other parts which do not feel there is any relevance to my own experiences of growing up. The part that relates to it is that part which just doesn't fit in. At the start of this year I decided not to socialise so much with Deaf people outside of my family. I consciously arrange to meet hearing people, but often I will cancel the arrangement and stay at home by myself because I feel guilty about trying to push the Deaf part of me to one side. It's nothing to do with Deaf and hearing not being able to mix, more that I don't always want to be the person that is assisting the mixing. I don't want to be that person, don't want to be involved because when you are in between you never get the full pleasures that Deaf or hearing people get when they are whole and separate. They say you can have the 'best of both worlds', but I feel you get the worst of both worlds as well. When I am on my own there is none of that. I feel more safe and secure. There is no arguing, no misunderstanding, no conflict and no guilt. I don't feel I am constantly having to sort out the conflicts. Sometimes I think I would rather be on my own without the emotional manipulation that happens and which makes me feel so angry about who I am and why I can't be valued as I am. When I have arranged to go out with a hearing person, I still feel I have to tell Deaf people what I am doing when they ask. If I don't, I feel that I am lying, I am covering it up – that's the manipulation. But maybe I am manipulating myself? If I don't tell them, I have this little feeling eating away at me, preying on the guilt. I don't see why I should feel guilty, but I do feel guilty. They don't say anything that makes me feel guilty, but I feel it. So I feel safe when I am on my own, and I am sometimes not sure if, when I am with other people, there *are* any places of safety? Even with other hearing children of Deaf parents there is not the meeting of minds I hoped for. I thought there must be others out there and that I can't be *that* different, but when I met them it just didn't happen for me, maybe because we are all different individuals with different perceptions, based on our own experiences of growing up. I sometimes feel that if I had been part of a smaller family, I could have merged more with them. But I can't. I can't stand in a room talking about it as easily as others seem to be able to. There is never really any release from the responsibilities that were placed on me as a child.

I feel lonely all the time, no not all the time, no, I think *alone* rather than lonely – that would be more appropriate – and for different reasons. Being with a group of hearing people who know nothing about deafness, for example, I don't feel alone as long as one person there has a level of interest in something which is similar to mine. If I am with Deaf people and the communication is superficial it's fine. But if it's a group of hearing people and it's superficial, I would rather be at home on my own because all I keep thinking of is why can't I fit in? Why can't I do something? All these very difficult feelings of self-doubt keep returning. Often other people don't believe me when I say that I have this self-doubt. It's almost as if they have to see me as being always in control, always problem-free, but that is the wrong thing to say to me. I don't have the heart to say 'Piss off, I am entitled to my feelings!', but that is what I feel like sometimes – angry because people don't want to look beyond what they see on the surface or beyond their views of that. I always thought people could read me like a book, but I have realised more recently that what they are reading is very different from how I am, what I am actually feeling.

Andrew

I feel acutely aware that a change occurred because many of the people who in the *before* phase were loving, supporting and offered friendship, suddenly became their alter egos in the *after* phase and withdrew all of these things. That was very traumatic for me, because I felt diminished, devalued, isolated and alienated by the fact that they couldn't see *me* any more, at least not the person I knew. It was as if the person who had been able to get what he wanted before without too much of a problem had suddenly been replaced with a person who was completely ineffective and received all of the things he didn't want, whether he asked for them or not.

When I got over the initial anger about knowing that the only thing that had really changed was that I could no longer hear, it was replaced with a new anger about what this meant for communication and relationships with people who could hear. That anger was very much more extreme, because, if I have one regret about becoming deaf, it is to do with how it has changed my perception of love. Once, I am sure that I was able to experience love and to give love, especially to love myself and feel proud of myself. But that changed as I watched my family grow distant from me along with the love I thought they felt for me. I could see people trying to love me but I didn't feel it. It didn't reach me anymore because I became scared that if I started to feel it, it would be withdrawn in the same way that my family's love seemed to be. I feel sure that this changed the way I acted towards my children. I was no longer carefree. I watched my children growing up and somehow every change that happened seemed to catch me by surprise, because although I had been seeing the changes over time, I wasn't *aware* of what was happening because they were not communicated to me in a way that I had access to or understood. So I felt all the time that I was missing out on my children growing up. I think I felt scared of this because a lot of the feelings reminded me of how my parents felt so distant from me. The feelings were the same, but the situation was not the same. I don't feel my parents loved me and that was the reason for *their* distance. They were embarrassed by the son that they could not parade as a success in front of their friends because he was deaf. They were embarrassed by the stigma I presented for the family, and I know that my mother always felt that she was responsible for my 'deviance' because she hadn't taken me seriously when I said I felt ill. I don't remember my parents ever asking me how I felt about anything, certainly not how I felt about being deaf, and I just learnt to be self-sufficient and get on with it by myself.

I can remember thinking even in those days that I would never distance my children in the way that my parents distanced me. I wanted to be a responsible parent who was respectful of and a friend to my children as well, and most of all, who never dismissed or questioned their feelings. I don't think I ever thought about the fact that good communication would be needed for that, and in the end, it feels as if it is that lack of thought which has denied me my dreams of fulfilled parenthood. I blamed myself for that. I know I certainly missed out on the humour of family life and those little quirks in relationship which make most people smile – they somehow always happened more fleetingly and could never be recaptured. The downside of being a parent, perhaps even of life, was always so *loud* and so *demanding* that the gentle, happy side happened without my knowing it. Most of the people around me were very good at getting my attention when they wanted to have a tantrum, or when they wanted me to sort out *their* problems and conflicts but they never thought that *I* might need them to grab my attention when there is some fun in the atmosphere so that I could join in. Perhaps my children got so fed up with me saying 'What is it *now*?' that they didn't bother me with the minor anecdotes which lighten up their experience of the world – they always went to my partner. It is not as if I didn't have a sense of humour. Actually, I often laughed at myself when my deafness meant that I get things all wrong because it *was* funny. I also enjoyed a bit of teasing. But that was not the same as wandering around with a ridiculous smile on my face which was frozen in time as other people enjoyed their own amusements. When I began to feel overwhelmed by the children's behaviour and feeling left out, I started to communicate these feelings to my partner, but I felt that put pressure on her to act as the leveller and tell me stories about the children's more amusing escapades and comments. I just felt so apart from everything because I didn't enjoy it when it happened, always later. I realised, too, from some of the descriptions, that I had actually been there when it *did* happen and it has been yet another of those occasions when I had laughed but not known what the joke was.

Karen

When I went to college, I really couldn't cope with being deaf at all. I didn't tell people I was deaf because there was no obvious evidence of it so there seemed no need. I used to say that I couldn't hear very well. I wouldn't say 'deaf' – I couldn't. I went to lectures and missed all the information and I just coped by reading. I wanted to read a foreign language, but it was impossible, so I had to give it up. I couldn't cope with trying to make out the language tapes. In the courses where I could read all the books, I was fine. But there was one lecturer, for example, who had no recommended books for his course and I failed that course because I hadn't a clue what he was talking about. I couldn't be assertive and say 'I'm deaf… I need this, this and this…' I couldn't at that time.

I had many different relationships at college as well, but there was one relationship in particular. It started in my first year, was very difficult and continued right though my time there. This man obviously wanted a younger woman, someone he could influence and who could give his ego a boost. In this relationship, we were both very stubborn. We used to have big rows, sometimes fights. He was jealous if I looked at other men. Once when we were at a dance, I began to dance with another man and he went berserk and he got violent. I decided, that's it! I didn't want to know him any more. But he kept coming back, coming back, and I just couldn't refuse him. Part of that was my feelings about myself. I couldn't say no to him because part of me needed to be in a relationship with him for affirmation. I feel really embarrassed about it. I got pregnant and I had another abortion on the NHS, and this time the attitudes were awful. I had to go into the hospital the night before and as I was sitting in the waiting room...the nurses' attitudes... I don't want to think about it. That night I lay awake tossing and turning, I couldn't sleep, and the next morning, more because of the attitudes I experienced than because I didn't want the abortion, I decided that I couldn't go through with it and I started to walk out. But the nurses, once they thought that I didn't want the abortion, changed their attitude and they were very sympathetic and supportive. It was an awful experience; it made me feel very bad about myself. In the end, I went home and arranged an abortion from there.

All these things were happening and it was like I was shutting them away – I just couldn't or didn't want to face them at the time. I was staying in this man's house at the time I got pregnant. He really wanted me to have his baby, his child, but I realised that I didn't even like him as a person because he didn't want me for who I was – for the person I was. He just wanted his ideal of what he thought a woman should be and that wasn't me – I was just his slave. When he had friends over, he just expected me to cook for him and then he and his friends would go out to the pub and I was furious, churned up inside, asking myself 'Why am I doing this?' I felt so stupid, but I didn't know what those churned up feelings were about. It was as if I wasn't clear about my own identity as a woman or something. I knew that instinctively I did not like the situation, but was not sure why, nor what I could do about it. Perhaps becoming deaf reinforced my image of myself as the stereotyped 'passive' woman, and I think it became worse because I still had a 'hearing' attitude about being deaf. It didn't feel right but I couldn't work out why and so I felt trapped. I always allowed other people to do what they wanted and influence me and I wasn't strong enough to defend myself against that. But I was in there somewhere, I'm sure of it.

Unravelling Narratives

As was suggested in the introduction, there are a number of things which are necessary for genuine intimacy, which relate to the individuals themselves and the qualities they look for in adult relationships. Essentially, most people, when seeking relationships, apply a number of *filters* (Perlman and Fehr 1987; Murstein 1986) to those that they meet in order to determine their suitability. These filters might include:

- external characteristics
- attitudes, beliefs and values
- role fit, or whether the person's ideas about relationships match our own

and many sociologists support the view that partnerships based on *homogamy*, or the selection of partners who are like ourselves in age, education, social class, ethnicity, religion, attitudes, interests or temperament, for example, are much more likely to endure than those in which the partners differ markedly (Murstein 1986). Obviously likeness must be consistent at different levels within the individual, and not just in those characteristics which are overtly expressed. If a gay or lesbian, or a deaf person has unresolved conflicts about their sexual orientation or their deafness submerged by denial, entering a relationship with someone who is heterosexual, homophobic, hearing or audist will be potentially destructive. This is why a degree of self-knowledge and self-understanding is another prerequisite for intimacy, and why Erikson (cited in Evans 1967) believed that genuine intimacy is not possible unless identity issues have been appropriately resolved. Intimate relationships are not the same as relationships which exist for the purpose of self-definition and this is what distinguishes them from the vertical and horizontal relationships encountered in adolescence, for example. Relationships which are formed for the purpose of finding ourselves through another person or living for another person, as might happen when we have committed ourselves to a diffused identity status, inhibit intimacy because they may be formed solely for the purpose of resolving our unconscious conflicts, including those which have resulted from our relationships with our parents. Thus, a third prerequisite for intimacy is that we have been able to detach ourselves from the affectional bonds with our parents and transfer our emotional and psychological energy to other central attachments:

> If children are eventually to form their own households, their bonds of attachment to the parents must become attenuated and eventually end. Otherwise independent living will be emotionally troubling. The relinquishing of attachment to parents appears to be of central importance among the individuation-achieving processes of late adolescence and early adulthood. (Weiss 1986, p.100)

Bee (1994) suggests that young people who have formed secure attachments with their parents have an easier psychological transition to independence and intimate relationships with peers than those who have anxious or ambivalent parent/child attachments. This is because we tend to recreate in our adult relationships the pattern that we carry in our internalised model of attachment. So, if we have learned that attachments with hearing people cause us pain, we would be unlikely to seek adult relationships with hearing people, and if we do form relationships with hearing people, it is more likely that we would find them inappropriate in some way.

This happened with Karen, who continued with her diffused model of attachment in her first adult relationships: 'I wouldn't say "deaf" – I couldn't... I couldn't be assertive and say "I'm deaf... I need this, this and this..." I couldn't at that time...I just couldn't refuse him. Part of that was my feelings about myself. I couldn't say no to him because part of me needed to be in a relationship with him for affirmation.' When she eventually realised that she was not getting the affirmation she thought she was, the impasse began to lift and she caught a glimpse of who she was: 'I was furious, churned up inside asking myself "Why am I doing this?" I felt so stupid, but I didn't know what those churned up feelings were about. It was as if I wasn't clear about my own identity as a woman or something. I knew that instinctively I did not like the situation, but was not sure why, nor what I could do about it. Perhaps becoming deaf reinforced my image of myself as the stereotyped "passive" woman, and I think it became worse because I still had a "hearing" attitude about being deaf. It didn't feel right but I couldn't work out why and so I felt trapped. I always allowed other people to do what they wanted and influence me and I wasn't strong enough to defend myself against that. But I was in there somewhere, I'm sure of it.'

Caroline, on the other hand, suggests that her initial work relationships with hearing people served to reinforce her Deaf identity still further: 'The first two weeks weren't bad because everyone was very excited and and trying to be helpful by writing down their names and things like that. Then that fizzled out – it never lasts, always too good to be true. I started trying to fit in their way, but that wasn't possible all the time because I was reliant on trying to lipread, and feeling a pull back in the direction of my sign, my natural place... I think I realised then that it was impossible to fit with hearing people. I know I'm Deaf and I belong in the Deaf community.' She sought and maintained intimate relationships with other Deaf people, remaining within the context she foreclosed her identity upon, but it is when 'hearing' invades these intimate relationships that she experiences a profound sense of shock at the realities she had to face up to but which she was unprepared for. The context foreclosed upon risks changing, and she finds it difficult to adapt: 'They said "She's fine!" I said "You mean she's Deaf?" "Oh no, no, she's hearing...hearing." And I thought "Hearing? But she can't be hearing."... I felt numb, as if a barrier had closed down around me and I was in the dark... I looked at Jane, my *hearing* baby, and I felt distant from her, that I didn't want her to be a hearing baby...I didn't know what to do that was best for her, I had no one I could ask, I hadn't even begun to think about such a situation because, for me, hearing had always been "out there" and not part of my family... It just hit me...so...hard.' This crisis has an influence on Caroline's sense of identity: 'I think I was starting to accept it, but inside I was still not with it, not myself. I was still very muddled and confused – very ambivalent.' Her ability to accept the situation was eventually helped through new relationships with people who were like Jane, but part of the Deaf context. The adaptation she finally made was still therefore very much based on her Deaf roots and her need for Jane to value Deafness, to preserve the Deaf context: 'But also I had sign language, and my identity was strong as a Deaf person – I was sure about who I was, and when I looked at Jane with these new eyes, all I felt was that I wanted her to grow up not regretting that she had a Deaf family because I know that is something that can happen – we are talking about two different worlds.' Paradoxically, Jane's birth also brought Caroline face to face with less desirable elements of the Deaf community which influenced her feelings about being a parent, as we will see in the next Chapter.

For Fiona, it is, ironically, her first long-term relationship with a *Deaf* man, who, importantly, comes from the opposite pole to her in terms of family background, that leads directly to forcing her to look at the contradictions in her life. The relationship is very competitive because, essentially, this man cannot affirm her Deaf identity as he sees her as 'hearing'. She feels forced into defending herself: '"This is me. If you don't like it, fine!" It felt as if I was constantly being pushed into making some choice, but even then I was not sure what the choices were and what they meant... I think that perhaps my partner couldn't accept the fact that I was more Deaf than him.' But the difficulty of integrating the two parts of the contradiction – 'I do wonder about whether its possible to integrate them at all, I mean integrate them inside of myself?' – and in abandoning one or the other – 'often I will cancel the arrangement and stay at home by myself because I feel guilty about trying to push the Deaf part of me to one side' – eventually throws her into a crisis: 'By the third year of the relationship I was so completely confused that my confidence in myself and in relating was lost. I didn't know who I was any more.' I feel there are clear statements here about intimacy and identity formation being inextricably linked, and if this is an accurate translation, it supports Marcia's view that women tend to co-develop them. Fiona is quite clear about the difficulties that this crisis means for her, however: 'I don't always want to be the person that is assisting the mixing. I don't want to be that person, don't want to be involved because when you are in between you never get the full pleasures that Deaf or hearing people get when they are whole and separate. They say you can have the "best of both worlds", but I feel you get the worst of both worlds as well... Sometimes I think I would rather be on my own without the emotional manipulation that happens and which makes me feel so angry about who I am and why I can't be valued as I am.' But there is also a growing realisation of the role of our personal histories in creating who we are, which means that when she tries to develop relationships with other hearing children of Deaf parents, she is disappointed – it doesn't feel right: 'I am sometimes not sure if, when I am with other people, there *are* any places of safety? Even with other hearing children of Deaf parents there is not the meeting of minds I hoped for...when I met them it just didn't happen for me, maybe because we are all different individuals with different perceptions, based on our own experiences of growing up... There is never really any release from the responsibilities that were placed on me as a child.' Clearly she finds it difficult to detach herself from her childhood 'responsibilities', which means that the feelings surrounding them are ever-present and difficult to resolve. The way she deals with this is to throw herself into a new exploration phase where she begins to examine the hearing world and what it means for her in an attempt, ultimately, to understand and affirm 'the new hearing person [she felt she] had become'.

In contrast to Fiona, Peter had entered adulthood with a less clear picture of where deafness fitted in his identity, and he retained a sense of unconscious conflict. As he begins to explore his identity further in adulthood, he experiences a psychological and emotional crisis brought on by sustained contact with Deaf young people which possibly mirrors some of his own conflicts as an adolescent. He finally affirms Deafness as part of his identity, though this affirmation is associated with emotional trauma: 'It felt like I had been visiting another planet, but it wasn't an alien planet, and then coming back to earth was a shock... I felt ill, and I went up to bed, and I started to cry – I howled and tore at the bed clothes. My partner came to try to comfort me, but I couldn't tell him – I was too wound up and upset. I became very depressed... I think it was that experience which made me realise that I had to own being Deaf, I had to take it in me and welcome it.' We can see the contrast to the position accorded to the gay part of his identity, which he is clearly committed to, at least in terms of the intimate relationships he seeks, and how he perceives his Deaf identity before and after this crisis. The relationship between Deaf and gay is more ambivalent. On the one hand he says that 'I don't see myself as Deaf-gay, not like some others', and on the other, he alludes to the fact that his chosen partner, at least at this time, is able to sign and so there is some acknowledgement of needing to be with a partner who understands his Deafness.

Krishna, like Fiona, experiences some difficulties with voices from her childhood which, she feels, attempt to undermine her growth: 'It was as if all [her mother's] fears from the past were informing her – the authority figures in education coming back and saying that I didn't have the potential – using her as a mouthpiece.' However, though she acknowledges that 'both Deaf and hearing education had failed her', she 'had become determined and single-minded in doing what I felt was right for me and I had to pursue this course despite her fears'. But there is a sense that these voices are distant, because of her experiences in relationships formed in adult life and particularly through work. The voices do not restrict her ability to learn about the conflicts in her life, as she is 'aware of how difficult it can be to integrate all the parts of me, and [the relationships she makes] have brought me face to face with the inner conflicts which society imposes on me'. Moving into different kinds of rela-tionships 'means that there is an important part of me – my deafness, disability and gender – that is being marginalised, unaddressed and subjected on occasions to appalling attitudes'. She is very realistic about these conflicts: 'I struggle with that – I struggle a lot with it actually. So I do have conflicts, I know that, and I really have to think about whether I am being two-faced sometimes when I want to express what's here in me, I want to say what's in me, but I also feel I have to go along with the flow. But I will only do that as long as I know I'm not hurting people. If the flow is authoritarian and insensitive, or if I'm being forced to label or put people into boxes, it is very difficult to relate to it'. We get a sense that her exploration of these conflicts will continue, even if she is concerned about her ability to effect 'change on an organisational and political level', and reluctant to be 'a pioneer'. For Sam, however, there is only bitterness. The relics of his abuse and betrayal are ever-present and, as he enters intimacy and adopts a parenting role, they rear their ugly heads: 'It was like the past coming back to haunt me. I put my son down because I was frightened I would hurt him, and I started crying with confusion – it wasn't fair on my son, but I couldn't stop the feelings welling up. It wasn't his fault. I was frightened at that moment that because I had been abused at school I would end up abusing my son. That was when I realised I had a lot of problems inside, a lot of unresolved feelings because over the years I had held on to these awful feelings and they had now got out of control.'

Andrew recognises that the transitions he has made have influenced his perceptions of intimacy – 'many of the people who in the before phase were loving, supporting and offered friendship, suddenly became their alter egos in the after phase and withdrew all of these things. That was very traumatic for me, because I felt diminished, devalued, isolated and alienated by the fact that they couldn't see me any more, at least not the person I knew... If I have one regret about becoming deaf, it is to do with how it has changed my perception of love' – to the point where it has become difficult to feel a real sense of relating, and he attributes this to the nature of the parent/child relationship he experienced: 'I could see people trying to love me but I didn't feel it. It didn't reach me anymore because I was scared that if I started to feel it, it would be withdrawn in the same way that my family's love seemed to be. I feel sure that this changed the way I acted in the parenting role. I was no longer carefree.' However, his becoming deaf adds another dimension to his adult relationships and his feelings about partnership and parenthood: 'I watched my children growing up and somehow every change that happened seemed to catch me by surprise, because although I had been seeing the changes over time, I hadn't been aware of what was happening because they were not communicated to me in a way that I understood.' This contradicts what he believed a good parent should be – the exact opposite to the parenting he experienced: 'I can remember thinking even in those days that I would never distance my children in the way that my parents distanced me. I wanted to be a responsible parent who was respectful of and a friend to my children as well, and most of all, who never dismissed or questioned their feelings.' This makes him feel a failure: 'I don't think I ever thought about the fact that good communication would be needed for that, and in the end, it feels as if it is that lack of thought which has denied me my dreams of fulfilled parenthood.' But, like Krishna, Andrew maintains a sense of perspective, a realism which enables him to make distinctions between self-blame and humour, for example: 'The downside of being a parent, perhaps even of life, is always so loud and so demanding that the gentle, happy side happens without me knowing it... Actually, I often laugh at myself when my deafness means that I get things all wrong because it is funny. I also enjoy a bit of teasing. But that is not the same as wandering around with this ridiculous smile on my face which is frozen in time as other people enjoy their own amusements.' He remains aware that there are possibilities which can be explored through honest communication: 'When I began to feel overwhelmed by the children's behaviour and feeling left out, I started to communicate these feelings to my partner, but I felt that put pressure on her to act as the leveller and tell me stories about the children's more amusing escapades and comments.'

Such communication is sometimes usefully carried out in our inner worlds, and just as intimate relationships can precipitate further changes to the initial identity configuration, so too can our first real awareness of what is happening to us through the dynamics of the relationships we have with ourselves, as five of our narrators describe in Chapter Six.

Underground Rivers

Man's main task in life is to give birth to himself, to become what he potentially is. The most important product of his effort is his own personality. (Fromm 1947)

I could give you a whole list of the persons I can be. I am an old peasant woman who thinks of cooking and the house. I am a scholar who thinks of deciphering manuscripts. I am a psychotherapist who thinks of how to interpret people's dreams. I am a mischievous little boy who enjoys the company of a ten-year-old and playing mischievous tricks on adults, and so on. I could give twenty more such characters. They suddenly enter you, but if you see what is happening you can keep them out of your system, play with them and put them aside again. But if you are possessed, they enter you involuntarily and you act them out involuntarily. (Boa 1988, p.241)

Introduction

When a safe environment is provided, and a certain level of trust is established between two people, it frequently happens that they will begin to share things which they would not share in any other circumstances. Looking back over such episodes of sharing on a deeper level I am always struck by how much information they contain about the potential that open and honest communication has for understanding and, ultimately, for healing. This is simply because we work from our own reality, rather than from the multitude of double binds and ambiguous messages that most of us live with in everyday life. But it is also often because in such circumstances, we are attending to each other more closely. We pick up flashes of feeling, the minute flickers of changing expression, the alteration of body posture and a subtle undertone to what is being communicated which give hints of underground rivers. If the safe environment is a counselling environment, or if one or more of the participants in a shared narrative has skills in counselling, it frequently happens that the narrative moves onto a deeper level when this was not necessarily the original intention. It is an almost unconscious process born out of empathy, a desire to understand the other person and to be fully open with them. In each of the narratives we look at in this chapter, something happened in the course of the interview which caught my attention and seemed to me to be particularly significant for the narrator. It was not always something that was overtly expressed, but it did hang in the atmosphere. For example, when we left Caroline in the previous chapter, the feelings of grief surrounding the birth of her first hearing child were very palpable. Though the actual feelings were experienced a number of years ago, I felt that those feelings were still very much there. There was a sadness in Caroline's eyes throughout the interview, even when she was laughing, and it was not until she began to talk about Jane that the sadness became overt. I do not want to suggest that the sadness could be wholly attributed to these experiences, but the depth of her feelings made me sense their importance. Her sobbing came from a place very deep within her. Similarly, with Sam, there was an immediacy when he began to talk about his reaction to his son crying, which was quite apart from the overpowering numbness present throughout his narrative. In this situation, however, I can accept that I may have noticed the change because a part of me was crying out for a release from the trap that Sam and I had become enmeshed in. For both Caroline and Sam, however, these episodes did mark a change in the content of their narrative and the way in which it was subsequently expressed. Caroline took on a new vulnerability, whereas Sam, as we shall see in the following chapter, moved on to resolutions.

Other episodes occurred which were not so much markers, as a change of direction and, as suggested above, this new direction was inwards towards exploration of *inner transitions* and the 'communities of selves' (Hobson 1989) referred to in the Preface. Here, I was not so much a passive observer of changes, but became a participant in the narrative, swimming with the rivers as they ran deeper. For this reason, some of the narratives in this chapter will be punctuated by questions and comments from me, as they were expressed in the original interview, and by the images I subsequently formed of the narrators, because I feel this gives a truer reflection of how the narratives developed.

Krishna

I started to explore myself more and to read as well – and I went to college. When I began to question, I was also conscious of going back into the past, starting to remember pictures of things that had happened then. For example, when I got access to all the things which could have helped me more such as loop systems and minicoms, which I didn't have before, I began to meet with more deaf people through my job, and experienced sign language for the first time since being at the Deaf school where there was fluent sign language being used. As I found myself remembering signing as a child, I remembered also being told that it was bad and I shouldn't communicate in that way, and feeling I had to accept this judgement because it was my family that was telling me this, and I respected their views. When I rediscovered all these buried feelings in myself I realised that I didn't feel signing was bad. It became bad only because it wasn't the right way to communicate in terms of society's 'norms'. I had dismissed it at the time it happened because I couldn't understand it, make any sense of it. But now I started to try to understand what these feelings meant, to find the language to describe them, and this activated more feelings about the past. I feel fortunate that I had the opportunity to discover who I am, what I am, to make sense of my life and what had happened, to discover what it all meant, to build up a picture of my life experiences so that I could make sense of where I am today and where I am going in the future. It was a bit like being allowed to be my own god, creating my own image.

   MC: Can you describe that image?

I discovered much about myself which enabled me to make sense of myself, to understand my feelings and experiences and to commence a spiritual learning and healing process within myself which is continuing. I found I was discovering quite a lot of the basic instincts I had before, the more self-demanding instincts maybe, which enabled me to assert myself as a deaf, Asian woman and to say clearly to myself that there was nothing wrong with being as I am. I now know and accept that everything that has happened is part of the 'divine right order'. And anything that may happen in the future – there is a reason for it. It is an opportunity for me to learn something. When I acknowledged myself positively, I was more

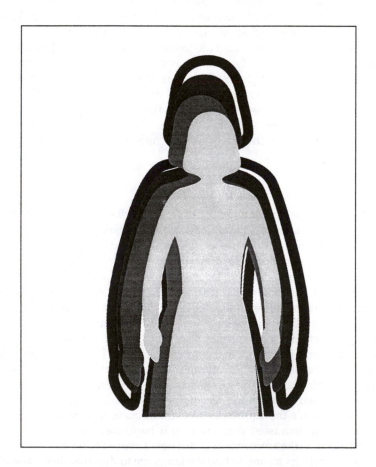

Figure 6.1 Krishna

able to acknowledge others positively. Also I realised the destructive power within a society which labels, stereotypes and devalues our experience in such a way that we actually believe in this less than positive view of ourselves. There's nothing wrong with who we are, it's how society views us and how we feel compelled to manifest their view of us. They impose their lifetime's values on us because they can't know or understand us, and they're sometimes afraid of us because we're different in some way from them.

> MC: *You describe a lot of very strong feelings about the different parts of yourself. So much strength…what does this mean for the relationships between them?*

Yes, I discovered that I do have strong feelings about being Asian, strong feelings about being deaf *and* strong feelings about being a woman. On one level, there is no conflict. On another, the strength of those respective feelings may appear to represent conflicts for me to those who do not understand. But those conflicts arise from society which places a 'valuation' on an individual's worth and creates hierarchies and divisions amongst people. Conflicts arise as society and the people in it make assumptions about you, label you, deny a part of you, perpetuate oppressive stereotypes of your Asian culture, disability, deafness or gender. But being an Asian deaf woman is what I *am* – the totality of my being and my experiences make me what I am. But the structures and systems operating in this society are not designed for viewing people in a holistic way, especially when the picture which is painted is *different* in some way. The system divides and rules. I cannot separate the different parts of myself and so I feel it is misguided for anyone else to try, especially when they don't have to live with the conflicts they create. When others don't view me as whole, they lose the totality of my experiences. Yes, it is true that at times, within this system, my race has become *more of an issue* than my deafness or my gender, and at other times my deafness or my gender has been at the forefront. But they all remain inextricably linked, so often I feel my multi-dimensional needs are submerged in this system, because of the way the system is structured.

Karen

Then something happened at work – it was linked to another person who was very difficult to cope with and that acted as a trigger to go for counselling. Something in me said 'Enough's enough.' But when I first started going – every two weeks – there wasn't much happening. A lot of that was to do with my resistance about my own attitudes and about my own need to judge myself, which I projected onto other people, thinking they were judging me. My resistance was in avoiding issues, talking about things at work or outside and avoiding exploring myself, and I couldn't make the links. A lot of it was about 'What does it mean?' It was all so confusing that I didn't understand what it meant. Eventually, I began to focus a lot on exploring who I was, what was my identity? I think I became aware that my 'child' has always been very strong in me and a big part of my identity. I felt my child was very strong and dominant in some situations, particularly those situations where I felt 'left out', and I would tend to respond to these situations by sulking, or demanding that *they* understand how I felt without giving them any understanding. This didn't improve things. When I learnt to have more balance, things generally felt better. Now, I'm thinking a lot more deeply about these issues, I can understand them better. Before it was just a jumble – I didn't have the awareness or the knowledge. My thoughts and feelings were going round and round in circles. I knew I wasn't happy, and I had these feelings of questioning why I was doing these things, but it wasn't clear enough for me at that time, or I couldn't do anything about it. I just knew I didn't like what I felt at that time. Because I had no boundaries, I was allowing other people's feelings to take me over and I couldn't focus on my own. I felt squashed. My expectations of myself were very high, and all the time I was mulling over and worrying about things.

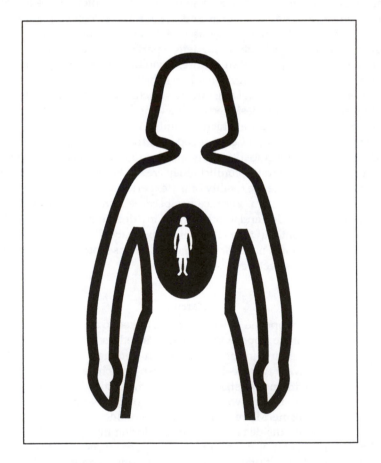

Figure 6.2 Karen

Fiona

I have changed. I hold myself back a lot more when I meet people. Now I start with finding out more about the person first, and try to establish whether we have interests in common that we can talk around. I don't talk about my Deaf background. If they ask about it, I will tell them, but I won't offer it up. Perhaps it's protecting myself from the hurt…

MC: What is the hurt about?

In a peculiar way I keep thinking I have been denied my right when I was growing up *to be a child*. I was always perceived as an adult because I was always the person who communicated with hearing people when they wanted to talk to my parents. They treated me like an adult when they should have remembered that I was a child. The adult in me now is trying to deal with the situation in the way that the child I was before couldn't – she couldn't look at a situation from a whole range of different perspectives. The child is very much associated with the Deaf part of me, very strongly associated with that. That child is feeling very stubborn right now… I think you have found the core of me…the child is definitely still very hurt and confused, still doesn't know for sure whether it's the real me that I am trying to cover up. I don't think I have found the real me yet because the child is still hurting, isn't in control, doesn't know how to solve the conflicts. She feels so vulnerable, not weak, just vulnerable, and that's what I feel now when I start talking about her. Sometimes I have tried to find out what she needs? But it's confusing – sometimes I think it's one thing and then it changes to something else and I can't get at it; I feel as if I am waiting for some indication. What I am thinking right at this moment is that I want to be that child, and that's a conflict because, at this time in my life, the rest of me is saying that I've got to grow up. Maybe *I* am now denying the child in me. But I just keep thinking I want to be a child, I want to behave like a child, I want to do silly things – but the adult me won't allow me to do those things.

MC: That sounds as if you don't want to be the child you were…

I don't. I want to be a *real child*, the child who was not allowed to be and still is not being allowed to be – a playful, child-like child. That is what I feel. I think real children are allowed to be silly. I don't have my own children, but I always say to the children I meet 'Behave yourself!' because when I was a child I always had to behave like an adult, I thought like an adult and I spoke like an adult. I played in the Deaf club, but I never played as a hearing child might play – I don't remember any humour. That's another thing I have had to learn. I wonder if I started to learn about the hearing world because I felt *the child* in me was oppressed rather than the deafness in me. They always say hindsight is a wonderful thing, but I don't like it. I have grown up now – I keep thinking the hindsight is too bloody late!

Figure 6.3 Fiona

    MC: You say that the Deaf part of you is very strongly associated with
    the child... I wonder which child?

I don't know. I have a kind of conversation between the Deaf and the
hearing voices... It's usually when I feel uncertain about the way the
hearing voice treats me, particularly when it is critical and makes me feel
I am wrong. I have a conversation with the Deaf voice, share with the Deaf
voice and get some feedback, it's like the sign gives me the reassurance I
want to carry on. But I need both of those people in me to give me the
reassurance that I am OK – that I am OK the way I am.

    MC: If those two people, Deaf and hearing, were in the room with you
    now, what would you want to say to them?

I would want their predominant characteristics to be that they both accept
me the way I am. Just two feelings, two words – reassurance and acceptance. I want them *both* to tell me, but I don't have that at the moment. I
need both to tell me. It is not good enough if it is just one or the other. It is

the same with that child and adult that keep coming back. I want them to be more equal, not just my adult telling my child that they mustn't do something. Sometimes I can feel my child rebelling even when it is something simple like a Deaf person asking me to help them make a phone call – I can feel my child saying 'No, I don't want to!'

MC: *(mirroring) 'No, I don't want to!'… That child is stubborn…!*

I feel like that! And then my adult says that I must do it! They argue all the time. But I want to be allowed to say 'No!' to that Deaf person sometimes. It's easy to say 'No!' to a hearing person and walk away because I know that is allowed, I know that I don't have to explain why. But a Deaf person? I have to explain, and I have to tell them why I am saying 'No!'

MC: *Are these conversations in sign or spoken?*

There are some things I can actually sign a lot better than I can speak. It just doesn't have the same quality if I try to say it, it doesn't have the depth. It's just like a bunch of words, it doesn't contain exactly what I want to say and when I am signing whatever it is *there*. I am trying to improve how I speak and what I say to achieve the same quality, but it's a slow process. I have conversations with myself in sign. I don't talk to myself. Having this inner conversation with myself is like a picture; it is not a sound thing, it is a picture. When I have tried to put an identity on that inner voice or that inner sign, I don't have the right language because it is a picture. One of the things I am actively doing – I don't know when I started it – is to stop signing to myself. I am trying to teach myself to speak to myself, but that still feels wrong. I don't feel stupid when I sign to myself even if I am walking down the street! It's interesting, when I am angry and I swear, I will always speak it. I won't sign it.

MC: *I wonder if the anger is associated with hearing and speaking?*

Maybe… Yes… I can see there is a connection. The kind of things that are coming up now are one of the reasons I wanted to go into counselling to try and start exploring it. I tried before, but the counsellor I saw was just hooked onto things that weren't there for me. It felt as if they were deciding for me where I wanted to go, but I wanted to decide for myself what I thought was important, what I thought was my problem, because I felt that once I got that out of the way I would be more open to looking at the situation. If I have something bothering me, I hold onto it. I just want to keep control for myself because everybody and everything else in my outside world is controlling. I only ever felt I had control in the family when I was looking after my brothers. But even then, I am not sure whether I was in control in the sense that I decided how they were to be cared for, or controlling in the way that I had been taught by my parents. I know that it often happens in large families that the elder children end up looking after the younger ones. But there may be a parallel with being a hearing child of Deaf parents, and the anger about the extra responsibility that brings.

Caroline

It's difficult in the Deaf community sometimes. When I'm asked if Jane is Deaf or hearing and I tell them she's hearing, there are celebrations because they think she's growing up to become an interpreter. It makes me angry really, because she's just a baby. I didn't have her so that she could become an interpreter. She was born as my daughter, to communicate with and to love, not to work for me! My reaction is always that we have minicom and Typetalk – she doesn't need to interpret for us. But they persist – it would be easier and faster if she interpreted for us. But I don't want that. I think I understand how they feel because many of them have hearing parents and always wanted help from their parents which they never got because there was no communication. I have a Deaf family and we always shared things with each other, talked things through and sorted it out. We didn't have to bring in help from outside, didn't want that intrusion. I can't put Jane up on the shelf like an ornament called HEARING and treat her like that. It's impossible.

I think the two situations are very different. Deaf adults with hearing families – they have a different identity – they want everyone to know that they have a Deaf identity and belong to the Deaf community, but sometimes it is as if their life hinges on the acceptance of this Deaf identity. They have to consciously decide that they want to be 'in' the Deaf community. It's not spontaneous or natural or because the community doesn't automatically accept them, but because they want to make themselves big, to make a statement about their power, to feel good about themselves. I understand that, but I find that very difficult. They are angry, yes. They're probably angry because of their upbringing with hearing parents who didn't relate to them properly – they never made a real bond – there was no communication, and they grow up late and realise that their parents could have done more for them. I understand they're angry, they want to become strong and powerful, and to oppress hearing people. But I'm different I don't have the same experience or background or upbringing and I am not hearing-focused in that negative way, not in that angry way, despite my experience with hearing professionals. And they don't have my experience and I can't help feeling sad about that. They transfer their experience of their own upbringing onto a hearing child of Deaf parents because of the communication issue I think.

Andrew

MC: What do you feel is central in you? What feels closest to you?

If you are asking me where my spirit is, I don't think I could tell you easily, I don't think I could explain it. Sometimes I get a feeling of it as being a little like the bee in that bees' hive I talked about earlier, busily moving from one cell to another, fertilising every cell and nurturing the development of every seed that is sown with some fundamental characteristic so that all the cells have the same roots and the ability to adapt and change which works for the whole hive. The image is an industrious one and that is important to me because inside I am very busy, very active.

MC: *Bees are very social insects. I've read somewhere that they dance to a perfect pattern.*

That makes me think of what I said before about not really being able to relate to having a social identity, that seems odd. But I think it is because I cannot look at myself as someone who is defined only in terms of how I relate to others – I can't easily dance with others, only with myself. I am a person with many aspects. So inside, I am busy with all these different 'people', building a rich and colourful inner life which more than compensates for a lack of a group identity, the acquisition of which seems to be out of my control.

MC: *Who are these people? What do you feel about them?*

...I think they are all the resources I need – the comfort, the wise counsel, the challenge, the courage, the power, the creativity, the sensitivity and so on, but *I* am somehow part of all of them. They help me relate to the world... It was as if, when I was forced to accept that it might also be more difficult for me to find and to establish relationships with new people who started from a different place, I began to find ways in which I could build support from within. Part of this is because I didn't want to become isolated, nor did I feel that I deserved to be isolated whatever the outside world was now saying. *I* hadn't actually changed in that all the experiences and the knowledge and the skills that I had accumulated in the *before* phase were still there in the *after* phase, they were just more difficult for others to access because of their own prejudices. I had also added new skills in the after phase, so, if anything, I eventually felt more expansive, more rounded when I acknowledged that I had grown with this new experience. Sometimes I wonder if these people, as part of the *after* phase, were conceived as some kind of substitute for the *before*? I wouldn't call it a conscious substitution, but at times it does feel like a substitution.

MC: *You make a distinction between inside and outside – talk about building support from within and having difficulty with relationships on the outside. What about the relationships between the people on the inside and the outside? What do these relationships mean for you?*

The worm which makes me feel so bad, the thing that made we want to defend myself in the first place, I suppose, has entered from *the outside* – it comes from all kinds of different sources and different people. When *I* feel it getting close to the nerve centre, something happens, some red light goes on somewhere – I *see* red and I get angry, but there is also someone in me who tries to rationalise, tries desperately to understand why the worm tries to get in in the first place. They act as some sort of reminder of the fact that I am what I am *now*, as I said before, the sum total of *all* my experiences, which *includes my experiences of being deaf and of being hearing*. And *some* of those experiences, some of my feelings about being deaf are very positive, because I am proud of that part of me too and it has helped me to get closer to who I am, to some of the things which I don't think I would have discovered about myself if I hadn't become deaf. But it feels as if I am not allowed to be Deaf, not allowed to be visual in my own way, not allowed to have the Deaf way that my hearing friends say is there and not able to be the 'hearing' person that many Deaf people say that I am.

> MC: *How do you see the deaf and hearing parts of you in relation to each other?*

There's a division between how I *want* to see them and how they *are* a lot of the time... I feel the Deaf and hearing parts within me want to be friends, to build bridges and to learn about each other. That is how I justify being able to be both Deaf and hearing. One enriches the other and that is how it should be. The two parts fit together very well on the inside, but I can see how they might not on the outside where history, prejudice and oppression have played such a strong role in driving them apart. I cannot easily tolerate any kind of separatism in the *after* phase even when I know that it may serve a purpose for the groups of people who wish to be separate. I feel a lot of separatism is imposed by inequality and that too sometimes crops up when the Deaf and hearing sides of me engage with each other. For example, when I am trying to work towards something which is important to me, I often find myself caught out by a lack of confidence in myself. This voice is saying 'But you can't do that' or 'You're not good enough for that' inside, but I am quite certain that voice has two sources and it depends very much on what I am doing. When I am trying to express something in sign language, for example, it is definitely a Deaf voice which is telling me that I look and feel stupid, and a hearing voice that says I am demeaning myself to gain acceptance. When I express myself in spoken language, the Deaf voice says I am on a power trip and the hearing voice often agrees, but for different reasons.

> MC: *It sounds as if they are censoring you in some way.*

Yes, that's it...they are both telling me that I am not good enough but in very different ways, and I don't know if there is a middle way on that one. I wish there was. I want to find it.

> MC: *I wonder if you already have. You talk about building bridges.*

Yes, but sometimes I feel they are made of matchsticks because it's so easy for the outside to demolish them.

> MC: *Only the outside?*

Maybe...maybe that's what stops me coming together...what smokes the bee out of the hive... I know that I have this rage inside of me and sometimes it feels separate from me... I don't like this angry person, but I can't seem to get rid of him because all the time society is saying to me that I am 'wrong' or 'bad' and I know I am not – at least not all of me is! Sometimes I feel he is trying to protect me and trying to give me some space to heal. I know what the anger is about. It's not only my anger about my own situation, but about other deaf people's situations as well. It's about the injustice in deaf people's lives and wanting to do something

Figure 6.4 Andrew

about it. It's not just hearing people – they're not the only worm. It's about this abuse of power, putting people down, not *caring* for them and *loving* them whatever they do or say. I find it difficult to understand how a community founded on pride in its difference hides a 'culture' which is so controlling. It seems to ignore the smile on the face that hides a deeply troubled deaf person who can only see themselves in terms of how much they can please hearing people, and think they can only do this by being happy. I've been there so many times! This kind of hypocrisy has made me feel that it is better not to trust anyone too readily if I am to hold on to myself enough to survive. I cannot see a clear system of beliefs and values or a solidarity which is all-embracing of all deaf people and holds them together, and so I cannot trust them. I certainly cannot see the mutual, unconditional support which I see in other cultures. Deaf people cannot be excused from this rejection on the basis of an ignorance of Deafness. I feel that the way in which they exclude people like me is a denial of our common history and oppression. Every time a deaf person is excluded or marginalised from Deafness by Deaf people, it is a kick in the teeth of all the suffering that has gone before. It's no better than this hearing mentality which is as good as saying to me that each of the words I use can only mean *one thing* and that is crazy. It feels as if I am being deprived of the opportunity to use my language creatively to define myself, because the meaning that other people give to what I communicate is always stereo-typed – they stereotype me.

When people say to me 'You must be positive' or 'stop being so negative', I can actually feel myself flinch inside – I want to shout at them; 'You don't know what the words mean!' All they are trying to do is to deny the fact that I may not feel positive at that moment in time because *they* can't cope with it. It makes me always want to ask what lies behind positivity, because I have learnt over time that it's so often false... I can no longer take things at face value when I have experienced so much betrayal in the after stage. I feel *very* angry about that. On a personal level, I feel angry because it says that my negative feelings or my anger are not valuable and not worthy of attention or love – that I am not allowed just to *be*. That reminds me of my family's view, and they are not deaf. I can 'hear' the rejection and the alienation of my family travelling through the Deaf community. I love my family as much as I have always done, if not more so because the distancing makes all my emotions so much more powerful. I watch them – all hearing – I watch their spontaneity and their laughter and the way in which they group together around being hearing, and no matter how hard I try or how much I want to, I cannot ever get back to the point where I can be a full part of that, and I won't be accepted by Deaf people without conditions either. I want them to show me that they care, and help me to be strong in myself again. But this too feels out of reach. So I live on a knife edge, on the outside looking in, watching the world go by and from time to time, I wonder if I am loved, or if I can be loved in this place between two worlds. That is my anger, and it sometimes takes over everything because all I want to do is to be...that's all...to *be*.

Unravelling Narratives

Looking at our inner worlds using subpersonalities is of course not a new concept, though I have not been able to find any references to its use in working with deaf people's identity issues. It is the foundation of some approaches to counselling such as *transactional analysis*, which hinges essentially on the exchanges which take place between three ego states and the resulting unconscious contracts that are made between them. These ego states are explained in Box 6.1 and are mentioned here specifically because some of the narrators refer to them. Psychosynthesis counselling also employs 'subpersonality conflicts and limited identities' in exploring the origins of the inner landscapes that people create for themselves (Whitmore 1991, p.77). She describes subpersonalities as:

Box 6.1 Ego states	
Ego state	Behaviours, thoughts and feelings
Parent	copied from parents or parent figures
Adult	direct responses to the here-and-now
Child	replayed from childhood

autonomous configurations within the personality as a whole. They are psychological identities, coexisting as a multitude of lives in one person, each with its own specific behaviour pattern and corresponding self-image, body posture, feelings and beliefs. Their unique characteristics form a relatively unified whole.

Rowan (1990, p.23) further suggests that Carl Rogers began to work with subpersonalities towards the end of his life, and cites a case example where Rogers talks to a woman about her fears. At one point in the interview, she says 'And whenever I want to get away with something, I would play the naughty little girl.' Later in the exchange, Rogers intuits 'that maybe one of your best friends is the you that you hide inside, the fearful little girl, the naughty little girl, the real you that doesn't come out very much in the open', and the client responds 'I've lost a lot of that naughty little girl. In fact, over the last eighteen months, that naughty little girl has disappeared' (Rogers 1986). At the most basic level, we know subpersonalities exist as part of the whole because when we refer to them, it is often in relation to the whole person that we are. So when we say 'I'm in two minds about this', 'I am not myself today', 'I don't like myself', 'I behave differently in different situations', and 'This is the real me', we are making statements about subpersonalities, though we may not be aware of it. It is this lack of awareness which can be the problem, because that is often linked to a corresponding blind spot to the controlling influences of environmental stressors and the demands we make of ourselves. This means that we get trapped in uncertainty, confusion and conflict. Often the subpersonalities come from some basic need which has arisen from unresolved conflicts in the past and which has been suppressed in some way. There is, moreover, a greater tendency to suppress or reject those subperson-alities which we and/or others perceive as 'bad' or 'weak' in some way:

> Rejecting a subpersonality creates a psychological block which stunts its growth and causes it to develop in a one-sided, distorted fashion increasingly at odds with the rest of the personality. Its useful qualities, its skills, its strengths are not available... Once a subpersonality is accepted, however, its real needs may be discovered and fulfilled in healthier ways; its positive qualities enhanced and its negative qualities dissipated. (Whitmore 1991, p.82)

Two of the above narratives may seem out of place in the above context, but I have included them here as they illustrate how a subpersonality might first be discovered and, to a certain extent, how it may be formed. Krishna, for example, talks about the healing process that can begin when 'buried feelings' are discovered: 'As I found myself remembering signing as a child, I remembered also being told that it was bad and I shouldn't communicate in that way, and feeling I had to accept this judgement because it was my family that was telling me this, and I respected their views. When I rediscovered all these buried feelings in myself I realised that I didn't feel signing was bad.' With this new-found awareness, she 'had the opportunity to discover who I am, what I am, to make sense of my life and what had happened, to discover what it all meant, to build up a picture of my life experiences so that I could make sense of where I am today and where I am going in the future. It was a bit like being allowed to be my own god, creating my own image.' This reflects how a counsellor might describe the value of working with subpersonalities. The subpersonalities do not get as far as having a name, but Krishna identifies them in terms of their associated feelings. Another aspect of Krishna's narrative which points to a healing process is that I feel she has successfully integrated the different parts of herself, has recognised that they are 'all' part of her and only become divided by the demands placed on her by a society 'which divides and rules'. This realisation enabled her to assert herself 'as a deaf, Asian woman and to say clearly to myself that there was nothing wrong with being as I am'. It also enabled her to 'relate more positively to others'. My image of Krishna was of a whole made up of integrated parts.

Karen, Fiona and Andrew show less integration, but a more developed understanding of their 'inner people'. Karen becomes a petulant, competitive and angry 'child' when faced with criticism or when confronted with power or authority. Yet, we may remember from previous parts of her narrative that in relation to her parents, she was always 'the good girl' who could get attention only by being 'bad'. Somewhere along the line, the 'bad' girl was suppressed, became 'guilt' and reached the point where she was expressed only in relation to particular challenges coming from the environment. For this reason, I felt that her 'bad' child was more deeply buried in her unconscious and cushioned from full awareness, and this resulted in my image of Karen. But I also sensed that somehow Karen acknowledged the neediness of that child, particularly her need for attention and intimacy which had not been satisfied by any of the relationships experienced so far. Fiona, on the other hand, developed a 'controlling' hearing parent subpersonality when she was quite young, ostensibly as a result of the responsibilities placed on her by her parents, but also, I suspect, to protect herself from the hurt directed at herself as a Deaf child: 'that child is very much associated with the Deaf part of me, very strongly associated with that... She feels so vulnerable, not weak, just vulnerable, and that's what I feel now when I start talking about her.' However, there came a point where the 'hearing' subpersonality became a reality, the adult in her who is 'trying to deal with the situation in the way the child I was before couldn't', which did not match the subpersonality she constructed in childhood, and this introduced a conflict. I say this because I got a sense that the real 'hearing' person might represent a *freedom* from responsibility, the person who was allowed to say 'No!' without feelings of guilt: 'I wonder if I started to learn about the hearing world because I felt the child in me was oppressed rather than the deafness in me.' The 'new hearing person [she] had become' also made her aware of the 'stubborn, hurt, confused and angry child' still buried, and her hidden need to be the playful, mischievous and happy *Deaf* child: 'I want to be a real child, the child who was not allowed to be and still is not being allowed to be – a playful, child-like child. That is what I feel. I think real children are allowed to be silly.' I felt this was important. Fiona acknowledges that her negative feelings are associated with 'hearing and speaking' because she cannot swear in sign language, for example. At this point, I also began to wonder if the two children Fiona described might actually be the two sides of the same child, the inordinate growth of the adult in a child's body who says 'Behave yourself!' and 'You must do it!' resulting in the suppression and denial of her basic need 'to be a child – a real child.' If these are the two sides of the same child, associated as they are with the Deaf and hearing parts of her, then it might explain why Fiona feels a very great need to have reassurance from *both* the Deaf and hearing people in her, 'that they both accept me the way I am.' My image of Fiona shows the two adults and the two children arm in arm.

Reading Caroline's contribution to this chapter, I wondered if some of the things she says might point Fiona in the direction of being able to feel that reassurance from within. Caroline faces some of Fiona's childhood struggles in the attitudes of some people in the Deaf community towards Jane. There is an expectation on Jane to become the hearing adult who is responsible towards and who supports her Deaf parents. But Caroline is vehement in her rejection of this suggestion: 'It makes me angry really, because she's just a baby. I didn't have her so that she could become an interpreter.' She wants to nurture Jane in exactly the same way that any responsible parent would: 'I can't put Jane up on the shelf like an ornament called HEARING and treat her like that. It's impossible... She was born as my daughter, to communicate with and to love, not to work for me!' Perhaps Fiona could gain reassurance through discovering and developing the nurturing parent in herself?

At this point in her narrative, Caroline was just beginning to ask questions about her relationships with other people which before she had taken for granted. Another reason I have included her narrative here is because of her perceptions of the origins of some Deaf people's anger and the relevance this has for Andrew's narrative. Caroline recognises that she is 'different; I don't have the same experience or background or upbringing and I am not hearing-focused in that negative way, not in that angry way, despite my experience with hearing professionals. And they don't have my experience and I can't help feeling sad about that.' She also has some empathy with Fiona's view about the competitiveness she experienced in her relationship with her first Deaf partner, described in the previous chapter: 'Deaf adults with hearing families – they have a different identity – they want everyone to know that they have a Deaf identity and belong to the Deaf community, but sometimes it is as if their life hinges on the acceptance of this Deaf identity.' She feels that 'They are angry, yes. They're probably angry because of their upbringing with hearing parents who didn't relate to them properly – they never made a real bond – there was no communication, and they grow up late and realise their parents could have done more for them…they transfer their experience of their own upbringing onto a hearing child of Deaf parents'.

Andrew, as one of the deaf people Caroline refers to, is very much aware of his anger, but whereas he accepts that some of this is linked to his upbringing, there is another dimension which comes from the Deaf community: 'It's not just hearing people – they're not the only worm. It's about this abuse of power, putting people down, not caring for them and loving them whatever they do or say. I find it difficult to understand how a community founded on pride in its difference hides a "culture" which is so controlling… Deaf people cannot be excused from this rejection on the basis of an ignorance of Deafness. I feel that the way in which they exclude people like me is a denial of our common history and oppression. Every time a deaf person is excluded or marginalised from Deafness by Deaf people, it is a kick in the teeth of all the suffering that has gone before.' What Andrew wants is affirmation from Deaf people: 'I want them to show me that they care, and help me to be strong in myself again.' But what he feels he gets is a double-edged censorship: 'When I am trying to express something in sign language, for example, it is definitely a Deaf voice which is telling me that I look and feel stupid, and a hearing voice that says I am demeaning myself to gain acceptance. When I express myself in spoken language, the Deaf voice says I am on a power trip and the hearing voice often agrees, but for different reasons.' Like Krishna, Andrew has felt the need to heal himself from within, in part because he cannot control what is happening on the outside. He has, by his own admission 'a rich and colourful inner life', with quite a large population of subpersonalities, but the more I listened to him, the more I felt that there was a hierarchy of people with anger and the two censoring characters uppermost in that hierarchy, and this is, in the end, how I arrived at the image of Figure 6.4. Yet there was also a sensitivity that he couldn't fully get in touch with and a strong sense of social responsibility towards other deaf people and towards the need for building bridges instead of creating conflicts. Perhaps, like Krishna, he is a 'pioneer' who is blocked by a very real concern about the further conflict that adopting that role might bring, and the self-centred judgements of others coming from an environment which is the exact opposite to that provided by counselling:

> The counsellor accepts and recognises the positive feelings which are expressed, in the same manner in which he has accepted and recognised the negative feelings. These positive feelings are not accepted with approbation or praise. Moralistic values do not enter into this type of therapy. The positive feelings are accepted as no more and no less a part of the personality than the negative feelings. It is the acceptance of both the mature and the immature impulses, of the aggressive and the social attitudes, of the guilt feelings and the positive expressions, which gives the individual an opportunity for the first time in his life to understand himself as he is. He has no need to be defensive about his negative feelings. He is given no opportunity to overvalue his positive feelings. And, in this type of situation, insight and self-understanding come bubbling through spontaneously. Unless one has thus watched insight

> develop, it is difficult to believe that individuals can recognise them-
> selves and their patterns so effectively. (Rogers 1942, p.40)

The final sections of the narratives, which form the focus for the following chapter, look specifically at the insight and self-understanding which has been gained from these journeys, and where, ultimately, our narrators 'rest their heads'.

CHAPTER SEVEN

Coming Home

This insight, this understanding of the self and acceptance of the self, is the next important aspect of the whole process. It provides the basis on which the individual can go ahead to new levels of integration. The individual seems to be saying 'This is what I am, and I see much more clearly. But how can I reorganise myself in a different fashion?' (Rogers 1942, p.40)

Previously when in deepest meditation, he was still his father's son, he was still a Brahmin of high standing, a religious man. Now he was only Siddharta...he was overwhelmed by a feeling of icy despair, but he was more firmly himself than ever. That was the last shudder of his awakening, the last pains of birth. Immediately he moved on again...no longer homewards, no longer back to his father, no longer looking backwards. (Hesse 1980, p.360)

Introduction

Every one of us, at some point in our life cycle, comes home to a place where we feel comfortable in who we are and with the feeling of belonging that this place gives us. Just as we can live in houses or flats, old and new, in the town or the country, alone or with others, in one room or many rooms, amongst neutral, blue, red or multi-coloured decor, and at the roadside or by the sea, so too can we inhabit a variety of inner worlds. This place that we come to rest in ourselves may feel 'right' for us but it may not be understood by or meet the approval of all those who visit it. But this place remains important to us because it is our new personalised base from which we can undergo further exploration and growth to consolidate our position in the wider scheme of things. Erikson described this final phase of exploration as the time when we must find a balance between *generativity* and *stagnation*. Generativity refers not only to procreation and rearing children, but also to developing a social conscience and sense of responsibility towards others. It is 'the desire of the autonomous "I", as part of the intimate "we" to contribute to the present and future well-being of other life cycles' (Kroger 1996, p.29), and to provide a role model for the next generation. Its natural counterpart is stagnation or self-indulgence, where our personal comfort becomes the overriding motivator for everything that we do, sometimes at the expense of that of others. Perhaps the psychosocial conflict could best be described as one between being complacent, and going where the flow takes us, exploring all its branches and tributaries until we reach the sea. At the extreme end of stagnation is being stuck in or consumed by the past, whereas generativity at its most exemplary is a liberation of the self for the good of others in the future, and this distinction gives rise to the image shown in Figure 7.1. It must be emphasised, however, that some attention to self-interest is crucial for perpetuating a generative life attitude, as is coming to terms with and accepting the 'unalterability of the past' (Erikson *et al.* 1986, p.56). Erikson (1964) suggested that identity at this stage is often *synonymous* with what we choose to care for or accept responsibility for, and this must be balanced with self-preservation:

> Our statement in declaring what we will stand for in life, our identity, in other words, is a statement about what we will look after. I would add that it is not just the *what* but the *who* that is central here. Because of our long tenure in childhood of being the object of care and solicitude, our longing is to grow into one who can be the source of what is so much valued. (Josselson 1994, p.100)

However, Rogers believed that when we take a further step away from the self, and from the clear approach to values that young children have, as we become more outward-looking we often come face to face with the reality of the world we live in. The shift in focus brings us a greater awareness of the demands that society places on us, the behaviour patterns which are acceptable or not acceptable, and what we have to do or be to 'fit'. This may bring with it additional challenges to our new-found sense of self:

> We seem to lose this capacity for direct evaluation, and come to behave in those ways and to act in terms of those values which will bring us social approval, affection, esteem... The modern individual is assailed from every angle by divergent and contradictory value claims. It is no longer possible, as it was in the not too distant historical past, to settle comfortably into the value system of one's forbears or one's community and live out one's life without ever examining the nature and assumptions of that system... To buy love we relinquish the valuing process. Because the center of our lives now lies in others, we are fearful and insecure, and must cling rigidly to the values we have introjected... One natural result of this uncertainty and confusion is that there is an increasing concern about, interest in, and a searching for, a sound and meaningful value approach. which can hold its own in today's world. (Rogers 1964)

In the final parts of their narratives, which form the body of this chapter, our narrators take us to their 'homes', the places where they are now in their lives, the value systems they have adopted, and which are a consolidation of what they have learnt from their past experiences and what they see for themselves and others in the future.

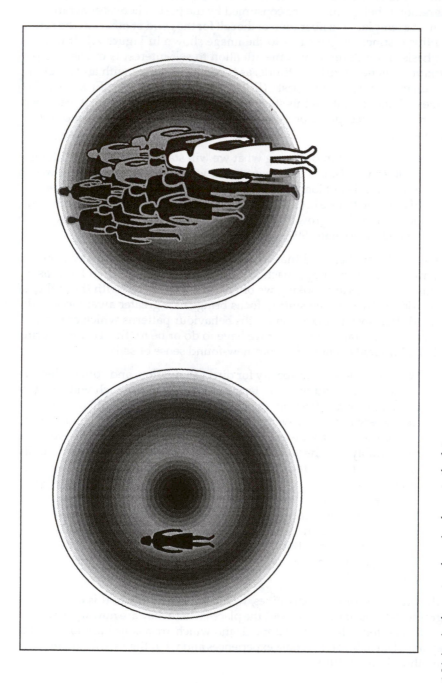

Figure 7.1 Living in the past and coming home to the future

Joseph

My identity is of Jamaican origin and I also have a strong Deaf identity. It is through the use of British Sign Language that I express my Deaf identity. However, at other times, I use pidgin sign language which is commonly used within the Black Deaf community. Because my identity reflects the culture and traditions, the way of life I have grown up with, and this includes my experience of oppression and dominance from hearing professionals in the field of deafness who make it difficult for Black Deaf people to develop their own consciousness. I think that it must be linked to internalised oppression as well. I feel that being Black and Deaf is a very important foundation for developing and maintaining the cultural identity in our community where we can share our values, beliefs and, most importantly, our pride. So I feel and believe in a 'community spirit' with Black and Deaf people – it's hard to separate them. I feel comfortable with this dual identity because I now have some understanding of who I am. But I only became aware of my bicultural identity through attending conferences focusing on deafness and race, through reading about Black history and Deaf culture, and in small discussions with deaf and hearing people in youth clubs. Sometimes I feel more Deaf than Black and sometimes the other way around, depending on the situation I am in – who I am with. For example, when I am in the hearing world, I feel I have to emphasise my Deaf identity to make hearing people accept who I am as a Deaf person. Most hearing people don't know anything about deafness, or have false or negative assumptions about deafness because of the media. So I feel it is important for me as a Black Deaf person to gain self-respect by educating hearing people to change their attitudes towards deafness and Deaf people. But Black people need to be educated about deafness as well. On the other hand, when I meet Deaf people, I feel that I have to emphasise my Black identity. The reason is that most white Deaf people don't know anything about Black identity and culture, I think because information about Black Deaf people in Britain is not accessible or available, and attempts to get together information about the experiences of Black Deaf people have met with a very little response.

I feel that there are both cultural differences and similarities between Deaf and Black culture, though because Black culture is expressed through food, clothing, drink, music, it feels richer and easier to define. I hold onto my identity as a Black Deaf person by maintaining my values and sense of self-respect and by involving myself in Black culture. For example, I go to a lot of discos and parties where they play Black music, especially reggae and soul. Dancing with Deaf women of my kind is very sensual and raunchy – when the music is slow and rhythmic and we dance very close, body to body, and squeeze very firmly but gently – that's really hot! This has been learnt from hearing Black people, but many Black Deaf people are excellent dancers, whatever kind of dancing is involved. Some white Deaf people might find that hard to understand, because Deaf culture has particular norms about touching, for example.

I feel that at the moment I belong more in the Deaf community at elite and grass roots levels, but, in fact I feel more comfortable in the Black community and with aspects of Black cultures and lifestyles. How accepted I feel tends to be related to how far I am able to adapt and adjust. So, for example, when I am with Black Deaf people at grass roots level, I feel I have to adapt my signing level to match theirs in order to feel accepted, and when I am with the elite part of the Deaf community, the political motivation to explore and discuss the issues affecting Deaf people takes over and so I adapt again. I want to maintain flexibility in my relationships with other Deaf and Black Deaf people, and in the way I communicate, but I feel that I can't always belong in the way I want to with everyone I am with and in every situation. I don't feel accepted for who I am unless I make a lot of adjustments. A lot of it is to do with popularity as well and how much respect I have in the Black Deaf community.

Caroline

Our reaction to a hearing child is different, because we know that it can be just as difficult for them being in a Deaf family and between that and the world outside – difficult because of trying to fit in and form a bond. I feel Jane's situation is better than most Deaf children who are born into hearing families, but I know she will have problems with the hearing community. I mean, I see Jane now – she's Deaf, she's not hearing, her culture, her behaviour are Deaf. Sometimes I feel sorry for her because I feel she's lonely in the hearing world. At her school it's difficult for her to fit in fully. With the childminder, it's fine because she has two children of her own and she can encourage Jane to take part and join in with their activities. It's also not just because she's half Deaf, half hearing, but because she's got no one to play with as all her brothers and sisters are much older than her or away at residential schools. I feel sometimes we're cruel to her, not intentionally of course, but it's very difficult. If I were in a different place, I would put Jane into a mainstream school where there's a unit for deaf children so that she can feel balanced if she wants to. Obviously she's older now, but sometimes I still have problems fully accepting that she's different, not Deaf like us. Up to about the age of three or four, Jane signed all the time and I was her interpreter. For example, when we went to the dentist to have her tooth looked at, the dentist spoke to her but he didn't understand, so she looked to me to translate for her. The dentist had to get someone to write so that I could read it and then translate into sign. Then Jane made the connection. She had an interpreter when she started school, but now she speaks and her sign has changed. I'm not worried because it means she will have two languages, she's bilingual but her sign, her BSL is not there so much now. It's English-based and sometimes made up. At the same time she has Deaf sign with her friends – it's fantastic. But though spoken language is taking over, I'm aware all the time that I just want her to grow up her own way without interference from me or anyone else, like any other child. The communication will always be an issue because I want to communicate with her like any mother and sometimes it's difficult.

Someone in my partner's family had a baby last year who was found to be Deaf and he feels it's not fair – why have they got a Deaf baby, why?

The mother of the child is from a hearing family, she's the only Deaf person in that family and he just doesn't understand why they have a Deaf baby and he doesn't. That feeling keeps coming back and back, and sometimes it feels as if it gets in the way of us seeing Jane as our 'perfect child'. It feels as if with the birth of this new baby, all the attention has shifted to him because he's Deaf. I am conscious that I don't want Jane to feel that the shift of attention is because she's hearing. But Jane is our daughter and we love her. I have to say, though, that it's difficult to think about having another baby now. It may be because I've had enough children, or because I'm just too busy to think about another baby. But, deep inside, I'm frightened that the baby will be hearing. Jane is definitely strong Deaf, but she's still hearing.

Fiona

Some people talk about Deaf and hearing worlds being quite separate and different and I do wonder about whether it's possible to integrate them at all, I mean integrate them inside of myself? The answer to that question is wide open. This is only my perception, but I can see changes happening amongst Deaf people. For example, whereas the Deaf were once oppressed, now I can see them being oppressive. Once people have been through that process and arrived at some sort of resolution, it may be possible to start to bring the two together. But at the moment, there is a very military attitude in some parts of the Deaf community which emphasises the separateness. They are oppressing hearing people, denying them the opportunity to go to a Deaf club, denying them the right of having a social life with Deaf people. Sometimes I get the feeling that there are very rigid boundaries around Deaf and hearing worlds. I know there are definitely boundaries with hearing people because I keep breaking them, and sometimes I feel that nobody will tell me what, when and why was something that I said yesterday acceptable then and today it is not acceptable. The boundaries keep moving but they are still rigid. I keep trying to find parallels with the way that Deaf people establish boundaries, but I end up thinking they really are very different. I feel that Deaf boundaries relate specifically to who Deaf people are meeting. So, for example, Deaf people's boundaries may be relaxed in their relationships with me but they won't be relaxed with other hearing people who can sign to the same level of fluency as I have or who don't have the 'culture'. At the same time, the Deaf boundary is fluid, if selective. It has to be, I suppose, because sometimes a boundary is like a sieve and only some things which fit the holes in the sieve can move in and out freely without damaging the boundary. At other times it is more like one of those three-way cat flaps where you can lock it to keep the cat out, keep the cat in, or allow complete freedom of movement in and out. There's more control then. When we talk about the differences between Deaf and hearing, I suppose we are looking at them in the same way that we might look at the differences between someone who is English and someone who is South American. A South American might observe that the English are very peculiar, they have their own ways and if you don't conform to these ways you are not easily accepted. And I think I can understand how that South American person might feel as a Deaf person living in a hearing body. I've bought books on English etiquette and I have read them, but I still feel that's not enough to tell me what I have to do to been seen as hearing in a meaningful sense, what it is I have to conform to.

I can go back to the family now, but I don't feel that I fit in *in the same way* – that's changed. I'm not sure what I feel about that. Before I would be too scared to join a group of hearing people and say something. Now, I remain anxious, but it doesn't frighten me in the way that it did. So it feels as if there has been an about-turn between the Deaf and hearing parts of me – not a competition with one coming out on top, just that both have changed the way that they operate. As I said before, I wanted to learn more about the hearing world, because people kept telling me *I am* hearing. I wanted to know what that meant for me. I wanted to be able to make a choice and actually have the proof which allowed me to say with confidence, 'Yes, I am hearing.' Perhaps this was related to being told by some Deaf people that I could have no idea what it was like to be Deaf? My experience of being Deaf was slightly different because I internalised the Deaf behaviour of my family. But I have never claimed to be Deaf in the same way that they are. I am hearing, I am me – but I am also different. Whatever *that* consists of at a particular time with particular people changes. I have felt that I am being denied the right to the reality of my own experience. I can understand why Deaf people respond in the way they do to that experience, but they can't deny me my experience and they can't deny my childhood. They can't deny my right to think and feel the way I do, when, as a child, that was the only way I *could* feel, it was the only thing I *knew*. I didn't feel Deaf, but I felt I was *one of them*. What do I feel about the divisions in my identity? For the most part I actually enjoy having experienced all the differences because of the wider opportunities it has brought. I am very glad I have had those opportunities. I often look at other people who have grown up in a particular life-style and a particular attitude or way of thinking and I am pleased I am not like them. I am pleased for that part but there is that other part – the doubt, the confusion and uncertainty that has become predominant in my life and which I think should have been sorted out a long time ago. I feel as if I am at the ambivalent stage in the development of my identity, but I think I should have gone through it when I was a teenager – I am like a teenager definitely – a late developer maybe? But I also wonder if those stages of development have any relevance for someone like me anyway. I have to say that whatever problems I may appear to experience, I like my life, it's wonderful and I wouldn't change it. I love it.

Karen

For a long time, I asked myself 'Who am I?', but, in reality, I wasn't asking this question specifically. I just had tremendous feelings of confusion and it was only really through counselling that I was able to explore that because I recognised that I was having problems coping. I mean, the things that have happened to me – they felt awful at the time – and I often wonder how the hell I have coped with them? For a long time, I was really only able to make sense of that feeling of being left out by talking to other people who became deaf, who described experiencing a similar feeling when they were with hearing. I now recognise there are two separate issues – those which are a result of my childhood experiences and those which are related to my feelings as an adult as a result of being deaf and feeling left out by hearing people – the kind of situation I experience at work, or if I mix with hearing people socially. For example, at work we have a policy that when everyone is in the office, we all use sign language. At one time, if people forgot to sign, I would feel angry and left out. Often I felt that the amount of anger was too much and through counselling, I started to understand it better and could remind people without getting so angry. I now find I am better able to understand the issues and separate them from the feelings I had when I was small. I got to my mid-twenties with all these churned-up feelings and then I met a really nice man at a party. There was just something that felt right. I didn't tell him I was deaf because he talked so clearly and I could lipread really well. But he knew. At that time, I couldn't use a voice telephone, so I was really deaf. But in a party situation, he talked so clearly that in some ways, it was easier for me above the noise than for him because I could lipread him, and that became a positive way of looking at what had been a difficult situation before I met him.

Now I don't see being deaf in a negative, medical way, but I did have to work through a lot of internalised oppression to arrive at that point in my life. I don't feel happy about the deaf/Deaf distinction. I am not Deaf because I wasn't born deaf and BSL is not my first language, but I do identify with the struggles of the Deaf community. There are many situations that are difficult and which I cannot participate in easily without an interpreter. I now tend not to get involved in such situations. The Deaf world can also present problems as they say 'Oh, you're hearing!' There is not much I can do about this. It can be very difficult to face oppression from both hearing and Deaf people, but it is more painful and more difficult to cope with when it comes from Deaf people. Logically, I know why it happens, but emotionally, it is very hard to accept. I have to continue working at that!

Peter

I am conscious of feeling more together now than before, but only because some parts of me had to go and some things had to be kept – a bit like a purging. I know, for example, that the Jewish religion does not readily accept gay people and, when I realised how important being gay was to me, I felt that I could no longer be a part of that, I couldn't go to the Synagogue any more. I think being Deaf and Jewish means something quite different from being hearing and Jewish – definitely – it's something to do with Jewish culture being linked to – just *being* hearing culture. It took me many years before my 'boxes' collapsed. Some Deaf gay Jewish seem to manage better than I do, I don't know why I can't. Maybe it has something to do with having to trust the people I know – I'm not sure. I know I feel different now. Obviously, I do feel I am hurt by it, but I can also at times be philosophical about it. I can't waste time being hurt forever-more. I have to move on. It makes me think of when I was at school – I used to blush easily – I would go bright red and people would look at me and I hated it. When I went to my last school I remember making a very conscious decision to stop blushing. And because I was able to control that I found that I could use my mind to control other things I wanted to. I made myself become more assertive. But I still think that if I had had all the answers, all the knowledge, the skills and the understanding earlier, my life would have been completely different. I would have made more progress, moved further ahead. But at the same time, I now realise that there are a lot of hearing people who have not had the same opportunities as I have had. So now, perhaps I feel that because I've worked really hard, never given up, sometimes I feel ahead of other Deaf people. But not ahead of hearing, because whatever the lack of opportunities, they always seem to know more or be able to do and understand more than me as a Deaf person. It's something about being able to keep a perspective – a broad perspective, not a narrow perspective – to notice what's happening and keep interested in it. So it's not just about being Deaf, or gay or Jewish. It seems to be much more about being able to see all of the parts and being more open to it.

I was able to say to someone I met recently that they must understand I am a Deaf person. Usually I can't say that to people in a way which is like making a political point. This friend said that in his friendships – when he has had so many bad experiences in the past, it's a bit like he felt the need to play 'the hard man' because that's what other men expect of him. There's a parallel feeling around being Deaf in a hearing world – the need to play the part of a hearing person, to be what they want you to be in order to gain acceptance. It was interesting to make that comparison about acting – though it also feels a bit like pandering to other people who are expecting things from you. But it made me think that if people don't accept what and who I am – tough! That's life. I can't please everybody and it's exhausting trying! But I feel I am still searching for something, though – that's interesting. For a long time I was asking my mother questions and wanting answers, questions like 'Who's God, where is He?' My mother really never gave me enough satisfactory answers – because she didn't know the answer or because she didn't understand the questions? I'm not sure. At that time, I was conscious of searching – trying to make sense of my world, needing to know whether my world was structured around being Deaf, knowing my identity and how to move forward with it. I now know the answer and that is really that I can't have all the answers anyway. So, I am still searching in a sense. I would describe myself as a very restless person, I don't relax very easily – I look relaxed on the surface, but I am not relaxed inside, there's a lot of changes. I want security, stability, but I also want change. I look for challenges because they give me excitement, so that I can ask myself questions like why am I doing this? I like change, I would hate it if everything were the same. I would find it difficult to get on with my life without change. But I still think of myself as a late starter.

Andrew

I have always felt divided in some way, and yet I sense that I don't need to feel divided – it is only the expectation that people have of how my experience might seem. They *want* me to be divided to satisfy their own expectations and prejudices. I know that other people see me as being divided, not clear about who I am, confused and so on. But somehow that doesn't reflect the division I feel, which is more a recognising that there exist within me two very important aspects which are seemingly irreconcilable – Deaf and hearing. But I wonder if they are. I mean if I look at characteristics that I have, such as strength and weakness, love and hate and so on, it is perfectly possible for me to have *both* strength and weakness and *both* love and hate, often in connection with the same things or the same people. We talk about love–hate relationships, don't we? So I have this very clear idea in my head that it must be possible for Deaf and hearing to live in harmony, and that is certainly how I want it to be. I need to have both deaf and hearing in the same way that I need friends and to work and to be organised in my life.

I was made with brown eyes and no one has yet tried to change their colour. Deaf and hearing are both valuable and just as fundamental to me, in very different ways. Why can't people see that because I have both, it is important that I can be free to explore them and to discover ways in which they can harmonise? Besides which, how can the *before* and the *after* be within themselves at opposite ends of the spectrum when each contains some of the other? But the expectations of the society in which I live seem to be that I must be one *or* the other because coexistence is impossible. These expectations feel like some force that is attempting to prevent me from creating my own meaning, and I can feel it damaging me if I let them too close. It feels as if they impose a difference between me – Andrew, and me – the label Andrew, and for me that also means a difference between *being Andrew* and being *the person called Andrew*. The latter is somehow alien, and perhaps that is because it only represents others' distorted and partial views of me rather than my own view of myself. The reality for me is very simple – deaf and hearing are *both me*, so rejecting one is like rejecting an important part of myself, like losing my right arm, and that doesn't feel right. That being said, I do not see myself as some kind of strange hybrid, and I resent attempts by others to imply this by suggesting that I have a confused identity or that I am muddled about who I am. I *am* clear. They just can't see me clearly, in part because they don't want to.

As a deaf person who grew up in the hearing world, I value my language in the same way that a Deaf person might value theirs. I worked very hard to learn that language, and I didn't have much help from anyone else either. But I feel so hurt when people call me an oralist, just because I am a deaf person who speaks, and especially when I can sign as well. I feel that forces me into a divided situation which threatens to destroy the bond between my language and my spirit because it introduces a split between them. I become 'not really "hearing" and not really "Deaf"' and neither condition is whole, neither condition is perfect, and in societies which hanker after 'purity', neither fits. *My* language is the language of my past and present learning experiences and it is the language which has now become a route to new future learning experiences in visual mode. It is the language which best expresses *all* of that for me, and so I want to be allowed to feel proud of it. I don't feel proud of the part of it that oppresses Deaf people or Black people, or women or gays and lesbians, but that doesn't mean that the language as a whole is bad or undesirable. And I don't feel proud of it when hearing people use their knowledge of it to change what deaf people feel and say, prevent them from giving their own view, and exclude deaf people from truth. I want to transform my language and the way I use it into something beautiful so that I can feel totally proud of it. It is not the only language, but it is for me *the* language, and I do not stress this in order to demean other languages which, for other people, are *their* languages and do for them what my language does for me. The point is that a language must allow me to express who I am – all of who I am – and to receive information from the world around me, and to explore inwardly and outwardly. A language which does not allow me to do all of these things is no good to me, and I actually think I would feel my sense of self diminish, maybe even die if I were forced to communicate in an alien language. I certainly find this when I am with hearing people who have no deaf awareness – I lose contact with myself and I don't feel that I have a real choice to be with them any more and feel good about it. I have also found that there are limits to what I can express in sign language, and I am sure this is because I am a late learner. But, more importantly, I am unable to express fully that part of my experience which is hearing, and I find it very difficult to conduct my inner conversations in sign language. I don't always dream in sign language but I don't hear intelligible voices all the time either – I am just aware of people communicating with me somehow. I do experience a wonderful quality of colour in my dreams.

It would be so easy to become a reservoir for all these viewpoints which present themselves as some kind of profound knowledge about who I am. But, in the end, are deaf and hearing not what I make of them, because they are a part of me? If this is the case, why should I choose between them? Besides which, how can I choose between them? On the one hand I have the memories and experiences of before and on the other I have the new treasures of after and both lay the foundation for future experiences. I think this is all about me – who I am and, more importantly, what makes me different from everyone else – my uniqueness if you like. To belong, I have to want to belong and that means that I have to see something which I can belong to or relate to. Relating often seems to me to be about constant friction, and I don't like conflict or stress – that is where the pain comes from, the cramps I feel in my spirit – the root of me that wants to understand who I am, to become strong in that, and not to reinforce something alien in myself because I cannot be in control of that. I want to understand my uniqueness so that I can always return to it when I need to for replenishment or whatever. It takes so much energy to be strong in who I am in the face of prejudice, that I gravitate towards people with whom there is a common soul. When I feel this 'soul' in the atmosphere it is a very profound experience. It has no label, certainly not the label 'Deaf' or 'hearing'. It brings both comfort and challenge. But most importantly it brings a sense of moving forward, exploring and growing. When part of this soul is under attack, I do feel driven to support and to defend it. And why not? It makes me feel good. I have, I think, learned from my experience of becoming deaf. It is not the kind of experience you can go through without developing some kind of understanding of how people communicate with each other and how communication can go wrong. I can't claim to be perfect, but the awareness of what people do to each other is extremely important to me and something I want to be at the heart of everything I do. To see all the verbal abuse and prejudice that people hurl at each other, all the misunderstandings that happen, all that waste – it really makes me want to do something about it. I just can't sit back and watch it happen when I think of all the deaf children and young people in the world. So, however much pain I have inside as a result of these stupid conventions that people have, and whatever my own personal circumstances, I have to look outward and try to see a way forward for others, to find a way to let them be who they want to be without all these judgements and conditions.

Sam

Eventually, I was able to tell my family about the things that had happened to me, though it was after my father had died. I think it was particularly difficult for my mother because, although she was very shocked of course, she is very religious and so this behaviour from the Christian brothers was very hard to accept in people who represented what she cared about. She hugged me and tried to pray for me but I couldn't pray with her. I told her that I no longer believed in God. I told her it was fine for her to pray for me, but to leave God out of it – I didn't feel I had any proof that God existed any more. If he did exist, he was associated with years and years and thousands and thousands of feelings of pain. Then I cried. All I needed now was to be hugged and hugged – for all that pain inside to be hugged away and replaced with support.

Because of all the damage that had been done to me in the name of 'religion' it seems I have opened my eyes a lot more to what else happened because of religion. It seems that every time I open the newspaper I read something about religion damaging people's lives, about wars being fought over religion. It seems so at odds with the stories of Jesus that we were taught about when we were young. And I ask myself now, is religion worth it? The word means nothing to me. I've lost interest in religion. I want to say to religious people, 'Tell me what to do about my anger with you', but I don't think their response will show tolerance and understanding of my anger and pain. I want to say, 'Tell me what to do when I go to Mass and I see people giving money to the Church and it reminds me of the brothers and the nuns of my childhood which are so strong that I can't pray and you all look at me as if there is something wrong with me.' 'Tell me what to do when I can't take communion because it reminds me of the toilet after breakfast.' Now I will go for a long walk rather than go to Mass, and some people in my family still say to me that God sees me as a bad person for not going. My response now is 'Does God see those nuns and Christian brothers as evil for what they did to me? I AM A VICTIM! Religion has invaded my life and damaged me. It has never supported me. I am only happy now when I can keep it at a distance.' I respect people who do have faith, but often their tolerance does not extend far enough to respect my suffering. If they want to go to church, fine. I can't.

I have learnt that I couldn't have explained to my family before because I didn't have the depth of language to explain in a way that they would understand. So my limited language was like another block to the expression of my feelings. That affected me so much because trying to find the language made me more angry and that in itself stopped me from communicating to my mother and father, who probably wouldn't have been able to understand me anyway. So now I feel I can't blame my mother and father. It wasn't their fault that our ways of communicating were so far apart and different. But the limited language also meant a lack of access to information about what was happening to me. I just didn't know whether all children experienced this treatment or whether it was normal or not. Without language and communication, I couldn't bond with my parents. One thing I was later able to share with the family was my feelings about them forcing me to put farm work and so on before my own needs for friendship of my own age, to get information from books and so on. It made me feel unimportant in their lives, unsupported and unloved. It wasn't fair to make children do these things so young. I think my mother realised then that all my time at home had been spent with family and that I had had no friends to play with and share with. I had no one who understood me. I just lived in a living hell. But my parents had no choice. They did what the experts told them to do.

For years, my identity was all over the place. I had no sense of direction and nowhere to go, and all the time I was searching for something. Now I know that I am stronger, more whole because when I am oppressed or feel I am being forced to do something I can resist it because I am able to respond and to turn it into something more positive by expressing how I feel. I also have found that because I have been through these painful experiences I am better able to understand other people who have experienced similar things. If I get angry and feel I want to hit or kick someone, I know I need to talk and share my feelings, not bottle them up, as that makes me more angry. I feel that all of this means that I am taking more care of myself and so that means I have now something I value in myself. I wonder if that is my identity. At the same time, when I do express feelings I still feel very nervous and worried about the response, so the vulnerability is still there. I am often close to tears with this terrible tension in my chest and a lump in my throat like I am approaching some deadline and under pressure to complete something on time or I will go over the edge. All of that happens when I start to talk about myself. But when I am able to express, I do feel calmer at the end of it, more settled, I do feel some relief from the pain. So I know that expression is important, and for a long time, I didn't have the language of feelings. For so long every path I tried to take was wrong or blocked. Now I feel I have found the right path and the future looks beautiful. The bad is getting less and less, and I feel happy, more whole because my confidence and self-esteem have grown. My attitudes have improved and the relationships I have are stronger I think because I recognise the boundaries between myself and others better and I have a clearer sense of who I am.

Krishna

There are so many facets, beliefs and values which come into play to determine what I make of my life experience. For example, I have a lot of relatives in India and visit India regularly. I have learned from these visits that my family's attitude towards my deafness was something to do with the conditioning they had had before, growing up in India where attitudes towards disability were, and in my view continue to be, very negative. Prejudice, discrimination and negative attitudes are shown in Asian communities in the same way as in many other cultures, but the particular way they are shown or expressed is part of the cultural set-up. Attitudes towards deafness in the Asian community are both easy and difficult to understand; they are easy if you understand the culture, customs and traditions and they are difficult for those who are not familiar with the Asian character. In the Indian subcontinent, there is a lack of social services and a scarcity of medical care and this dictates different attitudes to disability, most of which are based on ignorance, but some of which are based on religious beliefs such as the belief in 'a curse from God' which has come upon the house. Some of these attitudes are based on wider feelings of fear and revulsion or shame and guilt. Culturally, our people believe that any kind of 'abnormality' is a matter of shame and so it is not discussed and often hidden. Whatever form this prejudice or discrimination takes, however it manifests itself, a lot of people feel it to some extent, and it can be reflected in over-protection and under-expectation of disabled children. It feels a bit like the kind of attitudes that are held in respect of what is the 'perfect' woman and which are perpetuated in the media, but is there such a thing as a 'perfect' woman? Can perfection be achieved? There are a lot of views like that around and some of them are also very entrenched.

All this is very hard to describe in terms of culture because what is culture? Is it the values and beliefs of a particular group or is it something which is created by the people who live it? Hinduism, for example, is a way of life, a philosophy, rather than an organised religion; it is the culture of Indians – our spiritual heritage. It cannot be explained in one sentence because it is a mixture of so many things – a summation of all types of thoughts and all types of religions. It allows their coexistence. In Hinduism, on one side, woman is the object of worship of saints and seers and on the other, she is depicted as the cause of all problems in the world and looked down upon. As I said earlier, in my family my paternal grandfather held negative views and expectations of women's roles and these were handed down through the generations on his side of the family, whereas the women and many of the men on the maternal side hold the opposite view that women are esteemed – 'the light of the house.' Indian society is so full of contradictions that these different views must be allowed to coexist if they are not to become conflicts. As a disabled woman, I can feel trapped by such views or liberated and allowed freedom of thought and action. Sometimes I feel like I am different people in different circumstances because I have to go along with some things, because I can't disrupt the flow which has been there for centuries and is very important and fundamental to our spiritual and cultural heritage.

Very definitely I'm Indian, and proud of it. The feelings are very powerful. There are many positives about our culture. There are some negatives which I have taken a conscious decision not to take on board. Through my visits to India and through reading and attending workshops I continue to learn much about our way of life, which has in turn led me to ask questions about the meaning of life and why we are here. I believe in a higher power or consciousness – call it God, universal power or a spiritual dimension or perspective. For me it is a necessary perspective amongst others. I am conscious of using this perspective, but gaining understanding of it depends upon the level of interest and openness of others – it is of no meaning to those who are not interested or open to it. There is so much diversity in this world and I believe that all these differences must be valued and respected, striven for and, ultimately, transcended. Whether we are deaf, disabled, Black, female or whatever, we are all 'higher' than those differences – we are all part of one race, the human race, and we need to accept ourselves as well as others without judgement, criticism and prejudice. It is not easy to do, I know that, but I constantly strive to work in this direction.

The consciousness I describe is similar to an all-embracing spiritualism, it's about expanding ourselves, seeing ourselves as more than just our bodies, not narrowing ourselves or shutting ourselves off from what is out there. There is room for individualism within that consciousness. My deaf identity is part of my life more now than it was before. But I am conscious that my deaf identity is part of my other identities also, and it can't be separated that easily. Perhaps some people might say that I'm not deaf – as in Deaf community – but a lot of that is how they define deaf. The fact is that deafness is significant for me because it's in *here* – it's a part of me. I do feel *in the middle* – not fully BSL Deaf because BSL wasn't my first language. But then I don't really know what my first language was because at home I was exposed to Punjabi, later English, and then when I was at school, I was exposed to BSL. I do get a lot of comments like 'Oh you're not deaf' and I know it usually means *not Deaf and in the Deaf community*. However, again, it goes back to putting people in boxes and the important issue is how *I* see deaf people and *my* deaf identity. I have a lot of deaf friends and I am conscious of behaving in a *deaf way* when we get together and and socialise. Then there's deaf culture which is not so easily defined. Some say it's flashing lights, some people say it's sitting in a circle so that we can see each other, but that doesn't *feel like culture* to me. People say Deaf culture is *there*, but I wasn't really convinced it was *there* because of the way that they described it. What I do know is that part of *something* to do with being deaf can be felt deeply *here* in me, and it has to be a state of being to have meaning for me.

I remember when I was at the Deaf school I felt a tremendous sense of belonging, whereas before I had felt left out and as if I was on the outside of everything. I have many strong feelings of affinity with different groups, but with Asian deaf people there is a *greater* affinity – I am closer to *being whole* – which I am unable to express or measure. However at the same time, I am aware that it may not always be like this with *all* Asian deaf people because we have other aspects of ourselves which we do not share. Similarly, both the deaf and hearing worlds are important to me as I have disabled and hearing friends whom I can feel very at ease with, as they are accepting of me as I am and we share many similarities. When I think about those deaf people I have shared with over time, I somehow feel I have experienced something very powerful which I cannot express in words. The fact that each individual is deaf and each has their own diverse experiences which they have shared with me – there is a bond established through deafness, but it's more than that. I feel so privileged that I have been a part of their life and been with them for a portion of their life journeys. Of course some of these journeys have been painful but there is a kind of mental and spiritual growth that comes through pain and which gives greater self-understanding. Is that bonding what deaf culture is? Is it what deaf identity is? Or is it that there is a unity in the diversity of our deaf experiences?

Unravelling Narratives

The first thing that strikes me about all of these narratives is that despite the long and tortuous journeys that our narrators have taken, they have all arrived somewhere and none are stuck in limbo. There is a continued commitment to growth and to the search for individual and community meaning. Any confusion or ambivalence about the chosen course seems to be related to the oppressive expectations of the societies and communities to which our narrators want to belong. All acknowledge the role of their past in bringing them to where they are now, and some are quite explicit about this.

Joseph says: 'My identity reflects the culture and traditions, the way of life I have grown up with, and this includes my experience of oppression and dominance from hearing professionals in the field of deafness who make it difficult for Black Deaf people to develop their own consciousness. I think that it must be linked to internalised oppression as well.' He feels comfortable with his dual Black Deaf identity because 'I now have some understanding of who I am', and recognises that 'there are both cultural differences and similarities between Deaf and Black culture, though because Black culture is expressed through food, clothing, drink, music, it feels richer and easier to define. I hold onto my identity as a Black Deaf person by maintaining my values and sense of self-respect and by involving myself in Black culture.' He also makes very clear statements about social responsibility, the need to educate others in different ways, and how this influences who he becomes at any one moment. Interestingly, though, he makes a distinction between where he feels he belongs and where he feels comfortable: 'I belong more in the Deaf community at elite and grass roots levels, but, in fact I feel more comfortable in the Black community and with aspects of Black cultures and lifestyles.' He is aware of the pressures of a lack of socially conferred identity on his feelings of belonging: 'I want to maintain flexibility in my relationships with other Deaf and Black Deaf people, and in the way I communicate, but I feel that I can't always belong in the way I want to with everyone I am with and in every situation. I don't feel accepted for who I am unless I make a lot of adjustments'.

I feel that Joseph ends on a note of ambivalence, and in this respect he is similar to Caroline. Throughout her narrative, she has come across as the one person who has been able to settle comfortably into the value system of her family and community, and who maintains the clearest sense of who she is in spite of extreme pressures from outside. However, when she gives birth to a hearing child, she is forced not only to question some of her own values, but also to examine some of the assumptions prevalent in her community, as we saw in the previous chapter. She remains uncertain of how to manage the situation. 'Sometimes I feel sorry for her because I feel she's lonely in the hearing world... I feel sometimes we're cruel to her, not intentionally of course, but it's very difficult...sometimes I still have problems fully accepting that she's different, not Deaf like us.' This is reinforced by the difference in the attitudes towards Jane and those towards a new baby in the family, who has been born Deaf: 'That feeling keeps coming back and back, and sometimes it feels as if it gets in the way of us seeing Jane as our 'perfect child'. All the attention has shifted to him because he's Deaf. I am conscious that I don't want Jane to feel that the shift of attention is because she's hearing.' I was left with a sense of Caroline having been brought face to face with the fragility of her Deaf value system and the kind of attitudes which are needed to maintain it when it is faced with the contradictory values coming from the hearing world. She has moved from the position expressed in the previous chapter that she does not harbour anger towards hearing people to one of recognition that Deaf and hearing are after all, quite different and it may now be difficult to prevent them coming into conflict with each other because they have become part of her life. Before, these contradictions were very much 'out there'. The feelings coming from this realisation are powerful ones which mean that '...it's difficult to think about having another baby now. It may be because I've had enough children, or because I'm just too busy to think about another baby. But, deep inside, I'm frightened that the baby will be hearing. Jane is definitely strong Deaf, but she's still hearing.' I feel, however, that Caroline's commitment to the Deaf community as the place where she belongs will survive and remain the foundation for her search for the meaning of these new contradictions.

Andrew's present position is not so much one of feeling ambivalent about who he is, but more being clear about who he is and knowing that this identity is neither socially acceptable nor socially conferred. He is bewildered by and angry about the reasons for his lack of 'fit': 'I mean if I look at characteristics that I have, such as strength and weakness, love and hate and so on, it is perfectly possible for me to have both strength and weakness and both love and hate, often in connection with the same things or the same people. We talk about love–hate relationships, don't we? So I have this very clear idea in my head that it must be possible for Deaf and hearing to live in harmony, and that is certainly how I want it to be', whilst being certain that he needs 'to have both deaf and hearing in the same way that I need friends and to work and to be organised in my life. I was made with brown eyes and no one has yet tried to change their colour. Deaf and hearing are both valuable and just as fundamental to me, in very different ways. Why can't people see that because I have both, it is important that I can be free to explore them and to discover ways in which they can harmonise?' Andrew is also, like Joseph, aware of the conditions placed on his belonging by society: 'These expectations feel like some force that is attempting to prevent me from creating my own meaning and I can feel it damaging me if I let them too close. It feels as if they impose a difference between me – Andrew, and me – the label Andrew, and for me that also means a difference between *being Andrew* and *being the person called Andrew*.' This division between personal identity and socially conferred identity results in a need to defend his language choices and to ground them in his experiences: '*My* language is the language of *my* past and present learning experiences and it is the language which has now become a route to new future learning experiences in visual mode. It is the language which best expresses all of that for me, and so I want to be allowed to feel proud of it... I actually think I would feel my sense of self diminish, maybe even die if I were forced to communicate in an alien language.' He deplores the 'hypocrisy...in human terms' of a system which strives for the right to language but attempts to demean him in respect of *his* language choices, when he feels that he has no more choice than anyone else, but at the same time he is aware of the implications this might have for others: 'It is not the kind of experience you can go through without developing some kind of understanding of how people communicate with each other and how communication can go wrong...the awareness of what people do to each other is extremely important to me and something I want to be at the heart of everything I do... I have to look outward and try to see a way forward for others, to find a way to let them be who they want to without all these judgements and conditions.' Equally, he is clear that he wants to remain in control of his social identity: 'to belong, I have to want to belong and that means that I have to see something which I can belong to or relate to. Relating often seems to me to be about constant friction, and I don't like conflict or stress – that is where the pain comes from, the cramps I feel in my spirit – the root of me that wants to understand who I am – to become strong in that, and not to reinforce something alien in myself because I cannot be in control of that.' He describes this social identity as a search for a commonality which respects his uniqueness: 'I want to understand my uniqueness so that I can always return to it when I need to for replenishment or whatever. It takes so much energy to be strong in who I am in the face of prejudice, that I gravitate towards people with whom there is a common soul. When I feel this "soul" in the atmosphere it is a very profound experience. It has no label, certainly not the label "Deaf" or "hearing". It brings both comfort and challenge. But most importantly it brings a sense of moving forward, exploring and growing. When part of my soul is under attack, I do feel driven to support and to defend it. And why not? It makes me feel good.'

Andrew wants to continue growing, not to feel cramped, and he is aware of the kinds of conditions, and the kinds of people, who are needed for this growth. Karen, who also became deaf, shares some of Andrew's feelings about conflict and the different meanings attributed to the terms deaf and Deaf: 'I don't see being deaf in a negative, medical way, but I did have to work through a lot of internalised oppression to arrive at that point in my life. I don't feel happy about the deaf/Deaf distinction. I am not Deaf because I wasn't born deaf and BSL is not my first language, but I do identify with the struggles of the Deaf community.' She acknowledges that 'It can be very difficult to face oppression from both hearing and Deaf people, but it is more painful and more difficult to cope with when it comes from Deaf people. Logically, I know why it happens, but emotionally, it is very hard to accept. I have to continue working at that!' This is similar to the 'head and heart' distinction that Andrew makes in an earlier chapter, but it is not necessarily the focus of Karen's present life, as here she is preoccupied with a need to understand her childhood experiences and to differentiate these from her experiences as a deafened person: 'I now recognise there are two separate issues – those which are a result of my childhood experiences and those which are related to my feelings as an adult as a result of being deaf and feeling left out by hearing people – the kind of situation I experience at work, or if I mix with hearing people socially.' Though she has acknowledged that deafness is part of her identity, she expresses a need not to stop at this point. I am left with a feeling that, in this respect, she is similar to Fiona, particularly in her comment that: 'I can understand why Deaf people respond in the way they do to that experience, but they can't deny me my experience and they can't deny my childhood. They can't deny my right to think and feel the way I do, when, as a child, that was the only way I *could* feel, it was the only thing I *knew*. I didn't feel Deaf but I felt I was *one of them*.'

Fiona emphasises her personal history in the creation of who she is and also the fact that at some point she had to let go of some of this history: '…it feels as if there has been an about-turn between the Deaf and hearing parts of me – not a competition with one coming out on top, just that both have changed the way that they operate… My experience of being Deaf was slightly different because I internalised the Deaf behaviour of my family. But I have never claimed to be Deaf in the same way that they are. I am hearing, I am me – but I am also different.' Fiona, like Andrew and, in a different context, Joseph, refers to the difficulties that the boundaries between Deaf and hearing worlds pose for the integration of the two parts of herself: 'Sometimes I get the feeling that there are very rigid boundaries around Deaf and hearing worlds… The boundaries keep moving but they are still rigid. I keep trying to find parallels with the way that Deaf people establish boundaries but I end up thinking they really are very different…the Deaf boundary is fluid, if selective.' She feels that 'the doubt, the confusion and uncertainty that has become predominant in my life…should have been sorted out a long time ago. I feel as if I am at the ambivalent stage in the development of my identity but I think I should have gone through it when I was a teenager – I am like a teenager definitely – a late developer maybe?' Fiona is preoccupied with resolving past psychosocial conflicts and recognises that this has delayed her growth and self-understanding. Importantly, her positive attitude to life and the experiences she has been through will carry her forward.

Ironically, the same is true for Sam who, though his experiences were vastly different from Fiona's, ultimately found comfort through opening himself to the reality of past conflicts. He expresses the difficulty in explaining to his mother something which contradicted her devout faith, and in doing so, his new-found honesty came into direct conflict with the value systems he had been forced to adopt in childhood: 'I told her that I no longer believed in God. I told her it was fine for her to pray for me, but to leave God out of it – I didn't feel I had any proof that God existed any more. If he did exist, he was associated with years and years and thousands and thousands of feelings of pain... All I needed now was to be hugged and hugged – for all that pain inside to be hugged away and replaced with support. Because of all the damage that had been done to me in the name of "religion" it seems I have opened my eyes a lot more to what else happened because of religion... Religion has invaded my life and damaged me. It has never supported me. I am only happy now when I can keep it at a distance. I respect people who do have faith, but often their tolerance does not extend far enough to respect my suffering. If they want to go to church, fine. I can't.'

He is also able to recognise that his parents weren't totally to blame for his pain, and the role of language and communication in creating blocks to mutual understanding and bonding: 'So my limited language was like another block to the expression of my feelings. That affected me so much because trying to find the language made me more angry and that in itself stopped me from communicating to my mother and father, who probably wouldn't have been able to understand me anyway. So now I feel I can't blame my mother and father. It wasn't their fault that our ways of communicating were so far apart and different. But the limited language also meant a lack of access to information about what was happening to me. I just didn't know whether all children experienced this treatment or whether it was normal or not. Without language and communication, I couldn't bond with my parents.' He feels that being able to talk about his feelings has liberated his identity as something he values, even if some doubts still remain: 'I know that expression is important, and for a long time, I didn't have the language of feelings. For so long every path I tried to take was wrong or blocked... I feel that all of this means that I am taking more care of myself and so that means I have now something I value in myself. I wonder if that is my identity. At the same time, when I do express feelings I still feel very nervous and worried about the response, so the vulnerability is still there.' He feels that he has 'found the right path and the future looks beautiful. The bad is getting less and less, and I feel happy, more whole because my confidence and self-esteem have grown. My attitudes have improved and the relationships I have are stronger I think because I recognise the boundaries between myself and others better and I have a clearer sense of who I am... Now I know that I am stronger, more whole.' This is in contrast to his earlier position, where 'For years, my identity was all over the place. I had no sense of direction and nowhere to go, and all the time I was searching for something.' This echoes some of Peter's feelings about where he is now: 'But I feel I am still searching for something though –

that's interesting. For a long time I was asking my mother questions and wanting answers, questions like "Who's God, where is He?" My mother really never gave me enough satisfactory answers – because she didn't know the answer or because she didn't understand the questions? I'm not sure. At that time, I was conscious of searching – trying to make sense of my world, needing to know whether my world was structured around being Deaf, knowing my identity and how to move forward with it. I now know the answer and that is really that I can't have all the answers anyway. So, I am still searching in a sense.'

Peter also experienced deep disillusion with religion, though because it sprang from his commitment to being gay, the resulting conflicts meant that something had to be rejected: 'I am conscious of feeling more together now than before, but only because some parts of me had to go and some things had to be kept – a bit like a purging. I know, for example that the Jewish religion does not readily accept gay people and, when I realised how impor- tant being gay was to me, I felt that I could no longer be a part of that, I couldn't go to the Synagogue any more... Obviously, I do feel I am hurt by it, but I can also at times be philosophical about it. I can't waste time being hurt for ever more. I have to move on.'

He also acknowledges the effects of blocked communication on the path that his life took, 'I still think that if I had had all the answers, all the knowledge, the skills and the understanding earlier, my life would have been completely different. I would have made more progress, moved further ahead.' But he puts this into a wider perspective based on new-found knowl- edge: 'I now realise that there are a lot of hearing people who have not had the same opportunities as I have had.' Although he says that it 'took a long time before all the boxes collapsed', there is a sense that deafness has still to find its place in his inner world: 'I was able to say to someone I met recently that they must understand I am a Deaf person. Usually I can't say that to people in a way which is like making a political point.' He resents some of the role expectations imposed upon him by the hearing world: 'There's a parallel feeling around being Deaf in a hearing world – the need to play the part of a hearing person, to be what they want you to be in order to gain acceptance. It was interesting to make that comparison about acting – though it also feels a bit like pandering to other people who are expecting things from you. But it made me think that if people don't accept what and who I am – tough!' Like Fiona, however much he craves and values change, he feels he is 'a late developer'. Peter is clear that growth is 'something about being able to keep a perspective – a broad perspective, not a narrow perspective – to notice what's happening and keep interested in it. So its not just about being Deaf, or gay or Jewish. It seems to be much more about being able to see all of the parts and being more open to it.'

This parallels something that Krishna experiences, though she has trans- lated through a much deeper and more spiritual level: 'Hinduism, for exam- ple, is a way of life, a philosophy, rather than an organised religion; it is the culture of Indians – our spiritual heritage. It cannot be explained in one sentence because it is a mixture of so many things – a summation of all types of thoughts and all types of religions. It allows their coexistence... Indian society is so full of contradictions that these different views must be allowed to coexist if they are not to become conflicts. As a disabled woman, I can feel trapped by such views or liberated and allowed freedom of thought and action.' As part of her Hindu faith, she has embraced a clear system of beliefs and values: 'I believe in a higher power or consciousness – call it God, universal power or a spiritual dimension or perspective. For me it is a necessary perspective amongst others. I am conscious of using this perspective but gaining understanding of it depends upon the level of interest and openness of others – it is of no meaning to those who are not interested or open to it... The consciousness I describe is similar to an all-embracing spiritualism, its about expanding ourselves, seeing ourselves as more than just our bodies, not narrowing ourselves or shutting ourselves off from what is out there.' She feels that she is 'Very definitely... Indian, and proud of it. The feelings are very powerful. There are many positives about our culture. There are some negatives which I have taken a conscious decision not to take on board.' and has internalised the cultural traditions of her heritage through understanding their origins 'Sometimes I feel like I am different people in different circumstances because I have to go along with some things, because I can't disrupt the flow which has been there for centuries and is very important and fundamental to our spiritual and cultural heritage.' Moreover, through her belated education she has been able to understand that her 'family's attitude towards my deafness was something to do with the conditioning they had had before, growing up in India where attitudes towards disability were, and in my view continue to be very negative'.

Krishna's feelings about the deaf part of her identity are very much 'in relation to' the other parts. That is, though she acknowledges that deafness has been and is an important part of her life, it cannot be separated from other aspects of her identity, in particular what she calls the Asian 'character': 'My deaf identity is part of my life more now than it was before. But I am conscious that my deaf identity is part of my other identities also, and it can't be separated that easily...the important issue is how I see deaf people and my deaf identity...with Asian deaf people there is a greater affinity – I am closer to being whole – which I am unable to express or measure.' As with Joseph, this seems to be because she has difficulty with the concept of deaf culture when placed in the perspective of her cultural heritage: 'Some say its flashing lights, some people say its sitting in a circle so that we can see each other, but that doesn't feel like culture to me. People say Deaf culture is there, but I wasn't really convinced it was there because of the way that they described it. What I do know is that part of something to do with being deaf can be felt deeply here in me, and it has to be a state of being to have meaning for me.' But her sense of belonging with deaf people is strong, and she questions whether this bonding is what is meant by culture, and whether deaf people's unity is or can be based on a similar principle to the coexistence of Hinduism: 'When I think about those deaf people I have shared with over time, I somehow feel I have experienced something very powerful which I cannot express in words. The fact that each individual is deaf and each has their own diverse experiences which they have shared with me – there is a bond established through deafness, but its more than that. I feel so privileged that

I have been a part of their life and been with them for a portion of their life journeys. Of course some of these journeys have been painful but there is a kind of mental and spiritual growth that comes through pain and which gives greater self-understanding. Is that bonding what deaf culture is? Is it what deaf identity is? Or is it that there is a unity in the diversity of our deaf experiences?'

I will leave Krishna's questions open for the reader to respond to. It is left for me to try to pull the threads of these narratives together, and this I will do in the final chapter of the book within the framework of humanistic counselling.

Part 3

Narratives in Context

CHAPTER EIGHT

Images of Deaf Futures

I'm not perfect. I think more highly of snow and ice than of love. It's easier for me to be interested in mathematics than to have affection for my fellow human beings. But I am anchored to something in life that is constant. You can call it a sense of orientation; you can call it women's intuition; you can call it whatever you like. I'm standing on rock bottom and further than that *I* cannot fall. It could be that I haven't managed my life very well. But I always have a grip – with at least one finger at a time – on Absolute Space. (Hoeg 1992, pp.39–40)

To reach the clearing beyond, you must stay with the weightless journey through uncertainty. Whatever counterfeit safety we hold from over-investments in people and institutions must be given up. The inner custodian must be unseated from the controls. No foreign power can direct our journey from now on. It is for each of us to find a course that is valid by our own reckoning. And for each of us, there is the opportunity to emerge reborn, authentically unique, with an enlarged capacity to love ourselves and embrace others. (Sheehy 1974, pp.361–364)

In the Preface, I posed a number of questions which I hoped the narratives in the preceding chapters would provide responses to. These questions were in two groups. The first group concerned the process of counselling and, in particular, whether the process is different when working with deaf clients. By process, I mean what happens in the counselling relationship and what kind of narratives deaf clients bring to this relationship. I have emphasised in this context that I was the person who was present throughout the narratives and, to a certain extent, the connecting thread running through all of them. I have also stressed that though the interviews are not put forward as examples of counsellor–client interactions, there were many ways in which they were similar to such interactions, particularly in my attempts to create a safe environment and in the way in which I managed my part of the interactions and used counselling skills throughout them. I feel that my approach to the interviews may have been one factor which enabled the narrators to relate their experiences and respond to my questions on a deeper level. Because of this, I feel that it is legitimate to comment on process as if these were counselling interactions.

As I am deaf and was *not* working across deaf–hearing boundaries, certain characteristics of the dynamics of the relationships formed need to be highlighted. Deafness generally becomes an issue only when deaf and hearing people come into contact, and indeed this is one reason, additional to communication fluency and matching, which is cited for the value of using Deaf interviewers in social science research, as 'the cross-cultural variable' is reduced. How much of an issue deafness becomes when deaf and hearing people come together in the counselling situation depends on the level of deaf awareness of the hearing person, the hearing awareness of the deaf person and their ability to arrive at a common language which is sufficient for empathic understanding and the development of trust. These characteristics are additional to the skills and attitudes that we might expect any counsellor to have. It sometimes happens that when two deaf people meet, the commonality between them results either in a more open sharing of deaf-related experiences or the taking for granted of shared deaf-related experiences with a corresponding emphasis on the presenting issues. I do not want to make any assumptions about the level of empathy established between myself and the narrators, as I can give only my perspective on that. What I can say, however, is that deafness was not raised unless I asked a question which related directly to it, and I was careful in how I conveyed these questions. There is a difference, for example, in asking open questions such as 'Who are you?' and 'How would you describe yourself alone and in relation to others?' and more specific, closed questions such as 'Would you describe yourself as having a Deaf identity?' and 'Do you choose to affiliate with Deaf or hearing people?' The use of open questions did not preclude the possibility of deaf-related concerns being raised by the narrators, and in some cases they did focus on these concerns in parts of their narratives.

What is striking about these narratives is the different ways in which deafness is integrated. For example, Krishna really makes only incidental reference to her deafness and a dominant theme of her narrative is her exploration of her Asian culture and beliefs; Joseph focuses on his struggle to understand himself as a Black person and how deafness has constrained this. Sam's narrative is dominated by his abuse and later, by his disenchantment with religion; deafness is located in specific incidents for him, particularly incidents which aggravated his abuse. Peter moves fluidly between issues surrounding being Jewish, deaf and gay. For Caroline, Fiona, Andrew and Karen, being deaf is an important part of their narratives, but it is raised in very different contexts and clearly has a different qualitative meaning for each of them. This suggests to me that when deafness is not an issue within the counselling relationship, it cannot be assumed that it will be a presenting problem. The narratives reflect the kinds of narratives we might experience with any client, but because deafness is always 'in the air', the counsellor must be alert to the added dimension it brings without presuming what its effects may be. A misguided focus on 'deaf' can mean that the client's real concerns as human beings are obscured. Fiona refers to a counsellor that she met who kept to their own agenda rather than hers in the relationship, and how this made her feel uncomfortable. This illustrates the dangers of being presumptuous.

I will come back to the question of process below, but for the moment, I want to focus on the second group of questions which are primarily to do with the narrator's individual and varied responses to them. To recap, these questions were: 'Who am I?', 'Where do I belong?', 'What has supported me or constrained me on my journey to self-definition?', 'What is my identity in relation to my deafness?', 'What does being deaf mean in relation to other people?' and 'What additional tasks in the development of my identity have I had to take on board because I am different?' This is not the way in which the questions were framed in the interviews, but I hoped that the responses to the questions I *did* pose would throw some light on these areas.

Identity in Relation to Deafness

I have emphasised on a number of occasions that I view identity as something which is dynamic rather than static, and because, to a certain extent, it defines the boundary between self and others, it must be fluid, adaptable and constantly evolving over time. This gives me an image of identity as being similar to a solar system, which consists of a core planet around which orbit a number of other planets (Figure 8.1). The core planet generally provides all the conditions necessary to sustain the other planets, but because these planets vary in their configuration at any one moment, the influence of the core planet will vary. For this reason, some planets experience a more stable environment because the orbits they occupy bring them into regular contact with the core planet. Moreover, because the orbits themselves are made up of forces gravitating from the core planet, rather like the ripples of chapter one, the whole system is held together by the core planet. Sometimes the outer planets will move closer to the core planet, and, as astronomers will tell us, sometimes worlds collide. Using this image, then, what do the narratives tell us about core identity and identity configurations?

The core identity, which is closer to personal identity is, I feel, made up of gender, sexual and ethnic identities where any psychosocial conflicts surrounding these have been resolved satisfactorily. The grey area is perhaps sexual identity because someone who is gay or lesbian may not integrate this into their core identity until much later than someone who is heterosexual because of their experience of stigma and the lack of available role models with whom they can make positive identifications. But because of the necessity of sexuality for the core identity, developmental tasks surrounding its integration must be resolved and may take priority. Some might argue that the same is true of ethnicity, but I feel the process is different largely because one's ethnic identity is not always a source of stigma during the early stages of psychosocial development where positive identifications are possible *from within one's family of origin*. This view is supported by the evidence cited in chapter one that the proportion of *foreclosed* identities in adolescents from ethnic minorities is relatively large. A crisis commonly occurs later if, for example, racial discrimination against one's racial group is experienced. But it may occur earlier if there is another aspect of the developing child which challenges the belief and value systems of the racial or ethnic group. That is to say, each of the components of the core identity brings with it a belief and value system which has been part of the resolution of the psychosocial conflicts and may in itself act as a constraint to development of the core identity as a whole. We would expect someone who has successfully resolved the identity versus role confusion conflict to make clear statements about what they believe in and value as well as statements based on more concrete reasoning, and often these belief and value statements are linked to feelings about gender and sex roles and the cultural or religious views of our racial group. However, these statements may reflect 'the fundamental discrepancy' that Rogers (1964) highlights, in that they are statements of what we *ought* to value rather than what we feel we do value in today's changing society, and which I will return to below.

The point, here, is that the adoption of value systems which contradict our fundamental sense of ourselves is often part of the *negative* resolution of psychosocial conflicts. If there is a negative resolution of any of the tasks related to the parts of the core identity, the forces emanating from the core will influence the orbits of all the other parts of the identity configuration differently from where there is a positive resolution, because identifications that are made tend to reflect the initial 'inner schema' which has been developed in childhood. A positive resolution is one which results from an exploration period or crisis, and a commitment. A negative resolution frequently happens when there is no opportunity for self-exploration or environmental stressors result in unquestioning and uncritical adherence to what is socially acceptable as opposed to what feels right within the individual's structure of meaning.

I feel that this position is reinforced by the experiences of Krishna and Joseph, for whom the ethnic or racial identity of their family is a key determining factor in the initial identity construction. I also feel that, for them, this identity takes precedence over the integration of deafness into their identity configurations *in spite of* unhelpful parental attitudes towards their deafness rather than *because of* them, as both demonstrate evidence of substantial exploration and the commitment follows this. I feel a similar situation is true for Peter, who describes his core identity as 'gay' and demonstrates a commitment to this through his intimate relationships and his rejection of the core element of his family's identity – their Jewishness – because it conflicts with his gayness. Intimacy is an important indicator of the core identity, and Peter's particular way of explaining his situation is relevant here. He acknowledges that he has engaged in a long struggle to 'welcome deafness' and that he forms relationships with *hearing* gay men who are *sensitive to* his deafness. He can now tell others that 'they must understand that [he is] a Deaf person', but he describes this as 'making a political point' rather than as making a statement about his essence. If his *primary* commitment had been made to Deaf people, then I feel he would have sought relationships with *Deaf* gay men, because after the commitment had been made, his sexuality was not open to negotiation. Instead, he says that he 'does not see himself as Deaf-gay, not like some others', so he is clearly aware that such a group exists but feels he is different from them. It follows from this that if a white, heterosexual Deaf person from a Deaf family is prepared only to consider other Deaf people in their search for a life partner, Deafness then sets the precedent for intimacy and the final choice may be made on the basis of other less important characteristics.

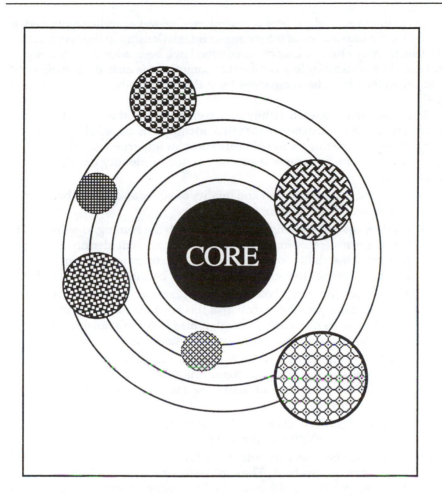

Figure 8.1 Identity configuration

This, in turn, raises questions about the existence of a 'deaf identity' and the position of deafness in the overall identity configuration. On the basis of the narratives explored in this book, and also, I have to say, on the basis of many years' participant observation in the deaf community and my experience in working with deaf clients in the counselling situation, I cannot confidently place deafness at the core of the identity configuration of any deaf person apart from those who have been exposed to the linguistic and cultural heritage of a Deaf *family* from birth. Moreover, I remain uncertain as to whether a deaf child's exposure to individual members of the Deaf *community* in the early years, when the parents are hearing, can substitute for this natural heritage, because the quality of bonds which can be formed will not be the same, nor will they be as visible or as constant as those established in natural parent–child interaction. Some may say that such interaction can never be 'natural' when parents and children are so different from each other, but I feel that to give in to this view and to focus on substitutes, however well-intentioned, is a denial of the importance of the parent–child relationship in the construction of identity. Why else is it that children who have been adopted often report that they live with a niggling feeling that something is missing in their lives, even when they have been removed from the birth mother at a very young age?

The distinction between family and community is therefore, I feel, the critical one in the construction of the initial identity. It is more helpful, because of this, to regard the integration of deafness as an important *additional* developmental task which becomes a primary factor in identity *development* for several reasons:

- it influences the formation and quality of affectional bonds between parents and deaf children;
- it influences and sometimes interferes with the coming together of all the factors necessary for the integration of personal identity, in particular, the ability to reason beyond the concrete operational level and the responses to social expectations to become more than a child;
- it is not socially or psychologically acceptable in hearing terms, and this means that *for most deaf children* it is not a viable option in the formative years of identity, though it may become available after initial identity constructions have been established;
- it disrupts patterns of both vertical and horizontal relationships through blocked or damaged communication, and therefore opportunities for trying out, accepting and rejecting different identifications;
- it may be negatively evaluated by the cultural and societal frameworks to which it is introduced.

These factors then become constraining factors, and all of them are referred to in the narratives of this book. The experience of stigma can bring deafness into a dominant position in the individual's identity configuration, perhaps even to such an extent that it collides with the core identity. When this happens the ripples of influence it exerts will tend to be destructive. Caroline describes lucidly the 'angry Deaf people' who need to become Deaf to prove themselves in some way, and Fiona uneasily questions whether they are actually 'more Deaf' than she is. I do not feel that any of the narrators are in this category of Deaf people, which might be described more accurately as 'a political identity' in the same way that feminism can be. This 'political identity' seems to be graded also from an identification with Deaf people's struggles without fully embracing the socio-cultural identity, which Karen refers to, to the 'angry Deaf' whose influence, Caroline suggests, is potentially destructive – not only self-destructive, but destructive of other deaf and hearing people. We can see evidence of this destruction in the narratives of Andrew and Fiona, who have become angry at the way they are alienated by militancy, and Karen, who seems to be rather more passive and to feel that she 'can't do anything about it'. The ripples of anger are far-reaching, but they change in quality.

Belonging – Family of Choice or Family of Origin?

For deaf people, the family of origin is the biological family. Whereas the characteristics of individual families of origin may vary, the key factor influencing the narrators' feelings of belonging to their families of origin lies in the quality of the affectional bonds formed, in particular how these are constructed around the family's attitudes towards deafness. For some of the narrators, the family of origin has been the source of identifications and patterns of bonding which have led to negative resolutions of psychosocial conflicts and a confused sense of personal and social identity. The family of choice is then seen as a place of retreat, where a sense of belonging, self-esteem and a positive self-concept can emerge. However, the family of choice may not always be available and the commitment cannot easily be predicted when there are several options to be selected from. Sometimes, there is no retreat, but rather a division between the family of choice and the family of origin in terms of the functions they serve for the individual.

Krishna, for example, views her family of origin as the home of her cultural heritage and her belief and value systems and I feel this is important to her because she makes a commitment to these systems *after having appraised them and recognising that they have flaws*. Her ambivalence about the flaws is not enough to shake her fundamental beliefs even when it impinges directly on two other aspects of herself which she views to be important – her deafness and her gender. She remains committed to 'the flow'. Joseph also feels committed to his cultural roots in the Black community, but he makes a distinction between where he belongs – the Deaf community – and where he feels comfortable – his family of origin, and as he moves between the two, the strength and location of his commitment is less clear. Peter's commitment, I feel, is eventually to the family of choice – the gay community, because, as was suggested above, it is arrived at after fundamental aspects of his family of origin have been rejected because they conflict with who he feels he is. However, he still enjoys a good relationship with his parents where he is now open about being gay, and so his adoption of a gay identity might be part of the process of separating from his parents as he moves into intimate relationships of his choice. Peter feels he is a 'late developer' and in this he is similar to Fiona. Whereas Peter has identified a place where he feels comfortable, Fiona remains torn between her family of origin and her family of choice. Denying her family of origin causes her a great deal of conflict, in part because the responsibilities placed on her by them as a child now act as a developmental stressor, producing feelings of guilt and conflicting with her current need to learn about and develop a sense of belonging in her current family of choice – the hearing community. For Andrew, and to a lesser extent for Karen, attitudes in the family of origin, coupled with the constraints on belonging imposed by the community boundaries and 'family values' of both Deaf and hearing communities, mean that the availability of a family of choice is limited. Part of this is because neither community fully accepts or reflects the duality of their personal identity and so this identity can only be a self-constructed one. Moreover, since it cannot easily be based on identifications with a group, social expression is complex. To a large extent, therefore, it must be explored and resolved within.

Removing Developmental Constraints – The Role of Humanistic Counselling

A summary of the factors influencing the development of identity in deaf people, together with the possible commitments which might be made and the outcomes of making these commitments is given in Figure 8.2. The task of this book has been to highlight where the blocks might lie to healthy commitments and what kinds of conditions are needed to enable deaf people to navigate their way around these blocks. As Figure 8.2 suggests, the most difficult and therefore the most important task is the avoidance of shame in relation to deafness or any other source of difference which is the subject of stigma. Marcia (1994) says that this task must be approached on three levels, which he calls *societal, educational* and *psychotherapeutic*. The role of society, and all the families and communities of which it is made, is to enable an exploratory period which is free from judgements and conditions and to provide multiple valid niches for commitment. Societies which value pluralism, which have fluid boundaries that allow free movement in and out, and which allow coexistence of diverse groups are more likely to achieve this role. The niches suggested in Figure 8.2 represent the minimum possibilities for deaf people, and there are still far too many deaf people who are channelled in the direction of shame or discouraged from developing new structures of meaning for themselves because of introjected negative value systems and moralistic inflexibility. The task of education is to be less prescriptive, more facilitative of psychosocial learning and rewarding of individual commitments, and more enabling of 'occupational and ideological experimentation'. Marcia suggests that this 'would represent a move beyond mere training to true education' (p.78), and I have explored what this might mean for deaf education elsewhere (Corker 1996). I will come back to societal and educational tasks in the conclusion to this chapter.

The Process of Counselling in Easing Transitions

The task of counselling involves the process of change as a means of achieving personal growth. Woolfe and Sugarman (1989) suggest that this involves recognising that clients are *developing* rather than developed and that change, whilst offering potential for development, is not a sufficient condition for development to take place *per se*. Clients who have experienced stigma or oppression have often encountered change in a way that inhibits or prevents development and creates the need for a number of additional transitions which will put them back on course. Hopson and Scally (1980, p.183) view development as being founded on the idea of the individual becoming more *self-empowered* – 'more proactive, less dependent upon others, valuing the integrity of others as well as themselves, more in charge of themselves and their lives'. They suggest five attributes which are needed for self-empowerment:

- goals
- life skills

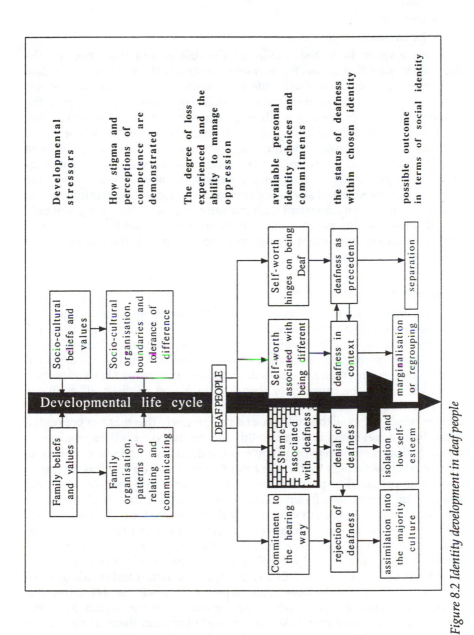

Figure 8.2 Identity development in deaf people

- values
- awareness
- information

I do not want to focus too heavily on the first two of these because the individual goals that clients have will vary enormously, and work with deaf people tends to over-emphasise life skills without looking at the systems which have created the need for such skills. In *counselling*, however, the primary goals are personal growth, increased self-responsibility and aware-ness of ourselves as developing, dynamic individuals which are consistent with maturity and self-actualisation. Individuals who experience stigma must develop coping skills, increase their self-awareness and clarify their values as they relate specifically to living in and developing appropriate challenging responses to a hostile and alienating environment. Accepting our lot without question is not often consistent with maturity, and, in many cases, amounts to self-abuse, but the power of such environments is that they act as very effective barriers to positive change in people who lack the self-esteem to challenge.

Information and Awareness

The first step to such resolution is for counsellors to recognise that all people, even people who lack self-esteem, have choices. This is central to the principle of self-empowerment. To be able to make realistic choices we have to know what the alternatives are, but when working with deaf clients, we are often dealing with people who have been deprived of a diversity of life experience, explanation and the capacity to absorb information through all available channels. Such clients lack information about or awareness of the range of choices which are available to them, and it is precisely this that has prevented them from developing. Sometimes this means that counsellors need to be aware both of their own experiences and the diversity of others' experiences – the kind of awareness that comes from listening and developing empathy, and being prepared to pass this on to clients when appropriate. Listening without judgement to different clients as they explore the life choices they have made and the different outcomes of these choices for them represents a range of possibilities or alternatives that counsellors can have available to them when working with any client on identifying which path is appropriate for them. So, for example, if we look back at the narratives we can pick up a number of different perspectives on a particular situation and in doing so we can see that the narrators have made different choices in resolving the situ-ation. This is another reason why the commentary on the narratives is pre-sented in such a way that links can be made between them. It shows the process of self-education that I went through as I listened, but it also shows how important it is that counsellors are open to many different 'ways of seeing'. For example, if I had not explored subpersonalities, I might not have been able to recognise the significance of 'underground rivers' in the devel-opmental process. Likewise, if I had not looked at Marcia's work on identity statuses, I might not have understood that these statuses have particular implications for the kind of safety I can create for different deaf clients in the counselling situation:

> A safe context is not the same thing for a Foreclosure as it is for a Moratorium. To attack frontally a Foreclosure's rigid defences and to successfully strip the person of internalised childhood ideals is to leave that person bereft of any internal guarantor of self-esteem and thence to risk an acute depressive episode. What must be done is to establish some connection based upon authentically shared values between therapist and client and then to slowly and gently disequilibrate the existing structure, providing plenty of time for the formation of new ego ideals. While a safe context for a Foreclosure is based on some alliance with existing ideals, this is not necessarily the case for the Moratorium who is already in a disequilibrated state. What is required here is a validation of the process of struggle itself as an ingredient necessary for psychosocial growth. To make an alliance with either pole of the ambivalences with which the Moratorium is wrestling is to make oneself a participant in that struggle, and not a benevolent and dependable observer. The alliance to be made here is with the Moratorium process itself, and not with any one value. (Marcia 1994, pp.78–79)

Counsellors need to be prepared to provide non-judgemental information to clients which assists them in meeting the goal of self-empowerment, in particular, information which gives what Grace (1992, p.44) describes as 'compassionate explanations' for the structures of meaning clients have constructed and safety for them to explore alternative structures. He says:

> Adult clients often report a great sense of relief and understanding when I suggest that they may have significant differences between their chronological and developmental ages. They quickly identify situations where they and others felt or acted like 'young teenagers.' Contemptuous and shaming responses to unidentified developmental lag can then be replaced with a more respectful, benevolent and responsible 're-parenting' of the younger parts of oneself.

Of particular importance in this process is being able to explore with clients how damaged communication may have contributed to developmental lag or delay. Many deaf clients will point to the inability of their parents to communicate with them or the way in which professionals forced them to communicate in a particular way when this prevented them from full access. I have found, however, that these comments often focus on the surface facts – that 'the school was oral', or 'it's my parents' fault because they couldn't sign' for example – rather than on the process of interpersonal communication itself, which lies deeper and is often the origin of the damage. It is in this area that I have found an understanding of cybernetic models of communication in constructing patterns of shared experiences (Dallos 1991; Watzlawick *et al.* 1967) to be extremely useful. In chapter one, for example, it was pointed out that in any situation where individuals come together – in the family, in the community or in the counselling relationship – they may be at different stages in their life cycles and have different perspectives on the developmental process which can provide mutual reinforcement of both positive and negative patterns of beliefs, behaviours and feelings. What kind of reinforcement emerges often depends on the characteristics of the different individuals in the interaction, and who holds the power in the interaction. If we start with one of the examples given above – 'It's my parents' fault because they couldn't sign' – we can create a simple circular model of what might be happening in the interaction between parents and deaf child (Figure 8.3).

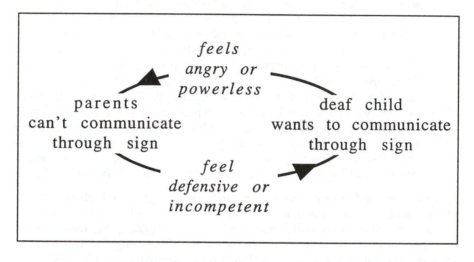

feels
angry or
powerless

parents
can't communicate
through sign

deaf child
wants to communicate
through sign

feel
defensive or
incompetent

Figure 8.3 'It's my parents' fault because they couldn't sign'

Both parents and child have become locked in particular ways of behaving and feeling, and, in the absence of alternatives, these patterns become what Dallos calls 'the dynamic equilibrium' of the interaction. Both parents and child take steps to correct any deviations from this equilibrium. This may happen at an unconscious level, so that no one in the interaction is aware of the patterns. Further, a third party entering the system may collude with one party and this may threaten the equilibrium, which sets the stage for further cycles of damage. Caroline gave us an example of this when she related how one of the peripatetic teachers contradicted her decision to behave towards her child in a particular way when they were 'naughty'. Caroline felt that not only was her parenting role being threatened, but also the pattern of communication she had built with her children which established the framework for the relationships they had with each other. To break these destructive patterns requires some understanding of the possible positions that each of the parties in the interaction are coming from. It is easy to allocate blame or to adopt other stereotyped ways of thinking if we don't have any knowledge of these possibilities, and sometimes, raising awareness of these possibilities can in itself relieve the tension of a damaging equilibrium.

If we look at each of the three participants in the kind of interaction that Caroline describes, using our understanding of life cycles and the different ways in which people behave, we have a more complex scenario, which is described in Figure 8.4. Hearing parents may, for example, be at different stages in coming to terms with their child's deafness, professionals may adopt a particular style in the work which they do with parents and children and children may behave in a reactive manner to the demands of parents and professionals if they have not yet established themselves as separate from their parents. Deaf children, because they are often overprotected and viewed as less competent than hearing children, tend to remain insecurely attached to parents for longer and so we might see these kinds of reactive behaviours in young teenagers and, if they are internalised, even in young adults, as Karen describes.

It is important, however, to recognise that if a parent is stuck at a particular stage in their cycle, and a professional adopts a way of working which increases the parent's feeling of being stuck and provides the child with the reverse of what they need at any one moment, the child will often react in a way which simply deepens the parent's sense of crisis and leads to a further, more frenetic cycle of repeated behaviours. Taking the example illustrated in Figure 8.4, if the professional were to *negotiate* with parents and not make assumptions about the child's competence, the parents might be able to break the deadlock imposed by that particular stage of their life cycle and move on, and the child, in feeling more valued, would establish different behaviour patterns. In this example the professionals are pivotal, because they hold both power and knowledge, and the capacity to influence change. When a deaf client comes for counselling, these patterns of behaving may already have become so deeply entrenched that they are repeated in the client's adult relationships. They need to understand that though the past cannot be changed, its influence on the present and the future can be. Karen refers to the deeper self-understanding that she gains from being able to separate behaviour which was appropriate to the situation she faced in her teenage years and behaviour which is appropriate to her current relationships. By showing the client how family behaviour patterns might have been constructed in a non-judgemental way, the client can then begin to identify the locus of power within themselves and to learn through the counselling relationship, alternative, more mature ways of communicating. This is what Grace describes above as 'responsible re-parenting of the younger parts of oneself', and it aims to take the place of the 'inner child abuse and neglect' that many clients have become accomplished in.

Challenging Distorted Value Systems

Different approaches to counselling practice and theory have their own sets of beliefs, assumptions, values, norms and standards – their own philosophical and moral foundations, and Woolfe *et al.* (1989, p.12) suggest that 'the term "counselling movement" is in fact a considerable over-simplification of a variety of approaches to working with people which have different origins, methods, objectives and values'. I have said, for example, that one of the reasons I am drawn to humanistic counselling is that it has done much to dispense with labels and stereotypes. As such, I see it as a force for freeing people from straitjackets and putting them back in touch with their ability to choose. Many of the constraints that people experience are due to belief and

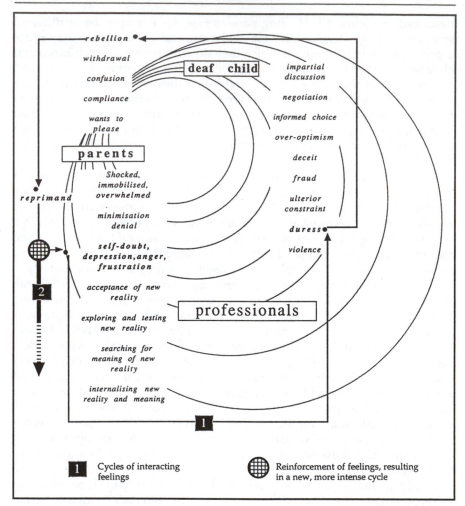

Figure 8.4 *Constructing patterns of feelings, behaviours and communication (see text for explanation)*

value systems in society which dictate what we have to do in order to 'fit', and this is reinforced by society's notion that some behaviours and feelings are 'right' and others are 'wrong'. Sam learnt very early on that he would be punished if he was not obedient, and later, that he would be punished even when he felt he was being obedient. He grew up believing that religion was 'good', only to learn that it was associated with behaviour and practice which he saw as 'bad'. Fiona had internalised the belief that to say 'no' to responsibility is 'wrong', whereas Andrew felt that he was being forced to accept that being both deaf and hearing meant that he was 'mixed up' when he believed that bridges can be built. These values, if we are not careful, can form the foundation of counselling. I spent a considerable amount of time in *Counselling – The Deaf Challenge* explaining why particular beliefs about deaf people can undermine the counselling process in exactly the same way that particular patterns of communication can. Counsellor values can reinforce positively or negatively client values; thus, although I have some reservations about Egan's (1994) eclectic framework, I do have considerable empathy with his comments about 'building a value orientation' into the helping process and the need for counsellors to be 'proactive in their search for the beliefs, values and norms that will govern their interactions with their clients' (p.48). Hopson and Scally (1980) stress that values must be consistent with self-actualisation or maturity and therefore be focused on self-respect and respect for others, responsibility for self, and the assumption that oneself, others and systems all have the potential to change. At this point, I want to draw attention to what Carl Rogers (1964) meant by values, with reference to the work of Charles Morris (1956). He says that we use the term *value* in three ways:

- *operative* values 'refer to the tendency of any living beings to show preference, in their actions, for one kind of object or objective rather than another';

- *conceived* or *conceptualised* values are the result of preferences held by individuals for 'symbolised objects' which include some anticipation of what might happen when we behave in a particular way towards that object;

- *objective* values are those based on our ideas of what is preferable, regardless of whether or not it is desirable.

When a deaf child is given the choice between learning something the easy way and learning something the hard way, the choice of the easy way might be based on operative values. When a parent of a deaf child says 'oralism is the best policy' this expresses an objective value (though the same statement from a professional might reflect a conceived value), but when a parent says that something is 'for the child's own good' it indicates a conceived value. Rogers says that young children work on the basis of operative values. He calls this 'an organismic valuing process' and suggests that somewhere along the path to adulthood it is exchanged for a 'more rigid, uncertain, inefficient approach to values', which has its origins in learning that 'what feels "good" is often "bad" in the eyes of others', and adopting the often highly contradictory attitudes which gain approval as part of our self-appraisal. Important aspects of the adult valuing system then become:

- values which are internalised from other individuals or groups who are significant to us, and which we view as if they are our own values
- values which mean that we will be more loved or accepted
- values which are not related or clearly related to our own experiences
- values which are 'right' usually because others tell us so

and this leads to the kind of questioning that one of my clients recently engaged in:

'Am I what I am?'

'Am I struggling at being what I want to be but am not able to be?'

'Why is it that I never vent my anger when it hurts me so?'

'How important is life to me now where am I taking myself? What's happening?'

'Am I hating myself because past experience of school made me hate everyone for their action?'

Box 8.1 summarises the transitions that our narrators made, the commitments and the resolutions that they arrived at and the suggestions they made for their futures. In working with deaf clients, the counsellor can usefully learn from this summary in the suggestion and demonstration of alternative behaviour patterns and roles which can help clients to break the vicious circle. But this must not be done in a contrived way, as it may come across as a lack of genuineness. For me this means that to enter into a counselling relationship with a deaf client is to enable them to become strong in who they are, to resolve any conflicts they might have, to recognise what they feel comfortable with, and to understand where and who they want to be. These are my values and they imply that I have to recognise my own vulnerabilities, that I am prepared, when appropriate, to use them in achieving this end, and that I must not present myself as someone who has all the answers, nor must I detach myself to such a degree that I am unknowable and therefore omnipotent. Part of being able to develop shared meanings with my clients comes from an ability to establish common ground and this cannot be done if I approach the client's situation from a perspective which is out of their reach. I know that in many ways I will be more knowledgeable than they are about other people's situations because I have opened myself to alternative experiences, and that I can use this knowledge to good effect in suggesting alternatives and exploring different routes. But I can never be more of an 'expert' about their lives than they are themselves. To present this knowledge in a way which says 'I know better than you' simply repeats the patterns and the habits that clients so often are trying to break:

> The therapist is positioned as all-knowing and wise – a model to which the client might aspire. This situation is all the more lamentable owing to the fact that in occupying the superior role, the therapist fails to reveal any weaknesses. Nowhere are the wobbly foundations of the therapist's account made known; nowhere do the therapist's personal doubts, foibles and failings come to light. And the client is thus confronted with a vision of human possibility that is as unattainable as the heroism of cinematic mythology... Under these conditions, the client confronts a relatively closed system of understanding. It is not only that the client's own reality will eventually give way to the therapist's, but all other interpretations will also be excluded. (Gergen and Kaye 1992, p.171)

It is not difficult to see the difference between this approach and the indiscriminate application of stereotyped labels described in chapter one.

Images of Deaf Futures

Carl Rogers believed that 'a common aspect of modern life is living with absolutely contradictory values'. I feel that far from being 'dated', as Woolfe *et al.* (1989) suggest, Rogers recognised *before his time* that counselling is 'a

Box 8.1 Deaf transitions

Narrator	Fundamental issues	From	To	Possible role of counsellor
Fiona	Resolution of deaf-hearing dichotomy; foreclosed identity removed from context	Resentful Deaf child with adult responsibilities	Hearing adult with internalised Deaf child	Encouraging discovery of 'nurturing' parent to liberate a happier child and exploration of developmental delay
Andrew	Societal attitudes which conflict with his inner reality	Division between deaf and hearing parts of himself	Building bridges between deaf and hearing parts; strong social conscience	Acceptance and support of inner reality and strengthening the bridges he has built
Caroline	Foreclosed identity removed from context by birth of hearing child; lack of sensitive community support	Strong foreclosed Deaf identity	Ambivalence and possibly psychosocial moratorium	Finding a connection based on authentically shared values; gentle introduction of alternatives
Karen	Diffused identity with diminished sense of self and living through others; low self-esteem	'Good', passive child experiencing sibling rivalry and feeling unloved by parents	Tentative exploration of relationships between inner child and adult relationships	Encouraging re-parenting of inner child to develop her self-esteem and exploration of developmental delay
Sam	Damaged trust resulting from sustained physical, sexual, psychological and emotional abuse; low self-esteem	Reasonably happy child, though isolated within the family	Very strong, frightened, damaged inner child projected onto current relationships; ambivalence about religion	Encouraging release of feelings about abuse; re-discovering the happy child through re-parenting; exploring developmental delay
Peter	Conflict between parental values and beliefs and own values and beliefs	Need to hide gay identity and ambivalence about deafness, Jewishness	Commitment to gay identity, rejection of parental belief systems; still searching for something	Further integration of deafness through exploring censoring 'distant voices' and exploration of developmental delay
Krishna	Cultural values; difficulty with integrating different parts of herself	Quiet, passive child; deafness and gender stigma	Proactive, more integrated adult with strong social conscience; commitment to Asian identity	Exploring cultural conflicts and coexistence
Joseph	Deprivation of Black cultural heritage; lack of education	Emphasis on deafness and racial stigma	Commitment to Black culture but still some remaining ambiguity about Deaf identity; strong social conscience	Exploring alternative ways in which splits can be managed and positive ways of adapting

social enterprise which cannot be divorced from the social, economic and political environment in which it is practised' (Woolfe 1982). The commitment of humanistic counsellors to the maintenance of organismic functioning and conditions of worth and the breaking down of stereotyped value systems, is a recognition that, in the end, when environmental stressors prevail, the person can come back only to their own structure of meaning for support and sustenance. It is better, then, that this structure of meaning is our own, rather than one which has been imposed upon us. Though most humanistic counsellors acknowledge that it is their basic trust in the individual that sets them apart from just about every institution in society, I believe that it is also what makes humanistic counselling a primary mechanism for social change, because however much society changes, the transitions depend on the maturity with which individuals adjust. The value systems underpinning different environments are often based upon the current 'moral framework', but just because this framework currently espouses money as a value, for example (Orbach 1995), it does not mean that the old adage 'the love of money is the root of all evil' is out of date. It may simply mean that the makers of current frameworks are out of touch with human values or believe them to be 'wrong'. The practice in large business conglomerates has been known to be based on the value system of the managing director, but this does not mean that the workforce is happy or fulfilled or guarantees optimum productivity, nor that the value system is perceived by them as 'right' (Morgan 1994). The human consequences of value contradictions are far-reaching. In a very basic way, we end up 'divorcing ourselves from ourselves'. Rogers felt that the origins of such ways of thinking could be counteracted by a counsellor attitude which values *all* client feelings and experiences without passing judgement, and enables them to rediscover the organismic value systems which were more in touch with their experiencing of the world.

I feel that the narratives of this book are a testimony to endurance – the endurance necessary for oppressed people to 'mould themselves in their own image'. They also leave me with a number of very real concerns about identity development in deaf people which make me acutely aware of my responsibility to challenge some of the societal and educational value systems which inhibit or prevent the development of a mature identity. A foreclosed racial identity can be psychologically mature, stable and adaptive because the context foreclosed upon has the benefit of being established, often culturally rich, and in some cases tolerant of coexistence of many diverse strands. This is not so of the Deaf context. The Deaf community shows fluid boundaries *within*, but its boundary with other communities is rigid and does not allow for easy movement in and out. This creates a very strong feeling of 'us and them', which is ultimately a consequence of oppression, though it may be attributed to 'cultural difference'. The community does not easily tolerate coexistence of diverse elements in the wider deaf community, as evidenced by the difficulty of gaining access to the Deaf community when in a state of transition or ambivalence about Deafness. This description is not intended to be critical of Deaf people, because it seems there are two main ways in which the Deaf community has developed which parallel the development of *undifferentiated* or *relational* collectivism described in chapter one. The core group of members are those with foreclosed identities, who because of the obvious difficulties in accessing society at large and a strong Deaf heritage in the family of origin have not achieved individuation and separation from the context foreclosed upon. To a certain extent, *because* of the lack of access and prevailing attitudes towards deafness, there has been no choice about the context foreclosed upon. As we have seen, however, when this context is challenged in some way, the foreclosed identity is more prone to crisis and much less adaptive. If I can just give an example here which is not the situation that Caroline describes but it is an example that I have come across in counselling in working with a Deaf parent of hearing children. This woman had become so dependent on her hearing children to communicate for her outside of the Deaf community, that when she was asked a question, she would automatically seek their view and defer all responsibility for a response to them. Although she worked in Deaf sector employment and knew that the hearing people she worked with were able to sign quite proficiently, she could not manage communication with these hearing people without an interpreter because she had no skills in negotiating her way around communication barriers. In counselling, she promptly labelled me as 'hearing' and demanded an interpreter. I said that I felt it was important that we tried to establish some ground rules for communication and that we should both try to be more explicit with each other when we felt that we were not being understood, because I had already sensed that the presenting problem was linked to her inability to take responsibility for herself in relationships. This particular client departed in anger, but I have since worked with other similar clients where we were able to explore the issue of self-responsibility and its links to lack of exposure to situations where different strategies could be tried out. The point I want to make here is that if identity is foreclosed upon a context *which is in itself marginalised or segregated*, then encounters, particularly chance or unexpected encounters, which take place outside of that context are likely to be much more difficult. Sometimes they will 'leave [the individual] bereft of any internal guarantor of self-esteem' (Marcia 1994).

I make this point not because I am trying to make a case for integrated education and socialisation. Deaf people must always have the possibility of a Deaf peer group and the opportunity to communicate and socialise with each other through sign language or any other means *if they so choose*. I am, however, extremely concerned about the potential psychological damage to such individuals since contact with the hearing world cannot be avoided completely and there are many unscrupulous hearing people who thrive on situations like this one. I feel, moreover, that it is more healthy for a commitment to a Deaf identity to be made after a period of exploration of real alternatives and real choices rather than as a result of the situation which defines the second, and much larger, group of Deaf community members. This consists of those Deaf people who have through their family of origin achieved a measure of contact with the hearing world and have experienced some individuation and separation, but who have been so damaged by the experience that they have given up their self-identity in order to immerse themselves completely in the in-group of the Deaf community. They do so, however, without first having resolved the psychosocial conflicts of their childhood and so, as adults, their dominant and sometimes coexisting behaviour patterns in relation to others might best be described as those of an 'authoritarian, controlling parent', 'an invisible child', an 'angry, unloved child' or a 'compliant, passive accepting child'. None of these personalities are mature and the first and third, as we have seen, can be both powerful and destructive forces.

We all have a responsibility for the situation whereby large numbers of children have been 'lost' or transformed into monstrous caricatures of themselves and I believe that we all have a responsibility to find them again and to learn how to nurture them. I remain convinced that the key to growth and empathy in deaf clients' relationships with their counsellors is how they resolve the *oppression/trust dichotomy* (Corker 1995), where oppression is the 'processing of the individual by the environment' and how this is reflected in the counsellor in a growth-producing climate, and trust is the outcome which must result from the deaf person's processing of the counselling environment which will enable them to find a mature 'way of being' for themselves and their relationships with others. There will be many obstacles to resolution which are exemplified in the following paradox:

> It is a strange paradox, which is nonetheless characteristic of identity, that the individual regards the environment with a subtle and sensitive gaze in which a wealth of psychic systems cooperate to refine this regard, enabling the person to distinguish the most delicate shades; and yet at the same time, the environment classifies the individual with the gross, shadeless platitudes of stereotypes. These have historical, sociocultural roots, and they are told to the individual like books are revealed to their readers according to laws that belong to another realm than psychology. (Grotevant *et al.* 1994, p.14)

Deaf futures hinge not only upon the recognition that stereotyped beliefs, values and attitudes are the scourge of minority communities, but upon an understanding that a restriction of diversity prevents growth and adaptability. Krishna puts forward a very strong case for the role of humanistic counselling in undoing some of the existing damage and in paving the way for brighter deaf futures when she says: 'There is so much diversity in this world and I believe that all these differences must be valued and respected, striven for and, ultimately, transcended. Whether we are deaf, disabled, Black, female or whatever, we are all "higher" than those differences – we are all part of one race, the human race, and we need to accept ourselves as well as others without judgement, criticism and prejudice.'

Bibliography

Ainsworth, M.D.S., Blehar, M., Waters. E. and Wall, S. (1978) *Patterns of Attachment.* Hillsdale, NJ: Lawrence Erlbaum Associates.

Alderson, P. (1993) *Children's Consent to Surgery.* Buckingham: Open University Press.

Allport, G. (1954) *The Nature of Prejudice.* Reading, MA: Addison-Wesley.

Anthony, S. (1992) 'The influence of personal characteristics on rumor knowledge and transmission among the deaf.' *American Annals of the Deaf 137,* 1, 44–47.

Basilier, T. (1973) *Horseltap og egentlig dovhet i socialpsykiatrist perspektiv.* Oslo: Universitetsforlage.

Baumrind, D. (1967) 'Child care practices anteceding three patterns of pre-school behaviour.' *Genetic Psychology Monographs 75,* 43–88.

Baumrind, D. (1971) 'Current patterns of parental authority.' *Developmental Psychology Monograph 4,* 1, Part 2.

Baumrind, D. (1973) 'The development of instrumental competence through socialisation.' In A.D. Pick (ed) *Minnesota Symposium on Child Psychology 7,* 3–46. Minneapolis: University of Minnesota Press.

Bee, H. (1994) *Lifespan Development.* New York: Harper Collins.

Bell, R.Q. and Harper, L.V. (1977) *Child Effects on Adults.* Hillsdale, NJ: Lawrence Erlbaum Associates.

Bernard, D. (1992) 'Developing a positive self image in a homophobic environment.' In N.J. Woodman (ed) *Lesbian and Gay Lifestyles: A Guide for Counselling and Education.* New York: Irvington.

Bertling, T. (1994) *A Child Sacrificed to the Deaf Culture.* Wilsonsville, OR: Kodiak Media Group.

Bion, W. (1961) *Experiences in Groups.* New York: Basic Books.

Boa, F. (1988) *The Way of the Dream: Dr Marie-Louise von Franz in Conversation with Fraser Boa.* Toronto: Windrose Films.

Bodner, B. and Johns, J. (1977) 'Personality and hearing impairment: A study in locus of control.' *Volta Review 79,* 362–368.

Bosma, H.A., Graafsma, T.L.G., Grotevant, H.D. and de Levita, D.J. (eds) (1994) *Identity and Development: An Interdisciplinary Approach.* London: Sage Publications.

Bowlby, J. (1969) *Attachment and Loss, Volume 1: Attachment.* London: Hogarth Press.

Bowlby, J. (1973) *Attachment and Loss, Volume 2: Separation, Anxiety and Anger.* London: Hogarth Press.

Bowlby, J. (1979) *The Making and Breaking of Affectional Bonds.* London: Tavistock.

Bowlby, J. (1980) *Attachment and Loss, Volume 3: Loss.* New York: Basic Books.

Bowlby, J. (1988a) 'Developmental psychiatry comes of age.' *The American Journal of Psychiatry 145,* 1–10.

Bowlby, J. (1988b) *A Secure Base.* New York: Basic Books.

Brown, R. (1986) *Social Psychology,* Fourth edition. New York: Free Press.

Burr, V. (1995) *An Introduction to Social Constructionism.* London: Routledge.

Carter, E. and McGoldrick, M. (1980) *The Family Life Cycle: A Framework for Family Therapy.* New York: Gardner.

Carty, B. (1994) 'The development of deaf identity.' In C.J. Erting, R.C. Johnson, D.L. Smith and B.D. Snider (eds) *The Deaf Way: Perspectives from the International Conference on Deaf Culture.* Washington DC: Gallaudet University Press.

Choi, S-C., Kim, U. and Choi, S-H. (1993) 'Indigenous analysis of collective
    representations: A Korean perspective.' In U. Kim and J.W. Berry (eds) *Indigenous
    Psychologies: Research and Experience in Cultural Context*. Newbury Park, CA: Sage
    Publications.
Clarkson, P. (1989) *Gestalt Counselling in Action*. London: Sage Publications.
Clay, H. (1834) 'Speech in the Senate, 14 March'. In C. Colton (ed) (1904) *The Works of
    Henry Clay*, Vol.5, p.627.
Corker, M. (1992) 'Models of deafness.' In *Roles and Relationships: Perspectives on Practice in
    Health and Welfare*. Open University Course K663, Workbook 3, 21–31.
Corker, M. (1994) *Counselling – The Deaf Challenge*. London: Jessica Kingsley.
Corker, M. (1995) 'Counselling and mental health services – Are they the same?' *Deafness
    11*, 3, 9–15.
Corker, M. (1996) 'Personal–social education for deaf children and young people:
    Changing concepts of need and creating caring communities.' *Journal of the British
    Association of Teachers of the Deaf*, in press.
Dallos, R. (1991) *Family Belief Systems, Therapy and Change*. Buckingham: Open University
    Press.
Davis, M. (1995) 'Deaf people and the counselling profession.' *Deafness 11*, 3, 3–4.
Denmark, J. (1994) *Mental Health and Deafness*. London: Jessica Kingsley.
Densham, J. (1995) *Deafness, Children and the Family*. Aldershot: Arena.
Dowaliby, F., Burke, N. and McKee, B. (1983) 'A comparison of hearing impaired and
    normally hearing students on locus of control, people orientation, and study habits
    and attitudes.' *American Annals of the Deaf 128*, 53–59.
Egan, G. (1994) *The Skilled Helper*, Fifth edition. Pacific Grove, CA: Brooks-Cole.
Eisenberg, N. (1992) *The Caring Child*. Cambridge, MA: Harvard University Press.
Erikson, E.H. (1956) 'The problem of ego identity.' *Journal of the American Psychoanalytic
    Association 4*, 56–121.
Erikson, E.H. (1959) 'Identity and the life cycle.' *Psychological Issues* (Monograph 1). New
    York: International Universities Press.
Erikson, E.H. (1963) *Childhood and Society*, Second Edition. New York: Norton.
Erikson, E.H. (1968) *Identity, Youth and Crisis*. New York: Norton.
Erikson, E.H. (1980) *Identity and the Life Cycle*. New York: Norton.
Erikson, E.H., Erikson, J.M. and Kivnick, H.Q. (1986) *Vital Involvement in Old Age*. New
    York: Norton.
Erikson, E.H. and Hall, E. (1987) 'The father of the identity crisis.' In E. Hall (ed) *Growing
    and Changing*. New York: Random House.
Evans, R.I. (1967) *Dialogue with Erik Erikson*. New York: Harper and Row.
Fong, M.L. and Cox, B.G. (1983) 'Trust as an underlying dynamic in the counselling
    process: How clients test trust.' In W. Dryden (ed) *Key Issues for Counselling in Action*.
    London: Sage Publications.
Forster, M. (1993) *Daphne du Maurier*. London: Chatto and Windus.
Fraiberg, S. (1974) 'Blind infants and their mothers: An examination of the sign system.' In
    M. Lewis and L.A. Rosenblum (eds) *The Effect of the Infant on its Caregiver*. New York:
    Wiley.
Fraiberg, S. (1975) 'The development of human attachments in infants blind from birth.'
    Merrill-Palmer Quarterly 21, 315–334.
Friel, B. (1994) *Molly Sweeney*. London: Penguin.
Fromm, E. (1947) *Man for Himself: An Enquiry into the Psychology of Ethics*. New York:
    Rinehart and Co.
Gergen, K.J. and Kaye, J. (1992) 'Beyond narrative in the negotiation of therapeutic
    meaning.' In S. McNamee and K.J. Gergen (eds) *Therapy as Social Construction*. London:
    Sage Publications.

Gibran, K. (1926) *The Prophet*. London: Heinemann (1974).

Gilligan, C. (1984) *In a Difference Voice: Psychological Theory and Women's Development*. Cambridge: Harvard University Press.

Goffman, E. (1963) *Stigma*. Englewood Cliffs, NJ: Spectrum.

Grace, J. (1992) 'Affirming gay and lesbian adulthood.' In N.J. Woodman (ed) *Lesbian and Gay Lifestyles: A Guide for Counselling and Education*. New York: Irvington.

Gregory, S. (1976) *The Deaf Child and his Family*. New York: Halsted Press. Republished as *Deaf Children and their Families*. Cambridge: Cambridge University Press (1995).

Gregory, S. and Bishop, J. (1989) 'The integration of deaf children into ordinary schools: a research report.' *Journal of the British Association of Teachers of the Deaf 13*, 1, 1–6.

Gregory, S., Bishop, J. and Sheldon, L. (1995) *Deaf Young People and their Families*. Cambridge: Cambridge University Press.

Grotevant, H.D., Bosma, H.A., de Levita, D.J. and Graafsma, T.L.G. (1994) 'Introduction.' In H.A. Bosma, T.L.G. Graafsma, H.D. Grotevant, and D.J. de Levita (eds) *Identity and Development: An Interdisciplinary Approach*. London: Sage Publications.

Gunter, P.L. (1992) 'Social work with non-traditional families.' In N.J. Woodman (ed) *Lesbian and Gay Lifestyles: A Guide for Counselling and Education*. New York: Irvington.

Guntrip, H. (1968) *Psychoanalytic Theory, Therapy and Self*. New York: Basic Books.

Haley, J. (1981) *Uncommon Therapy*. New York: Norton.

Hall, E. (1994) 'Deaf culture, tacit culture and ethnic relations.' In C.J. Erting, R.C. Johnson, D.L. Smith and B.D. Snider (eds) *The Deaf Way: Perspectives from the International Conference on Deaf Culture*. Washington DC: Gallaudet University Press.

Harter, S. (1988) 'The determinations and mediational role of global self-worth in children.' In N. Eisenberg (ed) *Contemporary Topics in Developmental Psychology*. New York: Wiley Interscience.

Harter, S. (1990) 'Processes underlying adolescent self-concept formation.' In R. Montemayor, G.R. Adams and T.P. Gullota (eds) *From Childhood to Adolescence: A Transitional Period*. Newbury Park, CA: Sage Publications.

Harter, S. and Monsour, A. (1992) 'Developmental analysis of conflict caused by opposing attributes in the adolescent self portrait.' *Developmental Psychology 28*, 252–260.

Hartup, W.W. (1989) 'Social relationships and their developmental significance.' *American Psychologist 44*, 8, 120–126.

Hawcroft, L., Peckford, B. and Thomson, A. (1996) *Visible Voices: Developing Deaf Service User Involvement in Local Services*. Carlisle: British Deaf Association.

Hesse, H. (1980) 'Siddharta.' In *Hermann Hesse: Six Novels with Other Stories and Essays*. London: Collins.

Higgins, P.C. (1980) *Outsiders in a Hearing World*. Newbury Park, CA: Sage Publications.

Hobson, R. (1989) *Forms of Feeling: The Heart of Psychotherapy*. London: Routledge.

Hoeg, P. (1992) *Miss Smilla's Feeling for Snow*. London: Flamingo.

Hoffman, L., Paris, S. and Hall, E. (1994) *Developmental Psychology Today*, Sixth edition. New York: McGraw-Hill.

Hofstede, G. (1991) *Cultures and Organisations: Software of the Mind*. London: McGraw-Hill.

Hogan, R.T. (1975) 'Theoretical egocentrism and the problem of compliance.' *American Psychologist 30*, 533–540.

Hopson, B. and Scally, M. (1980) 'Change and development in adult life – some implications for helpers.' *British Journal of Guidance and Counselling 8*, 2, 185–187.

Hui, C.H. and Triandis, H.C. (1986) 'Individualism-collectivism: A study of cross-cultural researchers.' *Journal of Cross-Cultural Psychology 20*, 296–309.

Hurwitz, T.A. (1992) 'Postsecondary education and political activisim.' In S.B. Foster and G.G. Walter (eds) *Deaf Students in Postsecondary Education*. London: Routledge.

Jones, J. (1995) 'Making the transition to being Deaf.' *Deafness 11*, 1, 4–8.

Josselson, R. (1994) 'Identity and relatedness in the life cycle.' In H.A. Bosma, T.L.G. Graafsma, H.D. Grotevant and D.J. de Levita (eds) *Identity and Development: An Interdisciplinary Approach*. London: Sage Publications.

Kagitcibasi, C. (1994) 'A critical appraisal of individualism and collectivism: Toward a new formulation.' In U. Kim, H.C. Triandis, S-C. Choi and G. Yoon (eds) *Individualism and Collectivism: Theory, Method and Applications*. London: Sage Publications.

Kannapell, B. (1994) 'Deaf identity: an American perspective.' In C.J. Erting, R.C. Johnson, D.L. Smith and B.D. Snider (eds) *The Deaf Way: Perspectives from the International Conference on Deaf Culture*. Washington DC: Gallaudet University Press.

Kaufman, G. (1980) *Shame: The Power of Caring*. Cambridge: Schenckman.

Keats, J. (1818) Letter to Richard Woodhouse, 27th October. In H.E. Rollins (ed) (1958) *Letters of John Keats*, Vol.1.

Kim, U. (1994) 'Individualism and collectivism: Conceptual clarification and elaboration.' In U. Kim, H.C. Triandis, S-C. Choi and G. Yoon (eds) *Individualism and Collectivism: Theory, Method and Applications*. London: Sage Publications.

Klein, M. (1932) *The Psychoanalysis of Children*. London: Hogarth Press.

Knights, B. (1995) *The Listening Reader*. London: Jessica Kingsley.

Kroger, J. (1996) *Identity in Adolescence*, Second Edition. London: Routledge.

Kubler-Ross, E. (1969) *On Death and Dying*. New York: MacMillan.

Ladd, P. (1995) 'Deaf people, disabled people and the future.' *British Deaf News*, December, 6–9.

Lane, H. (1992) *The Mask of Benevolence*. New York: Alfred A. Knopf.

Lederberg, A. (1993) 'The impact of Deafness on mother–child and peer relationships.' In M. Marschark and M.D. Clark (eds) *Psychological Perspectives on Deafness*. Hillsdale, NJ: Lawrence Erlbaum Associates.

Lee, J.A.B. (1992) 'Teaching content related to lesbian and gay identity formation.' In N.J. Woodman (ed) *Lesbian and Gay Lifestyles: A Guide for Counselling and Education*. New York: Irvington.

Leyens, J-P., Yzerbyt, V. and Schadron, G. (1994) *Stereotypes and Social Cognition*. London: Sage Publications.

Maccoby, E.E. and Martin, J.A. (1983) 'Socialisation in the context of the family: Parent–child interaction.' In E.M. Hetherington (ed) *Handbook of Child Psychology: Socialisation, personality and social development* 4, 1–102. New York: Wiley.

McCullers, C. (1946) *Member of the Wedding*. Boston: Houghton Mifflin.

Main, M. and Cassidy, J. (1988) 'Categories of response to reunion with the parent at age 6: Predictable from infant attachment classifications and stable over a 1-month period.' *Developmental Psychology* 24, 415–426.

Main, M. and Solomon, J. (1985) 'Discovery of an insecure disorganised/ disorientated attachment pattern: Procedures, findings and implications for the classification of behaviour.' In M. Yogman and T.B.Brazelton (eds) *Affective Development in Infancy*. Norwood, NJ: Ablex.

Marcia, J.E. (1966) 'Development and validation of ego identity status.' *Journal of Personality and Social Psychology* 3, 551–558.

Marcia, J.E. (1980) 'Identity in adolescence.' In J. Adelson (ed) *Handbook of Adolescent Psychology*. New York: Wiley.

Marcia, J.E. (1994) 'The empirical study of ego identity.' In H.A. Bosma, T.L.G. Graafsma, H.D. Grotevant and D.J. de Levita (eds) *Identity and Development: An interdisciplinary Approach*. London: Sage Publications.

Markides, A. (1989) 'Integration, the speech intelligibility, friendships and associations of hearing impaired children in secondary schools.' *Journal of the British Association of Teachers of the Deaf* 13, 3, 63–72.

Markus, H. and Kitayama (1991) 'Culture and self: Implications for cognition, emotion and motivation.' *Psychological Review 98*, 224–253.

Marschark, M. (1993) *Psychological Development of Deaf Children*. New York: Oxford University Press.

Mearns, D. and Thorne, B. (1988) *Person-Centred Counselling in Action*. London: Sage Publications.

Montgomery, G. and Laidlaw, K. (1993) *Occupational Dissonance and Discrimination in the Employment of Deaf People*. Edinburgh: Scottish Workshop Publications.

Moorhead, D. (1995) 'Knowing who I am.' In S. Gregory (ed) Deaf Futures Revisited. Block 3, Unit 10 D251 *Issues in Deafness*. The Open University.

Morgan, G. (1994) *Imaginization*. London: Sage Publications.

Morris, C.W. (1956) *Varieties of Human Value*. Chicago: University of Chicago Press.

Moss, J. (1987) 'Functional integration: the best of three worlds.' *Journal of the British Association of Teachers of the Deaf 11*, 1, 15–22.

Moustakas, C.E. (1974) *Portraits of Loneliness and Love*. Englewood Cliffs, NJ: Prentice-Hall.

Muncie, J., Wetherell, M., Dallos, R. and Cochrane, A. (1995) *Understanding the Family*. Buckingham: Open University Press.

Murstein, B.I. (1986) *Paths to Marriage*. Beverley Hills, CA: Sage Publications.

Ngugi Wa Thiong'o (1986) *Decolonising the Mind: The Politics of Language in African Literature*. London: James Currey Heinemann.

Nowell, E. (1989) 'Conversational features and gender in ASL.' In C. Lucas (ed) *The Sociolinguistics of the Deaf Community*. San Diego: Academic Press.

Orbach, S. (1995) 'Too tight to mention.' *Guardian Weekend*, 16 September.

Padden, C. and Humphries, T. (1988) *Deaf in America-Voices from a Culture*. Cambridge, MA: Harvard University Press.

Perlman, D. and Fehr, B. (1987) 'The development of intimate relationships.' In D. Perlman and S. Duck (eds) *Intimate Relationships. Development, Dynamics and Deterioration*. Newbury Park, CA: Sage Publications.

Phinney, J.S. (1990) 'Ethnic identity in adolescents and adults: Review of research.' *Psychological Bulletin 108*, 499–514.

Phinney, J.S. and Rosenthal, D.A. (1992) 'Ethnic identity in adolescence: Process, context and outcome.' In G.R. Adams and R. Montemayor (eds) *Adolescent Identity Formation*. Newbury Park, CA: Sage Publications.

Pollner, M. and Wikler, L. (1985) 'The social construction of unreality.' *Family Process 24*, 2, 241–259.

Rangell, L. (1994) 'Identity and the human core: The view from psychoanalytic theory.' In H.A. Bosma, T.L.G. Graafsma, H.D. Grotevant and D.J. de Levita (eds) *Identity and Development: An Interdisciplinary Approach*. London: Sage Publications.

Remvig, J. (1971) *Om sudo-mutitas og psyckiatri*. Kobenhavn: Mentalhygienisk forlag.

Rodda, M. (1966) 'Social adjustment of deaf adolescents.' In *Proceedings of a Symposium on the Psychological Study of Deafness and Hearing Impairment*. London: British Psychological Association.

Rogers, C.R. (1942) 'A newer psychotherapy.' *Counselling and Psychotherapy*. Boston: Houghton Mifflin.

Rogers, C.R. (1958) 'The characteristics of a helping relationship.' *Personnel and Guidance Journal 77*, 6–16.

Rogers, C.R. (1959) 'A theory of therapy, personality and interpersonal relationships, as developed in the client-centred framework.' In S. Koch (ed) *Psychology: A Study of Science, Vol 3. Formulations of the Person in Social Context*. New York: McGraw-Hill.

Rogers, C.R. (1961) 'Ellen West and loneliness.' *Review of Existential Psychology and Psychiatry 1*, 2 (May), 94–101.

Rogers, C.R. (1964) 'Toward a modern approach to values: The valuing process in the mature person.' *Journal of Abnormal and Social Psychology 68*, 2, 160–167.

Rogers, C.R. (1986) 'A client-centred/person-centred approach to therapy.' In I. Kutash and A Wolf (eds) *Psychotherapist's Casebook*. New York: Jossey-Bass.

Rose, P. and Kiger, G. (1995) 'Intergroup relations: political action and identity in the deaf community.' *Disability and Society 10*, 4, 521–528.

Rotter, J.B. (1966) 'Generalised expectancies for internal versus external control of reinforcement.' *Psychological Monographs 80*, 1, No. 609.

Rowan, J. (1990) *Subpersonalities*. London: Routledge.

Rowan, J. (1993) *Discover Your Subpersonalities*. London: Routledge.

Sheehy, G. (1974) *Passages*. New York: Dutton.

Sinha, J.B.P. and Tripathi, R.C. (1994) 'Individualism in a collectivist culture: A case of co-existence of opposites.' In U. Kim, H.C. Triandis, S-C. Choi and G. Yoon (eds) *Individualism and Collectivism: Theory, Method and Applications*. London: Sage Publications.

Sinha, J.B.P. and Verma, J. (1987) 'Structure of collectivism.' In C. Kagitcibasi (ed) *Growth and Progress in Cross-cultural Psychology*. Lisse, Netherlands: Swets and Zeitlinger.

Small, J. (1986) 'Transracial placements: conflicts and contradictions.' In S. Ahmed, J. Cheetham and J. Small (eds) *Social Work with Black Children and their Families*. London: Batsford.

Spence, J. (1985) 'Achievement American style: The rewards and costs of individualism.' *American Psychologist 40*, 1285–1295.

Spencer, M.B. and Markstrom-Adams, C. (1990) 'Identity processes among racial and ethnic minority children in America.' *Child Development 61*, 290–310.

Stephen, J.E., Fraser, E. and Marcia, J.E. (1992) 'Moratorium-achievement (MAMA) cycles in lifespan identity development: Value orientations and reasoning system correlates.' *Journal of Adolescence 15*, 283–300.

Stone, R. and Stirling, L.O. (1994) 'Developing and defining an identity: deaf children of deaf and hearing parents.' In C.J. Erting, R.C. Johnson, D.L. Smith and B.D. Snider (eds) *The Deaf Way: Perspectives from the International Conference on Deaf Culture*. Washington DC: Gallaudet University Press.

Street, E. (1989) 'Family counselling.' In W. Dryden, D. Charles-Edwards and R. Woolfe (eds) *Handbook of Counselling in Britain*. London: Routledge.

Swain, J. (1995) *The Use of Counselling Skills: A Guide for Therapists*. Oxford: Butterworth-Heinemann.

Taylor, G. and Meherali, R. (1991) The Other Deaf Community, Block 1, Unit 4, D251 *Issues in Deafness*, The Open University.

Tizard, B. and Phoenix, A. (1993) *Black, White or Mixed Race? Race and Racism in the Lives of Young People of Mixed Parentage*. London: Routledge.

Triandis, H.C. (1988) 'Collectivism and individualism: A reconceptualisation of a basic concept in cross-cultural psychology.' In G.K. Verma and C.Bagley (eds) *Personality, Attitudes and Cognitions*. London: MacMillan.

Walker, M. (1992) *Surviving Secrets*. Buckingham: Open University Press.

Wallerstein, J.S. and Kelly, J.B. (1980) *Surviving the Break-Up*. London: Grant MacIntyre.

Ward, J.V. (1990) 'Racial identity formation and transformation.' In C. Gilligan, N.P. Lyons and T.J. Hanmer (eds) *Making Connections*. Cambridge, MA: Harvard University Press.

Watzlawick, P., Beavin, J.H. and Jackson, D.D. (1967) *Pragmatics of Human Communication*. New York: Norton.

Weiss, R.S. (1986) 'Continuities and transformations in social relationships from childhood to adulthood.' In W.W. Hartup and Z. Rubin (eds) *On Relationships and Development*. Hillsdale, NJ: Lawrence Erlbaum Associates.

White, R.W. (1959) 'Motivation reconsidered: The concept of competence.' *Psychological Review 66*, 297–333.

Whitmore, D. (1991) *Psychosynthesis Counselling in Action*. London: Sage Publications.

Wood, D. (1989) 'Social interaction as tutoring.' In M.H. Bornstein and J.S. Bruner (eds) *Interaction in Human Development*. Hillsdale, NJ: Lawrence Erlbaum Associates.

Woodford, D. (1993) 'Towards a perception of a "hearing culture" and its relationships with a "deaf culture".' *Deafness 9*, 3, 13–15.

Woolfe, R. (1982) 'Counselling in a world of crisis: Towards a sociology of counselling.' *International Journal for the Advancement of Counselling 6*,: 167–76.

Woolfe, R. and Sugarman, L. (1989) 'Counselling and the life cycle.' In W. Dryden, D. Charles-Edwards and R. Woolfe (eds) *Handbook of Counselling in Britain*. London: Routledge.

Woolfe, R., Dryden, W. and Charles-Edwards, D. (1989) 'The nature and range of counselling practice.' In W. Dryden, D. Charles-Edwards and R. Woolfe (eds) *Handbook of Counselling in Britain*. London: Routledge.

Yu, A-B. and Yang, K-S. (1994) 'The nature of achievement motivation in collectivist societies.' In U. Kim, H.C. Triandis, S-C. Choi and G. Yoon (eds) *Individualism and Collectivism: Theory, Method and Applications*. London: Sage Publications.

Subject Index

Entries in italics refer to figures or boxed text.

Abuse 86–8, 121–2,
    129–30, 169–71, 177
  emotional 87, 100
  of inner child 195
  physical 86,98, 110–15,
    129
  psychological 86–7
  sexual 110–15
  suppression of feelings
    about 112, 122, 129,
    170
Actualising tendency 123
Affectional bonds 77, 135
  basic trust and 79
  need for fluent
    communication and
    170
Affectional needs 38
Altruistic behaviour,
    environment for
    96–97, *97*
Attachment, behaviours
    77, 78
  internal model of 84
  theory 77, 195;

Barriers to self-discovery
    13
Becoming deaf 30, 60,
    75–6, 107–9, 116–17,
    132–4, 148–52, 164–5,
    167–9
  and perceptions of love
    132, 138

effect on
    communication 116,
    125
Black culture 73
  Deaf identity and 56, 73,
    109, 120, 161, 184
  customs and traditions
    161–2, 173
  language and 73, 109
  racial identity and 50–1,
    109–10
  racism and 50, 85–6, 185
  youth clubs and 86
Boundaries, and
    self-management
    Chapter 4 *passim*, 119,
    Chapter 6 *passim*
  community 41–45,
    163–4, 176
  invasion of 122, *see also*
    Abuse
  personal 117;
Bullying, by peers 88–9,
    91, 98, 111
  by professionals,
    Chapter 3 *passim*,
    Chapter 4 *passim*, 101

Cochlear implants 95–6;
Collectivism 43–45, 200
  definitions of 41, *44*
  boundaries and 43–5, *44*
Communication,
  cybernetic models of
    193, *194, 196*
  importance of
    atmosphere for 69,
    72, 74, 80
  see also Language and
    Labels
Competence, and consent
    to surgery 45
  best environment for 60
  family expectations of 26
  professional
    expectations of 26, 46
  self-perception of 34,
    47–9
Conditions of worth 3,
    49, 151

Context, family 24–6,
    38–41
  socio-cultural 24–6, 41–5
Counselling, as a force
    for social change 195
  as a place of safety 19, 61
  as social construction
    14, 62
  common language in 8
  core values of 192
  deafness as part of 184
  environment 156
  ethical considerations
    15–17
  knowledge base of 11
  skills of 14, 78, 118, 122
  value base of 8, 192,
    195–8
  see also Humanistic
    counselling
Culture, *see also* Black,
    Deaf, Jewish,
    Hinduism
  belief and value
    systems of 38
  collective, *see*
    Collectivism
  individual , *see*
    Individualism
  manifest-prescriptive 10
  tacit 10

Deaf community,
  attitudes in 29, 136,
    148, 151
  boundaries of 59, 163,
    200–1
  confidentiality and trust
    in 16
  cultural expectations of
    34, 48, 59
  cultural reality of 151
  group loyalties of 16
  loss of acceptance by
    16–17
  self-determination in 34,
    59
  touching behaviour in
    104
  value attributed to
    counselling in 16

Deaf identity, evidence
    for existence of 53–7
    framework for
        development of 57–8
Deafness, affirmation of
    125, 137
    and normalcy 107, 119,
        141
    and second sight 104
    as defining
        characteristic 9, 18,
        101, 188
    club 126, 163
    culture 7, 29, 162–3
    meaning of 7, 105
    medical model of 29–32,
        76, 165, 176
    objectification of 81, 98,
        116
    personality
        characteristics of
        29–33
    pride in being 55, 101
    'pure' 66
Development see Identity
    formation
Developmental lag 49, 60,
    164, 166, 189
    compassionate
        explanations for 50,
        193;
Disability, as defining
    characteristic 9, 30, 129
    meaning of 30
    social model of 30
Discrimination,
    experience of 29–30,
    115, 121

Education, limits and
    restrictions to 34, 85,
    121
    mainstream 58, 162
    residential 33, 71, 85, 89,
        110–15
    teachers of the deaf and
        58, 86
Ego states 153
Emotional literacy 12

Erikson's psychosocial
    theory 12, 34
    and needs 34
    limits to 45–6
    development of 45–60;
Ethnic minorities 46,
    185–6
    identity development in
        50–52, 185, see also
        Hinduism
Eye contact, importance
    for deaf people 104, 108

Family 38–41, Chapter 2
    passim
    affirmation of
        experience by 66–8,
        79, 91–2, 98
    betrayal by 115, 170
    communication in 40,
        68–9, 93–4, 193–4
    cultural construction of
        39
    definition of 39
    denial of deafness in 75,
        79
    dynamics of 40, 82, 98,
        193–4
    fear of cultural split in
        58
    functions of 40
    life cycle of 10, 38, 195
    of choice 39, 189
    of origin 39, 185, 189, 201
    patterns of shared
        behaviour, beliefs
        and values of 8, 26,
        72, 106
    reaction to diagnosis in
        69, 73, 126
    safety in, 83, 115
    social rules in 67
    styles of parenting in 40
    synchronisation with
        individual life cycles
        38
    'the model parent' and
        65
    transitional stages of 39

Gay and lesbian 18, 46,
    88–9, 125–6
    homophobia
        experienced by 18,
        50, 52, 89, 115–16
    identity development in
        47–9, 106, 184, 186
    developmental lag in 50
    homosexual acts and
        homosexual identity
        in 52
    homosexual taboo and
        52
    finding community and
        52
    sexual object choice and
        52
    sexual orientation and
        52
Gender, identity 36, 46, 52
    role 52;
Gestalt, figure-on-ground
    4
Gossip, and anxiety 15
    problem of in Deaf
        community 15–16

Hearing, culture 56, 165
    modes of behaviour 105
    ways of thinking 105
Hearing children with
    Deaf parents 68, 104–6,
    126–8, 130–1, 145–148,
    162–3 childhood
    responsibilities of 91,
    137
    marginalisation
        experienced by 130–1
Hearing-impaired,
    meaning of 30, 55
Hinduism 73–5, 171–2,
    178–9
    and Deaf culture 172,
        184
    attitudes towards
        disability and 73–5,
        171
    beliefs and values of
        171–2, 178–9
    contradictions of 73, 171
    culture 73, 171, 178–9

extended family in 53
Humanistic counselling,
    and labels 17
    and self-empowerment
        190–1
    removing
        developmental
        constraints 190
    use of in easing
        transitions 190–198

Identification 12, 34, 55
    choices 58
Identity 12, 24
    ambivalence 56, 58, 59,
        116
    bicultural 50, 161
    Black 73
    composite 50, 119
    configurations 122, 185,
        187
    conflict and confusion
        29, 56, 59, 103, 107–8,
        115 129
    cultural 13, 38
    Deaf and deaf 53–60,
        108–9, 165
    'enmeshed' 45
    ethnic or racial 50–1,
        109, 185, 200
    gay or lesbian 47–9
    language 29, 54, 56
    mixed-race 50
    personal 9, 34, 54, 56, 60
    political 47, 59, 188
    self-constructed 37, 60,
        189
    social 9, 34, 54, 56, 60,
        174
    transitions 7, 141, 199
Identity formation 102,
        191
    additional tasks needed
        for 38, 50, 188
    and self-preservation
        159
    childhood and
        adulthood impasse
        in 103

chronological and
    developmental ages
    in 9, 45, 49
crisis 36, 57, 110. 120–1
commitment 36, 60, 106,
    110, Chapter 7 passim,
    186
factors needed for
    integration of 36, 58,
    119, 179, 188
negative resolution of
    102, 119, 125, 186, 188
over identification in 103
reactive 46
Identity statuses 36–37,
    37, 51, 192–3
    achievement 36–7
    diffusion 36–7, 120, 135
    foreclosure 36–7, 51, 98,
        185, 200
    moratorium 36–7, 118,
        121
Images, as mediators 7,
    24, 66, 71, 84, 103, 124,
    148, 160, 185
Individualism 42–3
    definitions of 41, 42
    boundaries and 42
In-group 9, 41, 45
    Deaf 201
Inner people see
    Subpersonalities
Integration, goals of 58
Intimacy, definition of 125
    prerequisite for 134–5,
    186

Jewish identity,
    anti-Semitism and 90,
    100
    conflict with gay 88–90,
        100, 165, 186
    customs 89–90, 100
    relationship to deaf 184
    symbols of 71, 100

Labels 17, 29–33, 47, 54
    as positive affirmation
        17

as a barrier to listening
    17
Language, and
    oppression 148
    functions of 56, 168
    importance of body and
        face in access 69, 73,
        78
    linked to client
        expectations of
        counsellor 18
    self-determination and
        147, 175
    value associated with
        147
Locus of Control 33–4
Loss 46, 48, 70–1
    and bereavement 48
    reactions to 48, 70–1, 73

Meaning, quest for 24
Moral framework 200
Mother–infant
    relationship 66
    blind babies and 77
    roots of self in 38, 77

Narrative, meaning of 12

Oppression 10, 19, 38,
    45–52, 53
    and 'coming out' 47
    internalised 29, 50, 106,
        161
    multiple and
        simultaneous 53
    oppression/trust
        dichotomy 202
Oralism 88, 92, 114
Out-group 41

Parent–professional
    collusion 72, 76
'Passing' 46, 166
Prejudice 9, 51

Professionals, *see also*
Education
Chapter 3 *passim*, 99–100
abuse of power by 82, 84
and compliance 45, 87
attitudes of 80
as role models 84
authority in 45, 82
control by 45, 82, 87,
93–96, 101
lack of consistency in
99, 110
lack of empathy from
86, 100, 127
racism in 86
style 45
Power, dimensions of 84

Recruitment 95
Relationships, and
homogamy 134
community 41–5
family 38–41, Chapter 2
passim
filters 134
horizontal 28, 33, 80, 85,
188
peer 33, 98, 201
vertical 28, 33, 188
Religion, damage caused
by 82, 100, 110–15, 169
disillusionment with
177–8
Rescue fantasies, of
parents 83

Scapegoat, counsellor as
archetype 18
Self, abuse of 81, 134, 192
alienation and 47, 56,
120, 148
and personality 26
defence of 169
definition of in
humanistic
psychology 12, 24
discrepancy between
ideal and actual 27,
46

emergence of in
children 26–27, 27
evidence for deaf 26, 32
independent view of 43
interdependent view of
38, 43
'lost' 101, 116–7, 134, 202
negative stereotypes of
10, 31–2
normative assumptions
about 10, 29, 32
private 15
Self-acceptance, need for
158, 202
Self-concept, and
self-evaluation 159
definition of 26–7
in mixed-race or mixed
parentage people 50
differentiation of 103
Self-esteem 97, 201
definition of 26–7
low 33, 117
Self-efficacy 47
Sex education and
counselling, lack of 100
Shame 49, 89, 171, 190
defences associated
with 49, 89
Sibling rivalry 71, 76
Sign language 141, 165
and Creole 109
British Sign Language
13, 67, 94, 162, 165
family signs 67, 94
Sign Supported English
13, 93
Social conscience, and
generativity 158, 161
Spoken language,
emphasis on 88, 90, 92
error analysis of 93
rigid teaching of 88, 92,
114
sign language
interference with 92
Stereotypes, and identity

Stigma 26, 46, 48, 82, 185
Stressors, environmental
10, 25
Structures of meaning 2,
19
Subpersonalities Chapter
6 *passim*, 192
and humanistic
counselling, 153
and psychosynthesis
counselling 152
and self-denial 145
and transactional
analysis 152
as inner resources 149
definition of 14, 153
images of 140, *142, 144,
146, 148, 151*
types of 154–7, 202
Systems, multi-layered
nature of 24–6, *25*
theory 24–6

Tinnitus 95
Transference 148
Trust, betrayal of 115, 170
client tests of 18

Values, contradictory
197–8, 200
organismic 197
types of 197
Voices, from the past 107,
128–9, 138, 141
inner 116, Chapter 6
passim, 127

Ways of seeing 4–7, 19